Prentice Hall
LITERATURE
Timeless Voices, Timeless Themes

PRACTICE BOOK

Selection Support: Skills Development

- **Build Vocabulary**

- **Build Spelling Skills**

- **Build Grammar Skills**

- **Reading Strategy**

- **Literary Focus**

COPPER

PRENTICE HALL
Upper Saddle River, New Jersey
Needham, Massachusetts

ISBN 0-13-436580-1

18 19 20 21 22 09

PRENTICE HALL

CONTENTS

UNIT 1: GROWING AND CHANGING

"The Sound of Summer Running" by Ray Bradbury
Build Vocabulary. 1
Build Spelling Skills: Words with *ie* and *ei*. 2
Build Grammar Skills: Nouns 3
Reading for Success: Literal Comprehension Strategies. 4
Literary Focus: Characters' Motives 6

"Stray" by Cynthia Rylant
Build Vocabulary. 7
Build Spelling Skills: Words That End in the "j" Sound 8
Build Grammar Skills: Compound Nouns 9
Reading Strategy: Read Sentences in Meaningful Sections 10
Literary Focus: Surprise Ending 11

"Saying Yes" by Diana Chang
"My Picture-Gallery" by Walt Whitman
"Dust of Snow" by Robert Frost
Build Vocabulary. 12
Build Spelling Skills: Adding Suffixes and Verb Tense
    Endings to Words Ending in *ue*. 13
Build Grammar Skills: Abstract and Concrete Nouns. 14
Reading Strategy: Reread to Clarify 15
Literary Focus: Images in Poetry 16

"Jeremiah's Song" by Walter Dean Myers
"Talent" by Annie Dillard
Build Vocabulary. 17
Build Spelling Skills: Adding Prefixes to Words. 18
Build Grammar Skills: Common and Proper Nouns. 19
Reading Strategy: Context Clues. 20
Literary Focus: First-Person Narrator 21

"Mummy No. 1770" by Patricia Lauber
Build Vocabulary. 22
Connect Nonfiction to Social Studies 23

"The King of Mazy May" by Jack London
Build Vocabulary. 24
Build Spelling Skills: Spelling the *oy* Sound 25
Build Grammar Skills: Pronouns and Antecedents 26
Reading Strategy: Recognize Signal Words 27
Literary Focus: Conflict Between Characters 28

"Books Fall Open" by David McCord
"O to Be Up and Doing" by Robert Louis Stevenson
"Change" by Charlotte Zolotow
Build Vocabulary. 29
Build Spelling Skills: Double Consonants in Two-Syllable Words . . . 30
Build Grammar Skills: Interrogative Pronouns. 31
Reading Strategy: Read According to Punctuation 32
Literary Focus: Word Choice 33

"The Circuit" by Francisco Jiménez
"Hard as Nails" by Russell Baker
Build Vocabulary. 34
Build Spelling Skills: Spelling Compound Nouns 35
Build Grammar Skills: Personal Pronouns 36

Reading Strategy: Break Down Long Sentences 37
Literary Focus: Theme 38

UNIT 2: REACHING OUT

"How to Write a Letter" by Garrison Keillor
    Build Vocabulary 39
    Build Spelling Skills: Words That End in *ence* 40
    Build Grammar Skills: Verbs 41
    Reading for Success: Literal Comprehension Strategies 42
    Literary Focus: Informal Essay 44

"Aaron's Gift" by Myron Levoy
"Water" by Helen Keller
    Build Vocabulary 45
    Build Spelling Skills: Adding Endings to Words Ending in *y* 46
    Build Grammar Skills: Verb Phrases 47
    Reading Strategy: Reread 48
    Literary Focus: Climax 49

"How to Write a Poem About the Sky" by Leslie Marmon Silko
"I'll tell you how the Sun rose—" by Emily Dickinson
"Wilderness Rivers" by Elizabeth Coatsworth
    Build Vocabulary 50
    Build Spelling Skills: Using *y* to Spell the Short *i* Sound 51
    Build Grammar Skills: Action Verbs and Linking Verbs 52
    Reading Strategy: Envision 53
    Literary Focus: Sensory Language 54

"The Great Flood" retold by Geraldine McCaughrean
    Build Vocabulary 55
    Connecting a Story From the Bible to Social Studies 56

"Zlateh the Goat" by Isaac Bashevis Singer
    Build Vocabulary 57
    Build Spelling Skills: Spelling the Final *s* Sound With *ce* 58
    Build Grammar Skills: Principal Parts of Verbs 59
    Reading Strategy: Summarize 60
    Literary Focus: Conflict With Nature 61

"Door Number Four" by Charlotte Pomerantz
"Count That Day Lost" by George Eliot
"The World Is Not a Pleasant Place to Be" by Nikki Giovanni
"The Children's Hour" by Henry Wadsworth Longfellow
    Build Vocabulary 62
    Build Spelling Skills: Spelling the *s* Sound With the Letters *sc* 63
    Build Grammar Skills: Verb Tenses 64
    Reading Strategy: Paraphrase 65
    Literary Focus: Speaker 66

"Old Ben" by Jesse Stuart
"Feathered Friend" by Arthur C. Clarke
"Childhood and Poetry" by Pablo Neruda
    Build Vocabulary 67
    Build Spelling Skills: Adding Suffixes to Words Ending in Silent *e* 68
    Build Grammar Skills: The Perfect Tenses 69
    Reading Strategy: Context Clues 70
    Literary Focus: Narratives 71

UNIT 3: PROVING YOURSELF

from *The Pigman & Me* by Paul Zindel

    Build Vocabulary 72

    Build Spelling Skills: Spelling the Sound *shun* at the End of a Word 73

    Build Grammar Skills: Adjectives 74

    Reading for Success: Interactive Reading Strategies 75

    Literary Focus: Internal Conflict 77

"Thunder Butte" by Virginia Driving Hawk Sneve

    Build Vocabulary 78

    Build Spelling Skills: Syllables 79

    Build Grammar Skills: Possessives as Adjectives 80

    Reading Strategy: Ask Questions 81

    Literary Focus: Atmosphere 82

"Be Like the Bird" by Victor Hugo

"Dream Dust" by Langston Hughes

"Stage Fright" by Mark Twain

"Alone in the Nets" by Arnold Adoff

    Build Vocabulary 83

    Build Spelling Skills: Spelling the Long *i* Sound With *igh* 84

    Build Grammar Skills: Articles 85

    Reading Strategy: Relate to Your Own Experience 86

    Literary Focus: Levels of Meaning 87

"The Dog of Pompeii" by Louis Untermeyer

    Build Vocabulary 88

    Connect a Short Story to Social Studies 89

"Mowgli's Brothers" by Rudyard Kipling

    Build Vocabulary 90

    Build Spelling Skills: Three Vowels in a Row 91

    Build Grammar Skills: Adverbs 92

    Reading Strategy: Predict 93

    Literary Focus: Animal Characters 94

"Names/Nombres" by Julia Alvarez

"The Southpaw" by Judith Viorst

    Build Vocabulary 95

    Build Spelling Strategy: Spelling the *k* Sound With the Letters *ch* 96

    Build Grammar Skills: Adverbs Modifying Adjectives and Adverbs 97

    Reading Strategy: Set a Purpose for Reading 98

    Literary Focus: Narrator's Perspective 99

"Adventures of Isabel" by Ogden Nash

"I'll Stay" by Gwendolyn Brooks

"Wilbur Wright and Orville Wright" by Rosemary and Stephen Vincent Benét

    Build Vocabulary 100

    Build Spelling Skills: Spelling Words That Use the Suffix *-ous* 101

    Build Grammar Skills: Adjective or Adverb? 102

    Reading Strategy: Use Prior Knowledge 103

    Literary Focus: Stanzas 104

UNIT 4: SEEING IT THROUGH

from "Lou Gehrig: The Iron Horse" by Bob Considine

    Build Vocabulary 105

    Build Spelling Skills: Adding Endings to Words Ending in *-ic* 106

    Build Grammar Skills: Prepositions 107

    Reading for Success: Strategies for Constructing Meaning 108

    Literary Focus: Biographical Narrative 110

"Lob's Girl" by Joan Aiken
"The Tiger Who Would Be King" by James Thurber
"The Lion and the Bulls" by Aesop
    Build Vocabulary 111
    Build Spelling Skills: *ie or ei?* 112
    Build Grammar Skills: Prepositional Phrases 113
    Reading Strategy: Compare and Contrast Characters 114
    Literary Focus: Foreshadowing 115

"Life Doesn't Frighten Me" by Maya Angelou
"Arithmetic" by Carl Sandburg
"Was Worm" by May Swenson
    Build Vocabulary 116
    Build Spelling Skills: Consonant Blends 117
    Build Grammar Skills: Adjective and Adverb Phrases 118
    Reading Strategy: Interpret Poetry 119
    Literary Focus: Rhythm 120

"The Friends of Kwan Ming" by Paul Yee
    Build Vocabulary 121
    Connecting a Short Story to Social Studies 122

"Greyling" by Jane Yolen
    Build Vocabulary 123
    Build Spelling Skills: The Sound *uff* Spelled *ough* 124
    Build Grammar Skills: Interjections 125
    Reading Strategy: Predict 126
    Literary Focus: Conflict 127

"Abuelito Who" by Sandra Cisneros
"who knows if the moon's" by E. E. Cummings
"The Open Road" by Walt Whitman
    Build Vocabulary 128
    Build Spelling Skills: Compound Connecting Words 129
    Build Grammar Skills: Conjunctions 130
    Reading Strategy: Make Inferences 131
    Literary Focus: Free Verse 132

"A Backwoods Boy" by Russell Freedman
"Jackie Robinson: Justice at Last" by Geoffrey C. Ward and Ken Burns
    Build Vocabulary 133
    Build Spelling Skills: The Suffix *-tude* 134
    Build Grammar Skills: Conjunctions Joining Sentences 135
    Reading Strategy: Identify Main Ideas 136
    Literary Focus: Factual Accounts 137

UNIT 5: MYSTERIOUS WORLDS

"The Strange Geometry of Stonehenge" by Katherine B. Shippen
    Build Vocabulary 138
    Build Spelling Skills: Using *cess* to Spell the Sound *ses* . . . 139
    Build Grammar Skills: Complete Subjects and Predicates . . . 140
    Reading for Success: Strategies for Reading Critically 141
    Literary Focus: Analytical Essay 143

"The Fun They Had" by Isaac Asimov
    Build Vocabulary 144
    Build Spelling Skills: Using *ch* to Spell the *sh* Sound 145
    Build Grammar Skills: Simple Subjects and Predicates 146
    Reading Strategy: Evaluate the Author's Message 147
    Literary Focus: Science Fiction 148

"A Dream Within a Dream" by Edgar Allan Poe
"The Spring and the Fall" by Edna St. Vincent Millay
"Ankylosaurus" by Jack Prelutsky
    Build Vocabulary 149
    Build Spelling Skills: The Sound *ow* Spelled *ough* 150
    Build Grammar Skills: Complete Sentences 151
    Reading Strategy: Make Inferences 152
    Literary Focus: Rhyme 153

from *Exploring the* Titanic by Robert Ballard
    Build Vocabulary 154
    Build Spelling Skills: The Sound *zhun* Spelled *-sion* 155
    Build Grammar Skills: Kinds of Sentences 156
    Reading Strategy: Fact vs. Opinion 157
    Literary Focus: Suspense 158

"Orpheus" by Alice Low
    Build Vocabulary 159
    Connecting a Myth to Social Studies 160

"Breaker's Bridge" by Laurence Yep
    Build Vocabulary 161
    Build Spelling Skills: *i* Before *e* Rule and Exceptions 162
    Build Grammar Skills: Direct and Indirect Objects 163
    Reading Strategy: Cause and Effect 164
    Literary Focus: Character Traits 165

"The Fairies' Lullaby" by William Shakespeare
"Someone" by Walter de la Mare
"Who Has Seen the Wind?" by Christina Rossetti
    Build Vocabulary 166
    Build Spelling Skills: Spelling the *awt* Sound With *ought* . . . 167
    Build Grammar Skills: Direct Objects 168
    Reading Strategy: Paraphrase 169
    Literary Focus: Repetition 170

"The Loch Ness Monster" by George Laycock
"Why the Tortoise's Shell Is Not Smooth" by Chinua Achebe
    Build Vocabulary 171
    Build Spelling Skills: Words Ending in *-ent* and *-ant* 172
    Build Grammar Skills: Subject Complements 173
    Reading Strategy: Author's Purpose 174
    Literary Focus: Oral Tradition . . . : 175

UNIT 6: SHORT STORIES

"Dragon, Dragon" by John Gardner
    Build Vocabulary 176
    Build Spelling Skills: Spelling the Long *i* Sound with a *y* . . . 177
    Build Grammar Skills: Clauses 178
    Reading for Success: Strategies for Reading Fiction 179
    Literary Focus: Plot 181

"Becky and the Wheels-and-Brake Boys" by James Berry
    Build Vocabulary 182
    Build Spelling Skills: *ace* and the *is* Sound 183
    Build Grammar Skills: Independent Clauses 184
    Reading Strategy: Predict 185
    Literary Focus: Conflict 186

"Overdoing It" by Anton Chekhov
"Eleven" by Sandra Cisneros
    Build Vocabulary 187
    Build Spelling Skills: Homophones with *r* and *wr* 188
    Build Grammar Skills: Subordinate Clauses 189
    Reading Strategy: Identify With Characters 190
    Literary Focus: Characterization 191

"Dentistry" by Mark Twain
    Build Vocabulary 192
    Connecting Fiction to Social Studies 193

"The Lawyer and the Ghost" by Charles Dickens
"The Wounded Wolf" by Jean Craighead George
    Build Vocabulary 194
    Build Spelling Skills: The Sound *shent* Spelled *cient* 195
    Build Grammar Skills: Simple Sentences 196
    Reading Strategy: Envision Action and Setting 197
    Literary Focus: Setting 198

"The All-American Slurp" by Lensey Namioka
"The Stone" by Lloyd Alexander
    Build Vocabulary 199
    Build Spelling Skills: The *k* Sound Spelled *qu* 200
    Build Grammar Skills: Compound Sentences 201
    Reading Strategy: Making Inferences. 202
    Literary Focus: Theme 203

UNIT 7: NONFICTION

"The Shutout" by Patricia C. McKissack and Frederick McKissack, Jr.
    Build Vocabulary 204
    Build Spelling Skills: Using the Prefix *ir-* With Words That Begin With *r*. 205
    Build Grammar Skills: Subject Pronouns 206
    Reading for Success: Strategies for Reading Nonfiction 207
    Literary Focus: History Essay. 209

"Letter to Scottie" by F. Scott Fitzgerald
"Letter to Joan" by C. S. Lewis
"Olympic Diary" by Amanda Borden
    Build Vocabulary 210
    Build Spelling Skills: Spelling the *g* Sound as *gue*. 211
    Build Grammar Skills: Object Pronouns: Direct and Indirect Objects 212
    Reading Strategy: Understand the Author's Purpose 213
    Literary Focus: Letters and Journals 214

"My Papa, Mark Twain" by Susy Clemens
"The Drive-In Movies" by Gary Soto
    Build Vocabulary 215
    Build Spelling Skills: Words with *-cess* 216
    Build Grammar Skills: Object Pronouns: Objects of Prepositions 217
    Reading Strategy: Author's Evidence. 218
    Literary Focus: Biography and Autobiography. 219

"Space Shuttle *Challenger*" by William Harwood
"Central Park" by John Updike
"Noah Webster's Dictionary" by Charles Kuralt
    Build Vocabulary 220
    Build Spelling Skills: Consonant Patterns. 221
    Build Grammar Skills: Apostrophes 222
    Reading Strategy: Set a Purpose 223
    Literary Focus: Media Accounts 224

"Restoring the Circle" by Joseph Bruchac
from "In Wildness is the Preservation of the World"
  by Henry David Thoreau and Eliot Porter
"Turkeys" by Bailey White
"How the Internet Works" by Kerry Cochrane
    Build Vocabulary 225
    Build Spelling Skills: Changing -ent and -ant to -ence and -ance 226
    Build Grammar Skills: Quotation Marks 227
    Reading Strategy: Identify Author's Main Points 228
    Literary Focus: Types of Essays 229

"Eulogy for Gandhi" by Jawaharlal Nehru
    Build Vocabulary 230
    Connecting a Eulogy to Social Studies 231

UNIT 8: DRAMA

The Phantom Tollbooth, Act I based on the book
  by Norton Juster, by Susan Nanus
    Build Vocabulary 232
    Build Spelling Skills: Spelling Words With tion and sion 233
    Build Grammar Skills: Subject and Verb Agreement 234
    Reading Strategy: Summarize 235
    Literary Focus: Elements of Drama 236

The Phantom Tollbooth, Act II based on the book
  by Norton Juster, by Susan Nanus
    Build Vocabulary 237
    Build Spelling Skills: The Sound shƏs Spelled cious 238
    Build Grammar Skills: Verb Agreement With Special Subjects 239
    Reading Strategy: Envision 240
    Literary Focus: Staging 241

Anne of Green Gables by L. M. Montgomery
    Build Vocabulary 242
    Connecting a Drama to Social Studies 243

Grandpa and the Statue by Arthur Miller
    Build Vocabulary 244
    Build Spelling Skills: Adding -er or -est 245
    Build Grammar Skills: Pronoun and Antecedent Agreement 246
    Reading Strategy: Predict 247
    Literary Focus: Dialogue 248

UNIT 9: POETRY

"The Naming of Cats" by T. S. Eliot
    Build Vocabulary 249
    Build Spelling Skills: Spelling the shun Sound With -tion 250
    Build Grammar Skills: Comparison of Adjectives and Adverbs 251
    Reading for Success: Strategies for Reading Poetry 252
    Literary Focus: Rhythm in Poetry 253

"The Walrus and the Carpenter" by Lewis Carroll
"February Twilight" by Sara Teasdale
"Jimmy Jet and His TV Set" by Shel Silverstein
"The Geese" by Richard Peck
    Build Vocabulary 254
    Build Spelling Skills: Long e Sound (ee and ea) 255
    Build Grammar Skills: Irregular Comparisons 256
    Reading Strategy: Identify the Speaker in a Poem 257
    Literary Focus: Narrative and Lyric Poetry 258

"The Sidewalk Racer" by Lillian Morrison
"Concrete Cat" by Dorthi Charles
Two Haiku by Matsuo Bashō and Muso-Soseki
Two Limericks Anonymous
    Build Vocabulary 259
    Build Spelling Skills: The *oo* Sound 260
    Build Grammar Skills: Comparisons With *more* and *most* 261
    Reading Strategy: Use Your Senses 262
    Literary Focus: Special Forms of Poetry 263

"Parade" by Rachel Field
"Cynthia in the Snow" by Gwendolyn Brooks
    Build Vocabulary 264
    Build Spelling Skills: *ei* and *ie* 265
    Build Grammar Skills: Double Negatives 266
    Reading Strategy: Read According to Punctuation 267
    Literary Focus: Sound Devices 268

"Simile: Willow and Ginkgo" by Eve Merriam
"Fame Is a Bee" by Emily Dickinson
"April Rain Song" by Langston Hughes
    Build Vocabulary 269
    Build Spelling Skills: Forming the Plural of Words that End in *o* 270
    Build Grammar Skills: Correct Use of *its* and *it's* 271
    Reading Strategy: Respond 272
    Literary Focus: Figurative Language 273

"Exclamation" by Octavio Paz
"Wind and Water and Stone" by Octavio Paz
    Build Vocabulary 274
    Connecting a Poem to Social Studies 275

"The Kitten at Play" by William Wordsworth
"Child on Top of a Greenhouse" by Theodore Roethke
"The Shark" by John Ciardi
Two Riddles by Ian Serraillier and Mary Austin
    Build Vocabulary 276
    Build Spelling Skills: Spelling the *ay* Sound as *ey* 277
    Build Grammar Skills: Correct Use of *good* and *well* 278
    Reading Strategy: Paraphrase 279
    Literary Focus: Poetic Image 280

UNIT 10: THE ORAL TRADITION

"The Emperor's New Clothes" by Hans Christian Andersen
    Build Vocabulary 281
    Build Spelling Skills: Spelling the *z* Sound With an *s* 282
    Build Grammar Skills: Commas in Compound Sentences 283
    Reading for Success: Strategies for Reading Folk Literature 284
    Literary Focus: Characters in Folk Literature 286

"The Ant and the Dove" by Leo Tolstoy
"He Lion, Bruh Bear, and Bruh Rabbit" by Virginia Hamilton
"Señor Coyote and the Tricked Trickster" by I.G. Edmonds
    Build Vocabulary 287
    Build Spelling Skills: Spelling the *j* Sound With *di* 288
    Build Grammar Skills: Commas in a Series 289
    Reading Strategy: Recognize the Storyteller's Purpose 290
    Literary Focus: Folk Tales 291

"The Gorgon's Head" by Anne Terry White
"How Coyote Stole Fire" by Gail Robinson and Douglas Hill
    Build Vocabulary 292
    Build Spelling Skills: Words Ending With -*ous* 293
    Build Grammar Skills: Commas With Interrupters 294
    Reading Strategy: Understand Cultural Background 295
    Literary Focus: Myths 296

"Why Monkeys Live in Trees" by Julius Lester
"Arachne" by Olivia E. Coolidge
"A Crippled Boy" by Tran My-Van
"The Three Wishes" by Ricardo E. Alegria
    Build Vocabulary 297
    Build Spelling Skills: -*cy* and -*sy* 298
    Build Grammar Skills: Varying Sentence Beginnings 299
    Reading Strategy: Predict 300
    Literary Focus: Oral Tradition 301

"Loo-Wit, the Fire-Keeper" retold by Joseph Bruchac
    Build Vocabulary 302
    Connecting a Myth to Social Studies 303

"The Sound of Summer Running" by Ray Bradbury (text page 5)

Build Vocabulary

Using the Root: *meter*

Words that contain the root *meter* have something to do with measurement. A *barometer*, for example, is an instrument that measures changes in the pressure of the atmosphere.

A. Directions: Match each description in the left column with the correct word in the right column. Write the letter of the word on the line next to its description. Use the clues in parentheses for help.

____ 1. an instrument that measures electric current

____ 2. an instrument that measures the speed of the wind

____ 3. an instrument that measures altitude

a. anemometer (found at a weather station)

b. altimeter (found in an airplane)

c. voltmeter (found in an electrician's toolbox)

Using the Word Bank

seized	suspended	loam	barometer
alien	limber	revelation	

B. Directions: Complete each sentence with a word from the Word Bank. Use each word only once.

1. We looked up at the model of the solar system that was _____ from the ceiling.

2. According to the _____, the air pressure had dropped only slightly since yesterday.

3. The little terrier had never seen a horse before, and he carefully studied the _____ creature before approaching it.

4. Because I had already guessed who the criminal was, the mystery story's ending did not come as a _____ to me.

5. These warm-up exercises are designed to help _____ the muscles and prevent injuries.

6. Just in time, Frannie _____ her little brother and prevented him from running into the street.

7. We admired the rich, fertile _____ in Mrs. Green's garden.

"The Sound of Summer Running" by Ray Bradbury (text page 5)

Build Spelling Skills: Words with *ie* and *ei*

Spelling Strategy A well-known rule states: "Use *i* before *e* except after *c* or when sounded as 'ay,' as in *neighbor* and *weigh.*"

Examples of words that follow this rule include *believe, receive,* and *freight.* In *believe, i* comes before *e.* In *receive, e* comes before *i* because the two letters appear "after *c.*" In *weigh, e* comes before *i* because the word is "sounded as 'ay.'"

Exceptions: The words *seized, either, leisure, weird, height,* and *protein* are exceptions to this rule. In all these words *e* comes before *i*, even though the letters do not follow *c* and are not sounded as "ay."

A. Practice: Choose the correctly spelled word to complete each sentence. Write the word on the line. Hint: The words below follow the i-before-e rule unless they are noted in the list of exceptions. You can use a dictionary to check your spellings.

1. We were invited to go camping, and we (siezed, seized) _____ the opportunity to enjoy the fresh mountain air.

2. I (recieved, received) _____ the package of supplies that you sent.

3. My (nieghbors, neighbors) _____, the Robinsons, enjoy birdwatching.

4. They go on field trips whenever they have some (liesure, leisure) _____ time.

5. This (peice, piece) _____ of cake is delicious.

6. I (believe, beleive) _____ that it is made with coconut.

7. The (frieght, freight) _____ company needs you to fill out this form.

8. Do you know the width, (hieght, height) _____, and (wieght, weight) _____ of the package?

B. Practice: Complete the paragraph by choosing the appropriate words from the box and writing them on the lines. Use each word once.

seized	perceive	conceives	believe

In "The Sound of Summer Running," Douglas _____ of a clever way to get a pair of Royal Crown Cream-Sponge Para Litefoot Tennis Shoes even though he doesn't have quite enough money to pay for them. He offers to run errands for Mr. Sanderson, the store owner, in order to make up for the dollar that he would owe for the shoes. First, however, Douglas must convince Mr. Sanderson to _____ in him and his plan. To do so, Douglas persuades Mr. Sanderson to try on a pair of the sneakers himself. With the help of Douglas's amazingly vivid descriptions, the middle-aged man is able to _____ the special qualities of the shoes and the reasons the boy wants them so badly. In fact, for a few moments, he is _____ with memories of what it is like to be Douglas's age and put on a brand new pair of sneakers.

"The Sound of Summer Running" by Ray Bradbury (text page 5)

Build Grammar Skills: Nouns

Look around. Name some of the sights that you see. The words that you will use are nouns. **Nouns** are words that name people, places, and things.

Now read the following sentences from Ray Bradbury's story. The nouns appear in italics.

Here *Douglas* stood, trapped on the dead cement and the red-brick *streets*, hardly able to move.

The *boy* looked down at his feet deep in the *rivers*, in the *fields* of *wheat*, in the *wind* that already was rushing *him* out of the *town*.

A. Practice: Identify the nouns in the following sentences. Write the nouns on the lines provided.

1. Douglas was coming back from a movie with his family.

   _____

2. The boy saw a fantastic pair of sneakers in a brightly lit window.

   _____

3. Douglas shared his thoughts and wishes with his father.

   _____

4. Douglas tried to describe how it felt to lace up a new pair of sneakers on one of the first days of summer and then go running through the neighborhood, feeling as if you could jump over fences, sidewalks, and dogs.

   _____

5. Mr. Spaulding advised his son to save up his money.

   _____

B. Writing Application: Write a sentence about each topic provided below, using the noun or nouns given. When you are finished, reread your sentences and underline any additional nouns that you used.

1. Write a sentence about the author, using the noun *Ray Bradbury*.

   _____

2. Write a sentence about the story's main character, using the nouns *Douglas* and *sneakers*.

   _____

3. Write a sentence about a hot day, using the nouns *sidewalk*, and *grass*.

   _____

4. Write a sentence about your favorite pair of shoes, using the nouns *shoes* and *feet*.

   _____

5. Write a sentence about "The Sound of Summer Running," using the nouns *story*, *sneakers*, *summer*, and *magic*.

   _____

Reading for Success: Literal Comprehension Strategies

The first step to understanding a work of literature is to grasp its literal meaning—the basic facts that the author is communicating. The following reading strategies will help to increase your literal comprehension of a selection:

- **Break down long sentences.**
  Read a sentence in meaningful sections, not word for word.

- **Use context clues.**
  When you come across an unfamiliar word, clues in the words and phrases around it can help you figure out its meaning.

- **Use signal words to identify relationships.**
  Signal words show relationships, such as time or importance, among ideas.

- **Reread or read ahead.**
  You may need to look back or ahead to clarify an idea, understand the cause of an event, or identify the relationship between people.

DIRECTIONS: Read "The Boy and His Grandfather" below, and use the reading strategies to increase your comprehension. In the margin, note where you break down long sentences, use context clues to determine meaning, use signal words to identify relationships, and reread or read ahead. On the lines that follow, write a paragraph summarizing your response to the tale.

"The Boy and His Grandfather" by Rudolfo Anaya

In the old days it was not unusual to find several generations living together in one home. Usually, everyone lived in peace and harmony, but this situation caused problems for one man whose household included, besides his wife and small son, his elderly father.

It so happened that the daughter-in-law took a dislike to the old man. He was always in the way, she said, and she insisted he be removed to a small room apart from the house.

Because the old man was out of sight, he was often neglected. Sometimes he even went hungry. They took poor care of him, and in winter the old man often suffered from the cold. One day the little grandson visited the grandfather.

"My little one," the grandfather said, "go and find a blanket and cover me. It is cold and I am freezing."

The small boy ran to the barn to look for a blanket, and there he found a rug.

"Father, please cut this rug in half," he asked his father.

"Why? What are you going to do with it?"

"I'm going to take it to my grandfather because he is cold."

"Well, take the entire rug," replied his father.

"No," his son answered, "I cannot take it all. I want you to cut it in half so I can save the other half for you when you are as old as my grandfather. Then I will have it for you so you will not be cold."

His son's response was enough to make the man realize how poorly he had treated his own father. The man then brought his father back into his home and ordered that a warm room be prepared. From that time on he took care of his father's needs and visited him frequently every day.

_____

_____

_____

_____

_____

_____

_____

_____

_____

_____

_____

_____

_____

_____

_____

_____

_____

"The Sound of Summer Running" by Ray Bradbury (text page 5)

Literary Focus: Characters' Motives

To understand the characters in a story, you must understand the **characters' motives**—the reasons for their actions and behavior. Early on in "The Sound of Summer Running," Ray Bradbury lets readers know about the factors that drive the behavior of the main character, Douglas Spaulding. Look at these excerpts from the story:

> Late at night, going home from the show with his mother and father and his brother Tom, Douglas saw the tennis shoes in the bright store window. He glanced quickly away, but his ankles were seized, his feet suspended, then rushed. The earth spun; the shop awnings slammed their canvas wings overhead with the thrust of his body running. His mother and father walked quietly on both sides of him. Douglas walked backward, watching the tennis shoes in the midnight window left behind.

> "Dad!" he blurted it out. "Back there in that window, those Cream-Sponge Para Litefoot Shoes . . ."

> His father didn't even turn. "Suppose you tell me why you need a new pair of sneakers. Can you do that?"

These passages, along with others in the story, clearly reveal the motive for Douglas's actions in the story: He wants the new sneakers.

A. DIRECTIONS: Read the following passage. Then explain what it reveals about Mr. Sanderson's motive or motives. Write your answer on the lines below.

> The boy . . . spun around like a whistle and went off. The door stood empty. The sound of the tennis shoes faded in the jungle heat.

> Mr. Sanderson stood in the sun-blazed door, listening. From a long time ago, when he dreamed as a boy, he remembered the sound. Beautiful creatures leaping under the sky, gone through brush, under trees, away, and only the soft echo their running left behind.

> "Antelopes," said Mr. Sanderson. "Gazelles."

_____

_____

_____

B. DIRECTIONS: Motives cause characters to act in a certain way. Use the lines below to name two actions that result from the characters' motives. Identify at least one action that Douglas takes and at least one action that Mr. Sanderson takes.

Douglas:_____

_____

Mr. Sanderson: _____

_____

Name _____ Date _____

"Stray" by Cynthia Rylant (text page 17)

Build Vocabulary

Using the Suffix -ly

Writers add the suffix -ly to a word when they want the word to describe how or in what way an action happens. For example, in the sentence, "Dennis jumped up suddenly," the word *suddenly* means in a *sudden way.* It tells how, or in what way, Dennis jumped up. Words that end in the suffix -ly can bring a sentence to life by telling more about the action.

A. DIRECTIONS: Add -ly to the following words; then use the newly formed words to complete each sentence below. Each word will be used only once.

furious   sad   contented   quick

1. Josh finished the test more _____ than anyone else.

2. Jenny stared in silent terror as the huge dog barked_____ .

3. Jamie opened the cage door, but the bird sat and chirped_____ on its perch.

4. Alana stared _____ out the window, watching the raindrops fall.

Using the Word Bank

timidly	trudged	ignore	grudgingly	exhausted

B. DIRECTIONS: In each sentence, replace the word or words in italics with a word from the Word Bank. Write your words in the space provided.

1. He did not want to share his candy, but he did it *unwillingly.* _____

2. The Scout troop had hiked for ten miles and felt *tired.* _____

3. If you *pay no attention to* the instructions, you will find it hard to put together the model

   plane. _____

4. The boy opened the door and peered *fearfully* inside, hoping that he had not come to the wrong house. _____

5. With a sigh, the man picked up the heavy suitcase and *walked with difficulty* down the long hallway toward the parking lot. _____

Recognizing Synonyms

C. DIRECTIONS: For each of the words in CAPITAL LETTERS, circle the letter of the word or phrase that is most nearly the same in meaning.

1. GRUDGINGLY
   a. happily
   b. resentfully
   c. pleasantly
   d. eagerly

2. EXHAUSTED
   a. grateful
   b. nervous
   c. weary
   d. hungry

3. TRUDGE
   a. march
   b. work
   c. wish
   d. run

"**Stray**" by Cynthia Rylant (text page 17)

Build Spelling Skills: Words That End in the "j" Sound

Spelling Strategy When a word, such as *trudge*, sounds like it ends with the letter *j*, it is actually spelled with the letters *ge* at the end.

A. Practice: Fill in the blank in each sentence below with a word that ends with a "j" sound. The first sentence has been filled in as an example.

1. It is better to forgive a friend than to hold a _____grudge_____.

2. Actors in the theater perform on a platform called a _____.

3. When people want to get across the river, they can walk across the _____.

4. Someone had torn out the last _____ of the book, so we never found out how it ended.

5. I grabbed a _____ to soak up the spilled water.

6. The driver stopped the car just before it went over the _____ of the cliff.

B. Practice: In the following paragraph, the missing words end with the "j" sound. Each one should be spelled with the letters *ge* at the end. Write each missing word in the space provided. The first space has been filled in as an example.

When Doris found the puppy, she did not know its _____age_____, but guessed

that it was about six months old. Even though her parents said she could not keep the pup,

Doris hoped that they would _____ their minds. Once the snow was gone,

however, Mr. Lacey took his car out of the _____ and drove the puppy to

the pound. As soon as he saw how the dogs were kept there, with ten of them locked in each

_____, he took the puppy back home.

Challenge: In the story, Doris finds a puppy. The word *puppy*, as you know, means a young dog. Many special words for young animals, such as *puppy*, do not sound like the word for the adult animal. Examples of such words are *colt*, meaning "young horse," and *faun*, meaning "young deer." Other words for young animals, however, sound similar to the words for the adult animals; for example, *chick / chicken*, and *duckling / duck*. In the spaces provided, write the word for the young animal on the right that goes with the name of the adult animal on the left. You may have to use a dictionary to look up some of the young-animal words.

	Adult Animals	**Young Animals**
1. _____	swan	calf
2. _____	bird	fledgling
3. _____	goose	piglet
4. _____	elephant	gosling
5. _____	pig	cygnet

"Stray" by Cynthia Rylant (text page 17)

Build Grammar Skills: Compound Nouns

Some nouns (words naming people, places, or things) are made up of two or more words. These are called *compound nouns*. These nouns can be spelled as single words, as hyphenated words, or as two or more separate words.

Examples:

Single word: cinderblock

Hyphenated word: ten-year-old

Two words: sweet potato

A. Practice: In each sentence below, underline the compound noun or nouns. Look for a single word, a hyphenated word, or two words.

1. Doris was holding a snow shovel when she first saw the puppy.

2. Mr. Lacey was cleaning his fingernails with his pocketknife.

3. The snow was keeping him home from his job at the warehouse.

4. The puppy was big for a six-month-old.

5. Mrs. Lacey looked into the room from the doorway.

B. Writing Application: Rewrite each sentence below, including a compound noun formed from the word *dog* plus the word in parentheses. If you are not sure whether a compound noun should be written as a single word or as separate words, use a dictionary to find out.

1. Doris gave her puppy a _____ as a treat. (biscuit)

2. She saved up to buy the puppy a _____ to wear. (collar)

3. She attached a _____ to the puppy's collar. (tag)

4. Doris's father built a _____ in the yard. (house)

5. The family thought the puppy might make a good _____, because it barked at the mail carrier. (watch)

6. Doris thought the puppy might be part _____. (sheep)

Reading Strategy: Read Sentences in Meaningful Sections

Long, complicated sentences sometimes contain too much information to take in at once. For this reason, it is a good idea to divide long sentences into smaller sections so that you can read and understand each section separately. Good places at which to divide a sentence are after a punctuation mark, such as a comma or semicolon, and before a connecting word, such as "and" or "but." For example, look at the following sentence from the story:

> Doris knew it had wanted some company and it had lain against the door, listening to the talk in the kitchen, smelling the food, being a part of things.

Using punctuation marks and connecting words as guides, you can divide this sentence into five sections:

1. Doris knew it had wanted some company

2. **and** it had lain against the door, [comma]

3. listening to the talk in the kitchen, [comma]

4. smelling the food, [comma]

5. being a part of things.

The first section of the sentence states that Doris knew the puppy wanted company. The second, third, and fourth sections describe what the puppy did to show it wanted company. The fifth section repeats the idea that the puppy wanted company, or to be "a part of things."

A. DIRECTIONS: Divide each of the following long sentences into smaller sections. Draw a line to show where each new section begins. Remember to use punctuation marks and connecting words as your guides.

1. The puppy had been abandoned, and it made its way toward the Laceys' small house, its ears tucked, its tail between its legs, shivering.

2. The puppy stopped in the road, wagging its tail timidly, trembling with shyness and cold.

3. She knew her parents wouldn't let her keep it, that her father made so little money any pets were out of the question, and that the pup would definitely go to the pound when the weather cleared.

4. By the looks of it, Doris figured the puppy was about six months old, and on its way to being a big dog.

B. DIRECTIONS: Choose one of the above sentences. On the lines below, write the information you learned from each section.

_____

_____

_____

_____

"Stray" by Cynthia Rylant (text page 17)

Literary Focus: Surprise Ending

A **surprise ending** to a story startles readers because it is not the ending they would have predicted. For a surprise ending to be effective, the author must trick readers by making them expect the story to end differently. In "The Stray," the author starts giving misleading clues about the story's outcome from the moment Mr. Lacey first sees the puppy.

"I don't know where it came from," he said mildly, "but I know for sure where it's going."

Shortly afterward, readers discover that Mr. Lacey plans to take the puppy to the pound. Further clues build up the reader's belief that Doris will not be allowed to keep the dog. The author does not reveal the happy surprise until very late in the story.

DIRECTIONS: In the space provided, explain why each of the following clues from the story makes the reader expect the ending to be sad for Doris and her puppy, rather than happy.

1. When Mrs. Lacey sees the puppy for the first time, she says, "Where did *that* come from?"

   _____

   _____

2. Mrs. Lacey allows Doris to feed the puppy table scraps only because she "was sensitive about throwing out food."

   _____

   _____

   _____

3. Even after a week had gone by, Doris didn't name the dog.

   _____

   _____

4. At dinner, Doris says: "She's a good dog, isn't she?" and "She's not much trouble. I like her," and, finally, "I figure she's real smart. I could teach her things." Her parents remain silent.

   _____

   _____

   _____

5. When Doris gets hungry for dinner, she doesn't want to go into the kitchen or past the basement door.

   _____

   _____

   _____

6. When Doris enters the kitchen, neither of her parents speaks to her, at first.

   _____

   _____

"Saying Yes" by Diana Chang (text page 26)
"My Picture-Gallery" by Walt Whitman (text page 27)
"Dust of Snow" by Robert Frost (text page 28)

Build Vocabulary

Homophones

The words *rued* and *rude* are homophones. So are the words *to, two,* and *too.* **Homophones** are words that sound alike but have different meanings. These similar-sounding words often have different spellings.

A. DIRECTIONS: Choose the correct homophone from Column A to complete each sentence in Column B. Write the word on the line.

A	B
won one	1. There is only _____ correct answer to this question.
	2. Do you know who _____ the song-writing contest?
rain reign	3. The _____ and sleet went on for days.
	4. The _____ of King Louis XIV of France lasted for 72 years.
so sew sow	5. The time to _____ these seeds is after the last frost.
	6. The skaters decided to _____ their own costumes.
	7. I was _____ tired that I fell asleep instantly.

Using the Word Bank

suspended	tableaus	rued

B. DIRECTIONS: Answer each of the following questions to demonstrate your understanding of the Work Bank words. Circle the letter of your choice.

1. Which of the following situations might someone have rued?

    a. He or she won the lottery.   b. He or she hurt another person's feelings.

2. Which of the following is an example of a suspended object?

    a. a crystal chandlier hanging in a ballroom   b. an antenna attached to a roof

3. Which of the following could be called tableaus?

    a. pictures of people dining, strolling, and dancing   b. heavy pieces of furniture

C. DIRECTIONS: Circle the letter of word or phrase that is closest in meaning to the Word Bank word.

1. TABLEAUS   a. tables   b. ovals   c. scenes   d. jewels

2. SUSPENDED   a. propped   b. hung   c. broken   d. erased

Name _____ Date _____

"**Saying Yes**" by Diana Chang (text page 26)
"**My Picture-Gallery**" by Walt Whitman (text page 27)
"**Dust of Snow**" by Robert Frost (text page 28)

Build Spelling Skills: Adding Suffixes and Verb Tense Endings to Words Ending in *ue*

Spelling Strategy Whenever you add a suffix or verb-tense ending to words ending in *ue*, drop the *e* if the ending to be added starts with a vowel.

Examples: glue + -ed = glued   true + -er = truer   rue + -ed = rued

glue + -ing = gluing   true + -est = truest   rue + -ing = ruing

A. Practice: Add the suffix indicated at the top of each column to the words at the left. Write the new words on the lines.

	-ed	*-ing*
cue	_____	_____
issue	_____	_____
argue	_____	_____
	-er	*-est*
blue	_____	_____

B. Practice: Complete the sentences by adding the indicated ending or suffix to each given word. Write the new words on the lines provided.

1. In "Dust of Snow," a crow (rescue +ed) _____ the speaker from his unhappy mood.

2. In "Say Yes," a series of questions is (cue + ing) _____ the speaker to reveal her thoughts about her heritage and identity.

3. In "My Picture-Gallery," Walt Whitman uses suprising images to create a (true + -er) _____ and more imaginative view of reality.

4. Poets sometimes enjoy (issue +ing) _____ challenges to their readers.

5. People have even (argue +ed) _____ about the meanings of poems.

Challenge: In "My Picture-Gallery," Whitman says that his gallery is full of "tableaus of life." The word *tableaus*, which means "dramatic scenes or pictures," comes from French. Another word that is French and whose ending has a similar spelling and pronunciation is *bureau*, meaning "a chest of drawers" or "a department or agency that performs a service."

On the lines below, write a sentence for the word *tableau*. Then write two sentences showing the two different meanings of *bureau*.

1. tableaus (pictures): _____

2. bureau (chest of drawers): _____

3. bureau (department or agency): _____

"**Saying Yes**" by Diana Chang (text page 26)
"**My Picture-Gallery**" by Walt Whitman (text page 27)
"**Dust of Snow**" by Robert Frost (text page 28)

Build Grammar Skills: Abstract and Concrete Nouns

Nouns are words that name people, places, and things. **Concrete nouns** name things that are touchable. **Abstract nouns** name things that exist but cannot be sensed by touch.

Notice the nouns in the following sentences. Which ones are concrete? Which ones are abstract?

Wildflowers add *beauty* to any *garden.*

Our *grandmother* takes great *pride* in her antique *furniture.*

Wildflowers, garden, grandmother, and *furniture* are concrete nouns. *Beauty* and *pride* are abstract nouns.

A. Practice: Read the following sentences. Decide whether each italicized word is an abstract noun or a concrete noun. Write your answer on the line.

1. The natural history *museum* draws many visitors. _____

2. My favorite gallery features dinosaur *skeletons.* _____

3. We looked with *fascination* at the ancient bones. _____

4. In our *notebooks* we sketched the skeletons. _____

5. The wide marble *staircase* led us to the Hall of Mammals. _____

6. The exhibit also increased our *knowledge* about threats that some species face.
_____

7. During lunch in the *cafeteria,* we discussed which department we should visit next.
_____

8. Our visit to the *museum* was a great success. _____

B. Writing Application: Complete the paragraph by writing an abstract or concrete noun in each blank, as indicated. Use the nouns below, or provide your own.

dissatisfaction	creativity	pride
paintings	tree	crow

Poets help readers view reality in new and surprising ways. For example, in "Saying Yes,"

Diana Chang demonstrates that a dual heritage can be a source of (abstract noun)

_____ rather than uncertainty or conflict. In "Dust of Snow," Robert Frost

captures a moment in which (abstract noun) _____ changes to happiness,

thanks to a (concrete noun) _____ in a (concrete noun)

_____. Walt Whitman displays his inventiveness and (abstract noun)

_____ in "My Picture-Gallery" by bringing to life a "little house" full of

(concrete noun) _____ that is unlike any typical art museum.

"Saying Yes" by Diana Chang (text page 26)
"My Picture-Gallery" by Walt Whitman (text page 27)
"Dust of Snow" by Robert Frost (text page 28)

Reading Strategy: Reread to Clarify

You may sometimes find it helpful to reread a phrase, sentence, or passage to clarify an author's meaning. Doing so can help you identify a significant detail or make connections between ideas.

Read and reread these opening lines from "Saying Yes."

"Are you Chinese?"
"Yes."

"American?"
"Yes."

"Really Chinese?"
"No. . . not quite."

"Really American?"
"Well, actually, you see . . ."

Did you note that the speaker is both Chinese and American the first time around? Did you realize that she is beginning to express the complexity of her personal identify as you reread? These are some of the ideas that may have occurred to you as you read and then reread.

DIRECTIONS: Answer the following questions, rereading as indicated.

1. Diana Chang ends her poem with the words "I'd rather say it / twice / yes." Reread the first four lines above. To what is the speaker saying "yes"? What do you think the deeper meaning of saying "yes" twice is?

   _____

   _____

2. Below is the opening line from "My Picture-Gallery." Consider your responses to the two statements within it. What do you picture when you read the first statement? How does your response to the second statement prepare you for the rest of the poem?

   In a little house I keep pictures suspended, it is not a fix'd house . . .

   _____

   _____

3. In the first half of "Dust of Snow," the speaker describes how a crow shook some snow onto him. In the second half, he describes how this action affected him. According to the speaker, the action

   Has given my heart / A change of mood / And saved some part / Of a day I have rued.

   Reread these lines several times. Then think about whether Frost's use of rhyme and rhythm is appropriate to the meaning of the poem. Why or why not?

   _____

   _____

"**Saying Yes**" by Diana Chang (text page 26)
"**My Picture-Gallery**" by Walt Whitman (text page 27)
"**Dust of Snow**" by Robert Frost (text page 28)

Literary Focus: Images in Poetry

Poets use **images**, words that appeal to the senses, to vividly re-create scenes and experiences. For example, the image of a hemlock tree in Robert Frost's "Dust of Snow" helps you see and smell a fresh outdoor scene on a winter day. Through imagery, poets also help readers understand the messages they are trying to communicate. Each image has its own special meaning within the poem.

The chart below shows how the image of the hemlock tree adds to the overall meaning of "Dust of Snow." Use this chart to explore other images in Frost's poem and in Walt Whitman's "My Picture-Gallery."

DIRECTIONS: For each image, note the senses that are involved. Then write a sentence or two about how the image helps you understand the meaning of the poem. The first one has been done as an example.

"Dust of Snow"		
Image	**Senses**	**Meaning in Poem**
1. Hemlock tree	sight, smell	This image suggests crispness and cheerfulness. It also suggests that nature has a refreshing quality.
2. Crow shaking snow onto speaker		

"My Picture-Gallery"		
Image	**Senses**	**Meaning in Poem**
3. A little house in which pictures are suspended		
4. A little house that is "not fix'd," round, only a few inches across, and can hold unlimited "shows" and memories		

"**Jeremiah's Song**" by Walter Dean Myers (text page 52)
"**Talent**" by Annie Dillard (text page 44)

Build Vocabulary

Using the Prefix: *dis-*

The prefix *dis-* means "the opposite of." When the prefix *dis-* is added to the beginning of a word, the new word means the opposite of the base word. For example, someone with a pleasant personality can be described as *agreeable*. A person who is not pleasant is *disagreeable*.

A. DIRECTIONS: Add the prefix *dis-* to each of the words below and write a sentence that uses the new word in the space provided. The first word has been done as an example.

		New Word	Sentence
1.	pleased	displeased	The displeased customer asked for his money back.
2.	order	_____	_____
3.	approve	_____	_____
4.	obey	_____	_____

Using the Word Bank

diagnosis	disinfect	precocious	uninspired	perpetual

B. DIRECTIONS: In the puzzle, write the words from the word bank that match the definitions below. The letters in the box will spell what some insects sometimes do.

1. not inspired 2. never stopping 3. unusually advanced 4. get rid of germs 5. medical decision

1. ___ ___ ___ ___ [ ] ___ ___ ___ ___ ___

2.   ___ ___ ___ ___ [ ] ___ ___ ___

3. ___ ___ ___ ___ [ ] ___ ___ ___ ___

4.   ___ ___ ___ ___ [ ] ___ ___ ___

5.   ___ ___ ___ [ ] ___ ___ ___

C. DIRECTIONS: Read each group of words. In the space provided, write the word from the word bank that fits in best with the words in the group.

1. matured, early-blooming, developed, _____

2. sterilize, clean, purify, _____

3. everlasting, eternal, constant, _____

4. boring, uninteresting, uncreative, _____

"Jeremiah's Song" by Walter Dean Myers (text page 52)
"Talent" by Annie Dillard (text page 44)

Build Spelling Skills: Adding Prefixes to Words

Spelling Strategy A prefix never changes the spelling of the word, even when the word begins with a vowel.

Examples: un- + inspired = uninspired / un- + necessary = unnecessary

dis- + interested = disinterested

A. Practice: Add the indicated prefix to each word. Write the new word on the line.

1. dis- + appear _____

2. dis- + honest _____

3. dis- + similar _____

4. dis- + connect _____

5. un- + prepared _____

6. un- + natural _____

7. un- + afraid _____

8. re- + enter _____

9. re- + heat _____

10. re- + inform _____

B. Practice: Complete the sentences below by adding the indicated prefix to each given word and writing each new word on the line.

1. Jeremiah's family is (un- + happy) _____ that he is ill.

2. He is so weak that he is (un- + able) _____ to do chores.

3. Ellie (dis- + trusts) _____ Dr. Crawford's medical opinions.

4. The boy thinks that Ellie (dis- + likes) Macon.

5. Grandpa Jeremiah (re- + tells) _____ his stories.

6. Ellie becomes (re- + acquainted) _____ with Macon.

Challenge: In the story, Dr. Crawford makes a *diagnosis* of Jeremiah's illness. The word *diagnosis* is formed from the prefix *dia-* and the ancient Greek word *gnosis*. One meaning for the prefix *dia-* is *completeness* or *thoroughness*. *Gnosis* means *knowledge*. Dr. Crawford's complete knowledge of Jeremiah's condition enables him to tell exactly what is wrong with him; that is, to make a *diagnosis*. Another medical term the author could have used in the selection is *prognosis*. The Greek prefix *pro-* means *before* or *beforehand*. When the doctor says that Jeremiah probably will not live long, he is making a *prognosis;* that is, a prediction, telling what will happen before it actually does happen. Many English words are based on one or more Greek words. Below is a list of words derived from Greek. The Greek words and their meanings are in parentheses. In the space next to each word, write the letter of the correct definition from the list of definitions on the right.

____ 1. biology (*bio* = life; *logy* = scientific study)

____ 2. tyrant (*tyrannos* = king)

____ 3. pharmacy (*pharmakon* = drug)

____ 4. philanthropist (*philos* = love; *anthropos* = human being)

a. powerful ruler

b. person who helps others

c. the study of animals

d. drugstore

"**Jeremiah's Song**" by Walter Dean Myers (text page 34)
"**Talent**" by Annie Dillard (text page 40)

Build Grammar Skills: Common and Proper Nouns

A **common noun** refers to any member of a group of people, places or things. For example, the word *composer* is a common noun. It refers to any person who composes, or writes music. *Mozart*, however, is a proper **noun**, because it refers to just one particular composer. Proper nouns always begin with a capital letter. If the proper noun is made up of two words, such as *Grandpa Jeremiah,* both words are capitalized. A common noun is not capitalized, unless it is the first word in a sentence or part of a title.

A. Practice: For each of the following sentences, indicate whether the underlined word is a common noun or a proper noun. In the space provided, write *C* for common noun or *P* for proper noun.

____ 1. He was a big <u>man</u> with a big head and had most all his hair, even if it was white.

____ 2. It rained the first three days of <u>August</u> .

____ 3. <u>Macon</u> sat slant-shouldered with his guitar across his lap.

____ 4. All the time Grandpa Jeremiah was talking, I could see Macon fingering his <u>guitar</u> .

____ 5. Apart from a few like Mozart, there never have been any great and accomplished little <u>children</u> in the world.

____ 6. If I had a little <u>baby</u> , it would be hard for me to rise up and feed that little baby in the middle of the night.

B. Writing Application: In each of the following sentences, you will find two errors in capitalization. Correct the errors on the lines below each sentence. The first sentence has been done as an example.

1. When Sister todd heard that Grandpa Jeremiah was ill, She became very upset.
   _____Todd_____   _____she_____

2. Annie dillard believes that Genius is very rare, and only a small number of people have it.
   _____   _____

3. Ellie goes to College in greensboro, North Carolina.
   _____   _____

4. The composer Mozart showed that he was a gifted Musician when he was a small Boy.
   _____   _____

5. The Doctor said that Grandpa jeremiah was very ill, and that he could only make him comfortable.
   _____   _____

6. Do you agree that enough education and hard work can make us all into great Writers and Artists?
   _____   _____

"Jeremiah's Song" by Walter Dean Myers (text page 34)
"Talent" by Annie Dillard (text page 40)

Reading Strategy: Context Clues

When you encounter an unfamiliar word while reading, you may not need a dictionary to learn its definition. There may be a hint in the *context*—the text just before and after the unknown word—that can help you figure out what the word means. The hint might be a word or phrase you do know, one that seems to have a similar meaning to the word you do not know. For example, in the following sentence from "Talent," the words following the word *discipline* contain a hint that could help you if you did not know what *discipline* means.

> People often ask me if I *discipline* myself to write, if I work a certain number of hours a day on a schedule.

Looking at the context, you can see that the word *discipline*, in this sentence, is connected to working "a certain number of hours a day on a schedule." A person who works this way makes rules for herself and follows them, so you know that *discipline*, in this sentence, means "work according to rules."

DIRECTIONS: Fill in the chart below to figure out the definitions of the italicized words in the following sentences. The first one has been done for you as an example.

1. Ellie thought that Dr. Crawford's medical knowledge was *obsolete* because he was out of touch with new developments in medicine.

2. Most people think that talent is *inherent* in great artists, but Annie Dillard does not believe that talent is an inborn gift.

3. Grandpa Jeremiah's illness had left him so *debilitated* that he was unable even to get out of bed.

4. Grandpa Jeremiah's *eerie* stories were enough to give you nightmares.

5. A writer who wishes to do good work must learn how to *persevere*, refusing to give up in spite of difficulties.

Unfamiliar Word	Context Clue	Definition
1. obsolete	"out of touch with new developments"	out of date
2.		
3.		
4.		
5.		

"Jeremiah's Song" by Walter Dean Myers (text page 34)
"Talent" by Annie Dillard (text page 40)

Literary Focus: First-Person Narrator

The **narrator** of a story is the teller of the story. Sometimes an author will use a character from the story as the narrator. That character calls herself or himself "I," and speaks directly to the reader, as if she or he were actually telling the story. Such a character is called **a first-person narrator**. It is important to remember that a first-person narrator does not know what other characters are thinking or planning, but only what those characters reveal through their words or actions. On the other hand, a first-person narrator can share with the reader private thoughts and feelings that only she or he would know. In "Jeremiah's Song," the first-person narrator is Grandpa Jeremiah's grandson. Referring to himself as "I," he tells you, the reader, what he, himself, thinks and feels. He also tells about events and actions he has experienced or heard about. In "Talent," the author acts as a first-person narrator. Annie Dillard refers to herself as "I," and communicates to the reader her inner thoughts and feelings about her work as a writer.

A. Directions: Show which of the following sentences is spoken by a first-person narrator by writing the letters *FP* on the line. Write an *X* on the line if the sentence is not spoken by a first-person narrator.

_____ 1. I was the one who loved Grandpa Jeremiah the most and she didn't hardly even know him so I didn't see why she was crying.

_____ 2. The boy loved Grandpa Jeremiah the most, and so he couldn't understand why people who hardly knew his grandfather would be crying.

_____ 3. All the time Grandpa Jeremiah was talking, the boy could see Macon fingering his guitar.

_____ 4. All the time Grandpa Jeremiah was talking, I could see Macon fingering his guitar.

_____ 5. The boy was glad when the rain finally stopped.

_____ 6. When the rain stopped, I was pretty glad.

B. Directions: In the space provided below, rewrite the following paragraph with the boy as the first-person narrator.

The boy sat by his grandfather's bed, listening to the old man's stories. He wondered if they were really true, but didn't ask. When he had asked in the past, his grandfather would just change the subject, so the boy didn't bother any more. The room was hot, and the boy felt perspiration trickle down his back. He could hear birds chirping outside and wished for a breeze. He thought about being old, and not being able to work or run around. He heard a knock on the door and Macon came in with a guitar. He was glad to see Macon, who smiled at him.

_____

_____

_____

_____

_____

Build Vocabulary

Using Forms of *fragile*

Recognizing different forms of a word can help expand your vocabulary. If you recognize the word *fragile*, an adjective meaning "easily broken or damaged," you may be able to figure out the word *fragility*, a noun meaning "the state of being fragile."

A. DIRECTIONS: Use the given form of *fragile* in a sentence of your own.

1. fragile: _____

_____

2. fragility: _____

_____

Using Words from the Selection

The words *parasite* and *fragile* are defined for you in the selection. Here are definitions of two other words from the selection:

technique	a specialized method used to accomplish something
fracture	a break, as in a bone

B. DIRECTIONS: Each of the following questions consists of a related pair of words in CAPITAL LETTERS, followed by four lettered pairs of words or phrases. Choose the lettered pair that best expresses a relationship similar to the one expressed in the pair in capital letters.

____ 1. TECHNIQUE : METHOD ::
    a. education : school
    b. road : map
    c. writing : pencil
    d. skill : ability

____ 2. FRACTURE : HEAL ::
    a. cloth : clothing
    b. rip : mend
    c. cut : bandage
    d. funny : laugh

____ 3. FRAGILE : STRONG ::
    a. broken : muscular
    b. calm : excited
    c. jump : pounce
    d. unfinished : fixed

____ 4. PARASITE : GUINEA WORM ::
    a. flea : dog
    b. catterpillar : butterfly
    c. dog : poodle
    d. flu : germ

C. DIRECTIONS: On the line, write the letter of the word that is closest in meaning to the numbered word.

____ 1. parasite
    a. organism
    b. umbrella
    c. bandage
    d. sailboat

____ 2. fragile
    a. skillful
    b. weak
    c. painful
    d. torn

____ 3. fracture
    a. factory
    b. part
    c. break
    d. section

____ 4. technique
    a. history
    b. study
    c. method
    d. mechanism

"Mummy No. 1771" by Patricia Lauber (text page 47)

Connect Nonfiction to Social Studies

Scientists who "dig up the past" are called *archaeologists.* They dig up ancient buildings, tools, and other objects and treat the things they find as clues to the lives of the people who made and used them. The findings and interpretations of archaeologists have given us valuable information about cultures of long ago. In fact, we owe much of what we know of ancient Egypt—religion, social customs, hairstyles and clothing, political structure, and more—from archaeological "detective work," such as that described in the selection, "Mummy No. 1770."

DIRECTIONS: Read the following quotations from "Mummy No. 1770," and answer the questions on the lines provided. The first one has been done for you.

1. What can we learn about the culture of ancient Egypt from this fact?

    . . . The hands had gold fingertip covers . . .

    The ancient Egyptians knew how to mine gold and knew how to make things out of it. Also, they

    probably considered gold valuable.

    Why do you think so? They were able to make fingertip covers out of gold. They used gold

    to cover the fingertip of a person who was probably important or from a royal family.

2. What can we learn about the culture of ancient Egypt from this fact?

    The inner organs had been removed . . .

    _____

    _____

    Why do you think so? _____

    _____

3. What can we learn about the culture of ancient Egypt from this fact?

    A small, hard object that had appeared in the x-rays proved to be a Guinea worm,
    a parasite that is taken in with drinking water.

    _____

    _____

    Why do you think so? _____

    _____

4. What can we learn about the culture of ancient Egypt from this fact?

    At times in ancient Egypt royal mummies were moved to new tombs. If they had been
    damaged, they were reparied at the time of the move.

    _____

    _____

    Why do you think so? _____

    _____

Build Vocabulary

Using the Suffix -or

The suffix -or at the end of a word indicates "a person or thing that does something."
For example, a person who *acts* is called an *actor*.

A. Directions: In the space provided, write the new word formed by adding the suffix -or to each of the following words. Then write a sentence using each word.

1. edit + -or = _____   4. profess + -or = _____

2. direct + -or = _____   5. sail + -or = _____

3. govern + -or = _____

6. _____

7. _____

8. _____

9. _____

10. _____

Using the Word Bank

toil	endured	prospectors	liable
poising	declined	summit	

B. Directions: Circle the letter of the description that best fits each word in CAPITAL LETTERS.

1. PROSPECTORS: a. people who work in factories   b. people who look for gold
   c. people who explore caves   d. people who climb mountains

2. TOIL: a. practice   b. rest   c. work   d. amusement

3. SUMMIT: a. top   b. crack   c. largest part   d. deep valley

4. DECLINED: a. took away   b. refused   c. rested   d. leaned to one side

5. LIABLE: a. useful   b. breakable   c. careful   d. likely

6. POISING: a. balancing   b. stopping   c. smiling   d. expressing

7. ENDURED: a. claimed to own   b. felt   c. suffered through   d. hardened

Recognizing Antonyms

C. Directions: Circle the letter of the word or phrase that is most nearly *opposite* in meaning to the word in CAPITAL LETTERS.

1. DECLINED: a. accepted   b. climbed up   c. stood up straight   d. refused

2. SUMMIT: a. beginning   b. middle   c. bottom   d. worst

"The King of Mazy May" by Jack London (text page 60)

Build Spelling Skills: Spelling the *oy* Sound

Spelling Strategy Whenever the *oy* sound occurs in the middle of a one-syllable word, spell the sound with the letters *oi*. Whenever the *oy* sound occurs at the end of a word, spell the sound with the letters *oy*.

Examples: poise (*oy* sound in middle)   boy (*oy* sound at end)

A. Practice: Complete each of the following words correctly using *oi* or *oy*.

1. ann____   2. c____n   3. j____   4. n____se   5. destr____   6. p____sing

B. Practice: Correct the misspelled italicized words in the following paragraph. Write a C in the blank if the word is spelled correctly.

Although Walt was still a *boi* _____ he was able to *spoyl* _____ the plans of the men who tried to jump the claims of the prospectors near his camp. The men planned to *destroy* _____ the stakes that marked the claims and take the claims for themselves. He did not want those men to *enjoi* _____ the wealth that others had *toiled* _____ for. Walt knew that there was nobody nearby to *joyn* _____ him in stopping these men, so he would have to act on his own.

Challenge: When Walt wants the dogs to begin pulling the sled, he shouts to them, "Mush!" and "Mush on!" You may know that the word *mush* in this context means, "Go!" However, you may be surprised to learn that the word comes from the French word *marchons* meaning, "Let's go!" The English word *march* comes from the same French word. Many English words are derived from French. Match each French word on the left with the English word derived from it on the right. Then, use each English word in a sentence. **Hint:** If necessary, use a dictionary to find the precise meaning of each English word.

____ 1. *chanter* (French for *sing*)   a. solely

____ 2. *arbre* (French for *tree*)   b. chant

____ 3. *beauté* (French for *beauty*)   c. fortify

____ 4. *fort* (French for *strong*)   d. beautiful

____ 5. *seul* (French for *only*)   e. arbor

6. _____

7. _____

8. _____

9. _____

10. _____

Name _____ Date _____

Build Grammar Skills: Pronouns and Antecedents

A **pronoun** is a word that takes the place of a noun or another pronoun. Common pronouns include *I, my, mine, you, your, yours, he, she, her, him, his, hers, it, its, we, us, ours, they, them, theirs, myself, ourselves, yourself, yourselves, itself, himself, herself,* and *themselves.* The **antecedent** of a pronoun is the noun or other pronoun to which the pronoun refers. Pronouns are useful because they make writing less repetitious.

Examples:

Walt saw eighteen dogs, and Walt chose ten of the best of the dogs.

Walt saw eighteen dogs, and he chose ten of the best of them.

Notice that the first sentence is repetitious. In the second sentence, however, the second occurrences of *Walt* and *dogs* have been replaced by pronouns, eliminating the repetition and making the sentence smoother. In the second sentence, *Walt* is the antecedent of *he,* and *dogs* is the antecedent of *them.*

A. Practice: In the following sentences, the pronouns are in italics. Draw an arrow from each pronoun to its antecedent, and underline the antecedent. The first sentence has been done for you.

1. When the claim-jumpers saw Walt, *they* ran after *him.*

2. Walt went to the men's camp, where *he* picked out the best of *their* sleds.

3. When the dogs heard Walt call to *them, they* raced away through the snow.

4. The sled bounced and slid along the trail, which made *it* hard to hold on to.

5. The Mazy May had followed a twisting course for miles, but *it* finally straightened out.

6. Because Walt was so brave, the miners called *him* the "King of Mazy May."

B. Writing Application: Rewrite each of the following sentences on the lines provided, replacing the repeated noun or nouns with the correct pronoun. The first sentence has been done for you.

1. By the time Walt was fourteen years old, Walt knew how to take care of Walt.

   By the time Walt was fourteen years old, he knew how to take care of himself.

2. As soon as the claim-jumpers reached their sled, the claim-jumpers began chasing Walt.

   _____

3. Walt saw the river in the distance, but the river was too wide for Walt to see the other bank.

   _____

4. The Klondike country attracted thousands hoping to make their fortunes, but the Klondike country proved to be harsh and dangerous territory.

   _____

5. The dogs ran faster when the dogs knew the right one was leading the dogs.

   _____

"The King of Mazy May" by Jack London (text page 60)

Reading Strategy: Recognize Signal Words

As you read, watch for signal words, such as *but, so,* and *on account of*. They are clues that tell you how one part of a passage relates to another part. For example, look at the following sentence from the selection:

Loren Hall was an old man, and he had no dogs, so he had to travel very slowly.

In the sentence above, *so* is a signal word that tells you that what happens in the last part of the sentence is the effect of what happens in the first part. What happens in the first part of the sentence is the cause. In other words, the fact that Loren Hall had to travel very slowly is the effect of his being an old man and having no dogs. Some other signal words and phrases that show cause and effect are *for* and *because*.

DIRECTIONS: Find the signal word or phrase in each of the following sentences. Then fill in the chart below. The first row in the chart has been filled in as an example.

1. Walt wanted to stop the men from taking away Loren Hall's claim because he knew that stealing was wrong.

2. Walt Masters's father had recorded his claim at the start, so Walt had nothing to fear.

3. Evidently the men had agreed with their leader, for Walt Masters could hear nothing but the rattle of the tin dishes that were being washed.

4. The sled almost tipped over on account of the curving trail and the inexperience of the lead dog.

5. The men would be returning to their camp soon, so Walt did not have much time.

6. Walt knew a lot about sleds and dogs, for he had lived around them all his life.

Signal Word or Phrase	Cause	Effect
7. because	he knew that stealing was wrong	Walt wanted to stop the men from taking away Loren Hall's claim
8.		
9.		
10.		
11.		
12.		

Name _____ Date _____

"The King of Mazy May" by Jack London (text page 60)

Literary Focus: Conflict Between Characters

In "The King of Mazy May," a group of men plans to steal another man's property. Walt Masters, who is only a young boy, is determined to stop them. This is the **conflict**, or struggle, that gives the story its tension and suspense. You, the reader, know that one side will win out in the end; the other will be defeated. As you read, you cheer for Walt because his thoughts and actions are good, kind, and honest. You root against the thieves because they think and act in an evil, cruel, and dishonest way. Often, in literature, as in this story, the conflict between characters is really a conflict between good and evil. Being aware of and understanding the conflict between characters in a story will increase your reading enjoyment.

DIRECTIONS: The following sentences from "The King of Mazy May" refer to either good or evil characters, thoughts, or actions. Under the appropriate headings, write the words in each sentence that let you know whether the sentence refers to the good or evil side of the conflict in the story. The first sentence has been done as an example.

	GOOD	EVIL
1. Last of all, he has a good heart, and is not afraid of the darkness and loneliness, of man or beast or thing.	he has a good heart	
2. But with the news of their discoveries, strange men began to come and go through the short days and long nights, and many unjust things they did to the men who had worked so long upon the creek.		
3. Yet, with the quickness of a cat, he had clutched the end of the sled with one hand, turned over, and was dragging behind on his breast, swearing at the boy and threatening all sorts of terrible things if he did not stop the dogs.		
4. In short, it was the old story, and quite a number of the earnest, industrious prospectors had suffered similar losses.		
5. They took greater care, and shot at him at the most favorable opportunities.		
6. He was only a boy, but in the face of the threatened injustice to old lame Loren Hall he felt that he must do something.		

© Prentice-Hall, Inc.

"Books Fall Open" by David McCord (text page 72)
"O to Be Up and Doing" by Robert Louis Stevenson (text page 73)
"Change" by Charlotte Zolotow (text page 74)

Build Vocabulary

Using the Prefix *un-*

The prefix *un-* means "not." This prefix reverses the meaning of words to which it is added. For example, the word *dissuaded* means "discouraged." The word *undissuaded*, which appears in the Word Bank, means "not discouraged."

A. DIRECTIONS: Add the prefix *un-* to each underlined word so that the following statements make sense. Write the revised sentences on the lines.

1. Harriet tripped and fell because her shoelace was <u>tied</u>.

   _____

2. Fortunately, she was <u>hurt</u>, and got up as if nothing had happened.

   _____

3. It's a good thing that she was walking in a relaxed and <u>hurried</u> manner when the mishap occurred.

   _____

Using the Word Bank

delver	venture	undissuaded	summons	crimson

B. DIRECTIONS: Answer each question with a word from the Word Bank. Write your answers on the lines.

1. Which word would you use to describe a fiery sunset? _____

2. Which word would you use to describe someone who likes to get to the bottom of something? _____

3. Which word would you use to describe a person who works for a cause even though other people tell him it's useless? _____

4. What would you do if you were willing to take a chance? _____

5. What would a person receive if she were called to appear in court? _____

Recognizing Antonyms

C. DIRECTIONS: Circle the letter of the word or phrase that is most nearly *opposite* in meaning to the word in CAPITAL LETTERS.

1. VENTURE: a. go forth   b. risk   c. prove   d. shrink from

2. SUMMONS: a. calls   b. adds to   c. dismisses   d. repeats

"Books Fall Open" by David McCord (text page 72)
"O to Be Up and Doing" by Robert Louis Stevenson (text page 73)
"Change" by Charlotte Zolotow (text page 74)

Build Spelling Skills: Double Consonants in Two-Syllable Words

Spelling Strategy When you spell most two-syllable words that contain a consonant sound in the middle and the vowel before the consonant has a short sound, double the consonant.

Examples: cattle   better   tissue   follow   puppy

A. Practice: Correct the misspelled italicized words in the following paragraph. If a word is correct, write C on the line.

This morning, we had breakfast at a nearby *diner* (1) _____. I ordered

wafles (2) _____, but Lucy ordered the *baccon* (3) _____-

and-egg special. It came on a large *plater* (4) _____ with fried potatoes

and *butered* (5) _____ toast. I said that the restaurant should *label*

(6) _____ the fat content of the special. After swallowing her last bite,

Lucy declared she'd have only salad for *super* (7) _____.

B. Practice: In the following sentences, correct the each misspelled italicized word by doubling the middle consonant. If the word is not misspelled, write C on the line.

1. David McCord celebrates the wonders *writen* _____ down in books.

2. What secrets have you found *hiden* _____ in the pages of a good book?

3. What facts, tips, and practical *maters* _____ can you learn about in a library?

4. A history book may unlock the mysteries of ancient *mumies* _____.

5. A science book may tell you about *radon* _____ gas or a certain snake's *ratle* _____.

6. You might look up the way to *padle* _____ a canoe or *pilot* _____ a small plane.

Challenge: The word *crimson* from the Word Bank means "deep red." It is one of hundreds of words that we use to name the many variations of basic colors such as red, blue, yellow, green, and brown. Here are more examples of words that name colors.

amber aqua chartreuse coral emerald magenta mauve violet turquoise vermillion

DIRECTIONS: For each topic given below, write a sentence that includes one or more of the color words in the above list. Check a dictionary to discover the shade of any colors that are unfamiliar to you. One example is provided.

1. (lilac bushes) The lilac bushes in the park ranged from pale mauve to deep magenta. _____

2. (grass) _____

3. (mountain lake) _____

4. (fiery summer sunset) _____

5. (maple syrup) _____

Name _____ Date _____

"Books Fall Open" by David McCord (text page 72)
"O to Be Up and Doing" by Robert Louis Stevenson (text page 73)
"Change" by Charlotte Zolotow (text page 74)

Build Grammar Skills: Interrogative Pronouns

What happened? Who was that? Which is correct? When you want to ask about something, you use special sentences called questions and special words called interrogative pronouns.

Interrogative pronouns are pronouns that introduce questions. The main interrogative pronouns are *who* (or *whose* or *whom*), *which*, and *what*.

Look at the following sentences. Which word in each one is an interrogative pronoun?

Which book have you selected?   To whom will you give it?
Who suggested that you select that one?   What will you write on the card?

In these sentences, the interrogative pronouns are *which, who, whom,* and *what.*

A. Practice: Choose the correct interrogative pronoun to complete each sentence.

1. (What, Who) _____ sorts of adventures do you dream of?

2. With (which, whom) _____ would you share your escapades?

3. If your imagined adventure were made into a movie, (what, why) _____ would the title be?

4. (Whom, What) _____ do you envision in the starring role?

5. (Who, Whose) _____ has been your most important role model?

6. (What, Which) _____ has this person done to inspire you?

7. (Whom, Which) _____ would you rather be—an explorer or a detective?

B. Writing Application: Read the following information about Robert Louis Stevenson. Then write a question about each topic suggested below, using the interrogative pronoun given.

The works of Robert Louis Stevenson appeal to readers of all ages. *A Child's Garden of Verses* is a collection of charming and simple poems that children and parents enjoy reading aloud. *Treasure Island* and *Kidnapped* are classic adventure stories popular with young adults. Stevenson's thriller, *The Strange Case of Doctor Jekyll and Mr. Hyde*, the story of a good man who becomes an evil fiend when he takes a mysterious potion, has intrigued both adult and young adult readers for over a hundred years.

1. Write a question about *The Strange Case of Dr. Jekyll and Mr. Hyde*, using the interrogative pronoun *who, whose,* or *whom.*

   _____

2. Write a question about *A Child's Garden of Verses* using the interrogative pronoun *what.*

   _____

3. Write a question about *Kidnapped* and *Treasure Island* using the interrogative pronoun *which.*

   _____

Name _____ Date _____

"**Books Fall Open**" by David McCord (text page 72)
"**O to Be Up and Doing**" by Robert Louis Stevenson (text page 73)
"**Change**" by Charlotte Zolotow (text page 74)

Reading Strategy: Read According to Punctuation

Punctuation marks are like familiar landmarks. They can help you find your way around a poem. A particular punctuation mark may signal that it's time to stop, take a long pause, take a short pause, or ask a question. Here are the functions of some of the most common punctuation marks:

Period (.) and Exclamation Mark (!) = FULL STOP

Comma (,) = PAUSE

Dash (—) and Semicolon (;) = LONG PAUSE

Question Mark (?) = ASK

A. DIRECTIONS: Answer the following questions about this excerpt from "Books Fall Open." Use the chart on this page as a reference.

Books fall open,	hear voices not	find unexpected
you fall in,	once heard before,	keys to things
delighted where	reach world on world	locked up beyond
you've never been;	through door on door;	imaginings.

1. After which words would you make a long pause? *Hint: Remember that you don't pause just because you come to the end of a line.* _____

2. After which words would you come to a shorter pause? _____

3. After which word or words would you come to a full stop? _____

B. DIRECTIONS: Answer these questions about this excerpt from "O to Be Up and Doing."

With voiceless call, the ancient earth

Summons me to a daily birth,

Thou, O my love, ye, O my friends—

The gist of life, the end of ends—

To laugh, to love, to die

Ye call me by the ear and eye!

1. Read the third and fourth lines quietly to yourself. What should you do after the words *friends* and *ends*?

_____

2. Should you pause after the words *earth* and *die*? Why or why not?

_____

Name _____ Date _____

"Books Fall Open" by David McCord (text page 72)
"O to Be Up and Doing" by Robert Louis Stevenson (text page 73)
"Change" by Charlotte Zolotow (text page 74)

Literary Focus: Word Choice

To get an important message across, you would choose your words carefully. For example, if you were writing a thank-you note or asking your mother if you could adopt a pet, you would choose words that are right for the situation, and that would help you achieve your purpose.

In a similar way, poets are careful about **word choice**. They select words with exactly the right sound and meaning so that readers can experience the scenes and grasp the ideas they have in mind. Notice how well the word *delver* works in these lines from "Books Fall Open."

> What might you be, / perhaps become, / because one book / is somewhere? Some /
> wise delver into wisdom, wit, / and wherewithal / has written it.

Delver, meaning "digger," helps to convey the richness that is found in books. Because the word is unusual, it also helps to make the sound of these lines more memorable.

A. DIRECTIONS: Answer the following questions about word choice in the poems.

1. In these lines from "O to Be Up and Doing," what do the words *uproar* and *press* mean? How do they help you picture a particular scene?

> O to be up and doing, / Unfearing and unashamed to go /
> In all the uproar and the press / About my human business!

_____

_____

2. Read the following lines from "Change." Then reread them, substituting the word *occurs* for the word *hangs*. Why is *hangs* a better choice?

> The summer / still hangs / heavy and sweet / with sunlight / as it did last year.

_____

_____

B. DIRECTIONS: Identify a word in the following lines from "Books Fall Open" that you think is an example of good word choice. Explain why you think the word works well within the passage.

> True books will venture,
> dare you out,
> whisper secrets,
> maybe shout,
> across the gloom
> to you in need,
> who hanker for
> a book to read.

_____

_____

_____

"**The Circuit**" by Francisco Jiménez (text page 80)
"**Hard as Nails**" by Russell Baker (text page 86)

Build Vocabulary

Using Compound Nouns

A **compound noun** is a noun that is made up of at least two words, such as *milkshake*.

A. DIRECTIONS: Use the following compound words from "The Circuit" and "Hard as Nails" to complete the paragraph below.

outside   overturning   backbone   doorstep   necktie   salesman   doorbell

The inexperienced _____, who didn't have much

_____ for his job, stood on the _____

_____ the house. Nervously, he straightened his _____

and rang the _____. When no one answered; he heaved a sigh of relief

and hurried back to his car, _____ a flower-pot along the way.

Using the Word Bank

drone	instinctively	savoring	embedded
exhaust	sublime	drawbacks	immense

B. DIRECTIONS: On the blanks, write the Word Bank word that matches each description.

1. _____ the sound that bees make

2. _____ very large

3. _____ the way you do something without having to think about it

4. _____ to use up

5. _____ disadvantages

6. _____ enjoying the taste of, relishing

7. _____ firmly fixed in the surrounding material

8. _____ wonderful, causing awe

Recognizing Synonyms

C. DIRECTIONS: On the line, write the letter of the word that is closest in meaning to the word in CAPITAL LETTERS.

____ 1. IMMENSE: a. angry   b. huge   c. difficult   d. messy

____ 2. EXHAUST: a. soak   b. work   c. enlarge   d. use up

____ 3. DRAWBACKS: a. disadvantages   b. handles   c. explanations   d. excuses

____ 4. SUBLIME: a. wonderful   b. funny   c. complicated   d. dull

____ 5. EMBEDDED: a. enlarged   b. cut in pieces   c. firmly planted   d. tied up

"The Circuit" by Francisco Jiménez (text page 80)
"Hard as Nails" by Russell Baker (text page 86)

Build Spelling Skills: Spelling Compound Nouns

Spelling Strategy To spell most compound nouns, combine the words from which they are formed into a single word.

Examples: draw + backs = drawbacks   gold + fish = goldfish

Exception: Some compound nouns use hyphens to link the words from which they are formed, and others are written as separate words.

Examples: brother-in-law   home run

A. Practice: On the lines provided, write the compound noun formed by combining each of the following pairs of words into one word. The first one has been done as an example.

1. ear + ring = _____earring_____

2. eye + lash = _____

3. dish + washer = _____

4. fire + place = _____

5. green + house = _____

6. smoke + stack = _____

B. Practice: Complete each of the following sentences by combining the words in parentheses and writing the resulting compound noun in the space provided.

1. Roberto in "The Circuit" wishes to be an ordinary (school + boy) _____.

2. But he is forced to begin work at (sun + rise) _____ each morning.

3. Instead of doing (home + work) _____, he spends his days picking grapes.

4. He cannot join other children while they have fun on the (play + ground) _____.

5. He does the same work as his father and (grand + father) _____ before him.

Challenge: In "The Circuit," Roberto calls his younger brother "Panchito." The father calls the family car "Carcanchita." In Spanish, the ending -*ito* or -*ita* is often added to a word to form an affectionate nickname. These endings, in Spanish, mean "little." A masculine word or name usually ends with the letter *o*, and a feminine word or name usually ends with the letter *a*. A family with a boy named Pablo is likely to call him Pablito, dropping the final *o*, and adding the ending -*ito*. If they have a girl named Teresa, they may call her Teresita, dropping the final *a*, and adding the ending -*ita*. In the space provided, write the Spanish nickname that can be made from each of the following names. Keep in mind that the names ending in *o* are masculine, and those ending in *a* are feminine.

1. Pedro _____

2. Carla _____

3. Sancho _____

4. Juana _____

5. Carmela _____

6. Manuelo _____

"The Circuit" by Francisco Jiménez (text page 80)
"Hard as Nails" by Russell Baker (text page 86)

Build Grammar Skills: Personal Pronouns

The following words are **personal pronouns**:

I, me, my, mine	he, him, his	she, her, hers
you, your, yours	we, us, our, ours	they, them, their, theirs

In a sentence, you can use a personal pronoun instead of a common or proper noun to refer to a person. For example, the second occurrence of the proper noun *Russ* in the first sentence below has been replaced by the personal pronoun *he* in the second sentence.

Russ's mother thought that *Russ* should have a job after school.

Russ's mother thought that *he* should have a job after school.

The second sentence sounds better than the first one, because using the pronoun *he* eliminates the repetition of the proper noun *Russ*.

One personal pronoun can replace more than one word. In the following example, notice that the words *the boy and his brother* in the first sentence have been replaced by the personal pronoun *they* in the second sentence:

The boy and his brother couldn't go to school because the boy and his brother had to work.

The boy and his brother couldn't go to school because they had to work.

A. Practice: Find the personal pronoun in each sentence; then write it in the space provided. Finally, underline the noun to which the pronoun refers. The first sentence has been done for you.

his 1. <u>Panchito</u> helped his father put the family's belongings in the car.

_____ 2. When Mama was ready, Papa helped her put the pot of beans in the car.

_____ 3. Mrs. Baker said that she did not see why children under twelve could not work.

_____ 4. The boys had to pick up their newspapers in front of Wisengoff's store.

_____ 5. Mr. Deems took some boys downtown and showed them the newsroom.

_____ 6. Russell watched the other people at the banquet to see how they ate.

B. Writing Application: Rewrite each of the following sentences on the line provided, replacing the italicized words with a personal pronoun. The first sentence has been done for you.

1. The younger children were happy that *the younger children* were moving.
   The younger children were happy that *they* were moving.
   _____

2. Panchito envied the other children when he watched *the other children* get off the school bus.

   _____

3. The man gave Mama work and showed *Mama* where the family would live.

   _____

4. Mrs. Baker wanted Russell to get a job because *Mrs. Baker* needed money.

   _____

"The Circuit" by Francisco Jiménez (text page 80)
"Hard as Nails" by Russell Baker (text page 86)

Reading Strategy: Break Down Long Sentences

All sentences contain a subject and a key idea about the subject. If you have trouble grasping the meaning of a long, complicated sentence, make the sentence easier to understand by breaking down the sentence into simple parts. First, identify the subject; then find the key idea. For example, look at the following sentence from "The Circuit."

> A few minutes later, the yelling and screaming of my little brothers and sisters, for whom the move was a great adventure, broke the silence of dawn.

To break this sentence down into simple parts, first find the subject. Here, the subject—what the sentence is about—is "the yelling and screaming of my little brothers and sisters." Next, find the key idea. Ask yourself questions such as the following: "What does the sentence say about the yelling and screaming?" "What did the yelling and screaming do?" "What effect did it have?" The sentence tells you that the yelling and screaming "broke the silence of dawn." You have now broken down the long, complicated sentence into a short, simple one: "The yelling and screaming of my little brothers and sisters broke the silence of dawn."

DIRECTIONS: In each of the following sentences from the selection, find the subject and the key idea. Then write them in the appropriate columns in the chart below. In the third column of the chart, combine the subject and key idea into a single short, simple sentence. The information for the first sentence has been written in the chart as an example.

1. That night, by the light of a kerosene lamp, we unpacked and cleaned our new home.

2. Slung around one shoulder and across the chest, the belt made it easy to balance fifteen or twenty pounds of papers against the hip.

3. I'd heard her talk of "a home of our own" all through those endless Depression years when we lived as poor relatives dependent on Uncle Allen's goodness.

4. When I solved the problem of the five extras by getting five new subscribers for home delivery, Deems announced a competition with mouth-watering prizes for the newsboys who got the most new subscribers.

SUBJECT	KEY IDEA	SHORT SENTENCE
1. we	unpacked and cleaned our new home	We unpacked and cleaned our new home.
2.		
3.		
4.		

"The Circuit" by Francisco Jiménez (text page 80)
"Hard as Nails" by Russell Baker (text page 86)

Literary Focus: Theme

A story usually has a **theme**, or central idea; it may be a thought or a belief about life that the story suggests. In many stories, such as "The Circuit" or "Hard as Nails," the author does not state the central idea directly but gives readers clues that they can use to figure it out. The clues may be found in the title of the story, in descriptions and explanations provided by the author, or in words spoken by the characters.

DIRECTIONS: For each of the following paragraphs, write the theme on the appropriate line. On the other lines, write three details from the paragraph that helped you to grasp the idea.

1. Whenever a school bus stopped near a field where Panchito was working, he had to hide. The law said that a boy of Panchito's age should be in school, but his family needed the money he earned working in the fields. From his hiding place he would watch enviously as the other children got on or off the bus, carrying their books and talking happily. Francisco had been to school. He had gone to several schools during the short periods of time when there was no farm work for him to do. He thought he could be a good student because he learned quickly and he enjoyed reading. But a boy did not get paid for going to school. So, after riding on a school bus for a few days, hoping to make some friends, Panchito would come home to find his family packing to leave once again.

Central Idea:

_____

Clues:

a. _____

b. _____

c. _____

2. Russell Baker was only twelve years old when he went into newspaper work. Baker did not mind having to work at the age of twelve; he was proud to be able to help his mother and sister by bringing some money home. Being a newsboy was not easy work. A newsboy had to get up very early in the morning, make deliveries in all kinds of weather, and constantly find ways to sell more papers. For four years, he sold newspapers, doubling the number of his subscribers. Over the years since that time, Russell Baker has remained in the newspaper business, becoming an award-winning columnist whose writing is read by millions. He is still proud of being in the newspaper business.

Central Idea:

_____

Clues:

a. _____

b. _____

c. _____

"How to Write a Letter" by Garrison Keillor (text page 107)

Build Vocabulary

Using the Suffix *-ory*

The suffix *–ory*, which means "having the quality or nature of," turns a noun into an adjective. Something that is *obligatory* has the quality or nature of an *obligation*. Here are some other examples:

satisfaction	⟶	satisfactory
explanation	⟶	explanatory
migration	⟶	migratory
preparation	⟶	preparatory

A. DIRECTIONS: Complete each sentence with one of the above words ending in *-ory*.

1. Sandy traveled to South America to complete her study of _____ songbirds.

2. Elena plans to take some _____ courses before applying to medical school.

3. Mike was relieved to see that he had received a _____ score in the competition.

4. There are no directions for filling out this form because everything is self- _____ .

Using the Word Bank

confidence	anonymity	obligatory
episode	sibling	

B. DIRECTIONS: Use each of the Word Bank words in a sentence according to the instructions given.

1. Use *confidence* in a sentence about the members of a basketball team.

   _____

2. Use *anonymity* in a sentence about a movie star.

   _____

3. Use *obligatory* in a sentence about everyday chores.

   _____

4. Use *episode* in a sentence about a letter.

   _____

5. Use *sibling* in a sentence about your family or someone else's family.

   _____

"How to Write a Letter" by Garrison Keillor (text page 107)

Build Spelling Skills: Words That End in *ence*

Spelling Strategy The *ens* sound at the end of words is often—but not always—spelled *ence* as it is in the Word Bank word *confidence*. Because the *ens* sound can be spelled in different ways, you may need to memorize the spelling of words that end in *ence*. Here are some other words in which the *ens* sound at the end is spelled *ence*.

intelligence	evidence	experience	occurrence	preference
residence	permanence	absence	correspondence	

A. Practice: Fill in each blank with a form of the underlined word ending in *ence*.

1. Ms. Waters was <u>confident</u> that we would raise enough money to buy new uniforms. Her _____ was reassuring.

2. <u>Evidently</u>, a crime had been committed. Therefore, the detective began to collect _____ .

3. I can understand why you would <u>prefer</u> to see Sam rather than Tony as class president. Just make sure that you express your _____ by voting.

4. Of course, my dog Sparky is <u>intelligent</u>. In fact, I think that he shows above-average _____

B. Practice: Complete the sentences by adding *ence* to each word part in parentheses. Write the new words on the lines.

1. Writing letters can be a wonderful (experi) _____ .

2. A letter from a far-away friend can make up for the person's (abs) _____ .

3. You can tell your friend about any (occurr) _____ , big or small.

4. The Postal Service delivers letters to your (resid) _____ daily.

Challenge: The word *anonymity* from the Word Bank means "the condition of being a stranger, not known by name." *Anonymity* is formed from a combination of the word root *-nym-*, meaning "name," the prefix *an-*, which means "without," and the suffix *–ity*, which means "state or condition." Here are two other words that contain the word root *-nym-*.

anonymous: given or written by a person whose name is unknown

pseudonym: a fictitious, or made-up, name used by an author

DIRECTIONS: Complete the following sentences using the word *anonymous* or the word *pseudonym*. Use each word once. Write your answers on the lines.

1. Mark Twain, the _____ of Samuel Clemens, is one of the most famous names in American literature.

2. Because no one knows who wrote this poem, the editors listed the author as "_____" in the table of contents.

"How to Write a Letter" by Garrison Keillor (text page 107)

Build Grammar Skills: Verbs

A **verb** is a word that shows an action, a condition, or existence. Look at the following sentences from Garrison Keillor's essay. The verbs are underlined. To be sure if a word is a verb, you can ask yourself if you can change it to show differences in time.

So a shy person <u>sits</u> down and <u>writes</u> a letter.

Few letters <u>are</u> obligatory.

<u>Remember</u> the last time you <u>saw</u> each other and how your friend <u>looked</u> and what you <u>said</u> and what perhaps <u>was</u> unsaid between you.

In the examples above, the verbs *sits, writes, remember, saw,* and *said* show action. The verbs *are, looked,* and *was* show a condition or existence.

A. Practice: Identify the verbs in the following sentences. Write the verbs on the lines provided. The first one has been done as an example.

1. When you write, Keillor advises, be sincere. _____ write, advises, be _____

2. According to Garrison Keillor, letters are a gift. _____

3. Shy people escape from anonymity when they write to others. _____

4. Some letters thank people, some invite people over, and some inform people of important events in our lives. _____

5. Instead, think of a friend, and imagine a conversation between the two of you.
_____

6. Start with a simple sentence and then let one thought lead to another. _____

7. If you make a mistake, just plunge ahead. _____

B. Writing Application: Write a sentence about each topic provided below, using the verb or verbs given.

1. Write a sentence about Garrison Keillor, using the verbs *write* and *tell.*
_____

2. Write a sentence about the essay "How to Write a Letter," using the verb *describe.*
_____

3. Write a sentence about the weather, using verbs that show existence, such as *is, was, seems, looks.*
_____

4. Write a sentence that states your opinion about something, using the verb *think.*
_____

5. Write a sentence about what you did last week, using three verbs that show action.
_____

Unit 2: Reaching Out

Reading for Success: Literal Comprehension Strategies

The first step in understanding a work of literature is to grasp its literal meaning—the basic facts and details the author is communicating. Apply the following strategies to understand the literal meaning of the selection.

- **Apply word identification strategies.** Divide unfamiliar words into syllables to find familiar word parts.

- **Paraphrase.** Restate a sentence or paragraph in your own words to be sure you understand it.

- **Envision.** Use details that the author provides to help you picture in your own mind the places, people, and events in a piece of writing. Try to experience sounds, tastes, smells, and physical sensations, as well.

- **Summarize.** Pause occasionally as you read to think about and sum up the main points or events in the work.

DIRECTIONS: Read the following passage from "Lakshmi" by Vasanthi Victor, and use the reading strategies to increase your comprehension. In the margin, note where you break down sentences, use context clues, and reread or read ahead. Finally, write your response to the selection on the lines provided.

from *Lakshmi* by Vasanthi Victor

The following passages describes the author's time in India when he was a child.

My grandfather had passed away. It said so in this letter from home, in black and white. It was written by Mother, who matter-of-factly moved on to other news about the rest of the family in India. This unexpected jolt took me back into the past—his death had triggered some old memory long since wiped out by the conscious present. My parents had come from the state of Kerala, and I remembered visiting there in my childhood. On these occasions I visited my grandfather and step-grandmother as well as innumerable uncles, aunts and cousins.

It was a great change for us those days to go from our house in the city to a remote village in Kerala. There was no electricity or running water in the homes. But almost every household had its pond which supplied water for washing and bathing. Some of these ponds were used to breed fish. We children enjoyed playing at the pond's edge since none of us dared to swim in its murky waters. Or we played in the sand that covered the front yard. It was freshly swept in the early hours of the morning by a woman who came in each day to do the chores.

The sound of the ocean could be heard in the distance, and a ten-minute walk brought one to the beach. Here fishermen still lived in huts made of woven palm leaves that were dried and tied together. Their floor was nothing but sand on which they spread mats on which to sit and sleep. Their livelihood depended on the catch of the day. These sturdy men left in their long canoes to spread their nets in the predawn hours and returned at midmorning with gleaming, slithering fish which their wives carried in baskets balanced on their heads to the gates of surrounding homes. Sometimes their children ran ahead to announce the catch of the day. I remember old women saying, "Twenty years ago there were more fish than you could eat in a week on any single day. Now you can count the fish on your fingers, just like those coconuts hanging on the palms."

(continued next page)

Coconut was used for everything—as oil for frying or as hair oil on our heads. Nothing like fish curry done in coconut milk or meat fried with coconut slivers. My aunts grated it to mix with vegetable dishes. Some men carried out the task of climbing palms to gather the nut. Grandfather usually had them climbing for tender young coconuts as a special treat for us. We delighted in feasting on the big bananas, the jackfruit and mangoes that grew nearby.

In Grandfather's house the main room where visitors were received also contained his bed. This is where he was to be found when he was not out working or tending to business. At night, after the evening meal, we congregated around his bed and listened to stories in the semidarkness of the oil lamps. The glow of the lamps attracted bugs and mosquitoes so that we could never sit still but kept slapping our bodies to kill the insects. One of our favorite stories was about the man returning home at nightfall, on foot, by way of the beach. There was no transportation so most people walked ten to fifteen miles a day while they went about their business. At the time there was a tale going around about a crooked lawyer who had met a violent death. His ghost was supposed to frequent this particular stretch of oceanfront. He waylaid unsuspecting travelers and scared them out of their wits. Some said that he wore his lawyer's robe; others, that he appeared headless or with a walking stick. Whatever his attire, they swore they had seen him and came back frightened and panting from running.

This man was more skeptical than others and, refusing to be scared by such tales, set out as usual. On his journey home he carried a sack of dried peppers on his back. As he made his way in the falling twilight, alone with no soul in sight, he was reminded of the lawyer's ghost. Except for the sea there was no other sound, maybe a solitary gull or two. In the growing stillness he suddenly heard a rustling sound; the faster he walked, the louder it grew. He began to think it was the swish of a cape behind him and turned a few times to see who was following. He saw nothing. All the same, as he approached the spot of the last sighting, he hurried even quicker. Louder and louder was the swish behind his back, until he was running, sure that the ghost was chasing him. He reached home in a state of anxiety and fear and ran a high fever during the night. It was only later—after he had recovered and in the light of bright day—that it dawned on him: He had been scared witless by the sound of the dried peppers on his back.

_____
_____
_____
_____
_____
_____
_____
_____
_____
_____
_____
_____
_____
_____

© Prentice-Hall, Inc.

Unit 2: Reaching Out

"**How to Write a Letter**" by Garrison Keillor (text page 107)

Literary Focus: Informal Essay

An **informal essay** is a brief, casual discussion of a topic. The writer of this type of essay uses conversational language to create a relaxed and friendly feeling. Sometimes, as in "How to Write a Letter," humorous ideas and details—exaggeration, surprising analogies—help to create the informal feeling. In addition to creating a sense of casualness, Keillor uses contractions such as *we'll* and *it's* to create a sense of casualness.

A. DIRECTIONS: Read the following passage from "How to Write a Letter." Circle three words, phrases, or details within the passage that help to create a relaxed, informal feeling. On the lines below, write a sentence explaining what makes each of the items informal.

A blank white eight-by-eleven sheet can look as big as Montana if the pen's not so hot— try a smaller page and write boldly. Or use a note card with a piece of fine art on the front; if your letter ain't good, at least they get the Matisse. Get a pen that makes a sensuous line, get a comfortable typewriter, a friendly word processor—whichever feels easy to the hand.

_____

_____

_____

B. DIRECTIONS: Look for more informal, humorous, and familiar words and phrases as you read, as well as other details that add to the essay's casual style. Use the organizer below to record your findings.

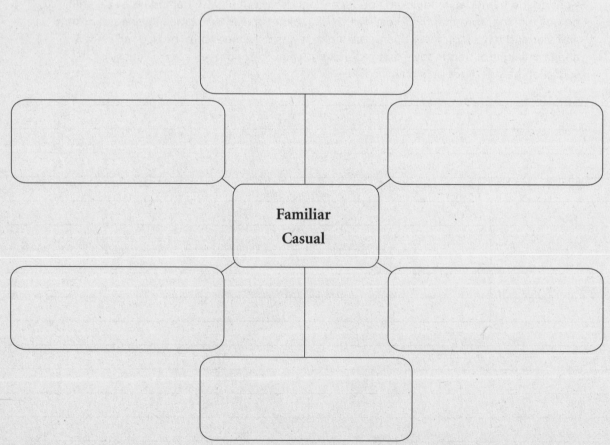

Familiar

Casual

"Aaron's Gift" by Myron Levoy (text page 116)
"Water" by Helen Keller (text page 122)

Build Vocabulary

Using Related Words: Forms of *console*

The Word Bank word *consoled* means "comforted." As you can see, the following words are forms of the word *console*. All three words are related in meaning.

Consolation means "comfort."
Inconsolable means "unable to be comforted."

A. DIRECTIONS: Use one of the forms of *console* to complete each sentence.

1. The little boy cried for a long time after losing his favorite toy; he seemed to be

   _____

2. Losing the game was a disappointment, but knowing that we had enjoyed our best season ever was a _____

3. Tanya's friends _____ her when her beloved cat Rusty died.

Using the Word Bank

frenzied	mascot	coaxed	consoled	drawing

B. DIRECTIONS: Answer each of the following questions to demonstrate your understanding of the Word Bank words. Circle the letter of your choice.

1. Which of the following might be a school's mascot?

   a. a cartoon-character bulldog   b. a football team

2. Which of the following would need to be consoled?

   a. someone who had just won an election   b. someone who had just lost an election

3. Which of the following would a young child need to be coaxed to do?

   a. clean up his or her room   b. watch his or her favorite video

4. Where would you see someone drawing water?

   a. at a pump connected to a well   b. at a table at a restaurant

5. When might a crowd of spectators at a race become frenzied?

   a. while waiting for the race to begin   b. while watching the finish of the race

Recognizing Antonyms

C. DIRECTIONS: Circle the letter of the word or phrase that is most nearly *opposite* in meaning to the word in CAPITAL LETTERS.

1. FRENZIED: a. frantic   b. surprised   c. calm   d. unharmed
2. CONSOLED: a. soothed   b. upset   c. repaired   d. greeted

"Aaron's Gift" by Myron Levoy (text page 116)

"Water" by Helen Keller (text page 122)

Build Spelling Skills: Adding Endings to Words Ending in y

Spelling Strategy When adding an ending to a word that ends in y, follow these strategies:

- If a consonant precedes the final y, change the y to i. However, if the ending begins with i, the y does not change.

  try + ed = tried   try + ing = trying

  study + ed = studied   study + ing = studying

  happy + est = happiest   happy + ness = happiness

- If a vowel comes before the y, just add the ending.

  enjoy + ed = enjoyed   enjoy + ing = enjoying   enjoy + ment = enjoyment

  journey + ed = journeyed   journey + ing = journeying

A. Practice: Add the indicated ending to each word. Write the new word on the line.

1. buy + ing _____

2. fry + ing _____

3. apply + ed _____

4. weary + ness _____

5. scary + er _____

6. employ + er _____

7. spy + ed _____

8. survey + ing _____

9. sturdy + ness _____

10. annoy + ing _____

B. Practice: Complete the paragraph by adding the indicated ending to each given word. Write the new words on the lines provided.

With the help of her teacher, Annie Sullivan, Helen Keller went on to live a life of remarkable

achievement. She continued (apply + ing) _____ herself to learning new

words and soon learned to speak, read, and write. She (study + ed) _____

hard and gained entrance to Radcliffe College, from which she graduated with honors in 1904.

In the years that followed, she (enjoy + ed) _____ a distinguished career

as a writer, lecturer, and civil rights advocate, (play + ing) _____ an

important role in winning public recognition for the needs and rights of visually disabled

people. The person who had, in her own words, been the wildest and (unruly + est)

_____ of children grew up to become one of the most famous and

influential people of our time.

"Aaron's Gift" by Myron Levoy (text page 116)
"Water" by Helen Keller (text page 122)

Build Grammar Skills: Verb Phrases

A **verb phrase** is a group of words that is made up of a main verb and one or more helping verbs. In a verb phrase, the main verb is the most important verb. There are many different helping verbs. The most common ones are shown in the chart below.

Common Helping Verbs	
Forms of *have*	has, have, having, had
Forms of *be*	am, is, are, was, were, being, been
Other helping verbs	do, does, did, may, might, must, can, could, will, would, shall, should

Look at these sentences. The verb phrase in each one is underlined. The main verb is in bold type.

The pigeon <u>was **trying**</u> to fly.

Aaron was not sure what his mother <u>would **say**</u> about his new-found pet.

Aaron's mother told him that all the family from Brooklyn and the East Side <u>would be **coming**</u> to their apartment for dinner and a celebration.

A. Practice: On the lines, write the verb phrase or phrases in each sentence. Then underline the main verb in each phrase.

1. Aaron had come to the park with his roller skates. _____

2. If you had seen him, you would have said that he is a fantastic skater.

   _____

3. Before coming to the U.S., Aaron's grandmother had lived in the Ukraine.

   _____

4. Cossacks had attacked her village, but she and her family survived.

   _____

5. Aaron thought that those must have been terrible times. _____

B. Writing Application: Complete the paragraph by writing a verb phrase in each blank. Use the verb phrases below or provide your own. When you are finished, underline the main verb in each verb phrase that you wrote.

> would bring   did bring   had made   had brought   will recall   could become

About a month after Aaron _____ Pidge home, Carl, the gang leader, told him that he _____ a member if he _____ the bird to be the gang's mascot. Aaron _____ the pigeon to the club house, but he soon realized that he _____ a terrible mistake. The boys intended to throw Pidge into the fire while making Aaron swear a loyalty oath! As you _____, however, Aaron and Pidge managed to escape.

"Aaron's Gift" by Myron Levoy (text page 116)

"Water" by Helen Keller (text page 122)

Reading Strategy: Reread

You don't have to read a story straight through from the beginning to the end. Often, as you are reading, you may find it helpful to go back and reread an earlier passage in order to clarify a word, idea, character, or event. Once you see how all the details fit together, you can continue to make your way through the story.

Suppose that you came to this passage in "Aaron's Gift." What word, idea, character, or event might you want to clarify by going back and rereading an earlier passage?

> With the pigeon gone, the boys turned toward Aaron and tackled him to the ground and punched him and tore his clothes and punched him some more. Aaron twisted and turned and kicked and punched back, shouting "Cossacks! Cossacks!" And somehow the word gave him the strength to tear away from them.

According to the passage, Aaron thinks of "Cossacks" when the boys attack him. You might want to reread an earlier part of the story to clarify who or what "Cossacks" are and why Aaron shouts this word.

DIRECTIONS: Read the following excerpt from "Aaron's Gift," noting that it comes before the scene described above. Then explain how it clarifies Aaron's use of the word "Cossacks." Write your answer on the lines below.

> Often, in the evening, Aaron's grandmother would talk about the old days long ago in the Ukraine, in the same way that she talked to the birds on the back fire escape. She had lived in a village near a place called Kishinev with hundreds of other poor peasant families like her own. . . .
>
> One day, a thundering of horses was heard coming toward the village from the direction of Kishinev. *The Cossacks! The Cossacks!* someone had shouted. The Czar's horsemen! Quickly, quickly, everyone in Aaron's grandmother's family had climbed down to the cellar through a little trapdoor hidden under a mat in the big central room of their shack. But his grandmother's pet goat, whom she'd loved as much as Aaron loved Pidge and more, had to be left above, because if it had made a sound in the cellar, they would never have lived to see the next morning. They all hid under the wood in the woodbin and waited, hardly breathing.
>
>   *   *   *
>
> But they had been lucky. For other houses had been burned to the ground. And everywhere, not goats alone, nor sheep, but men and women and children lay quietly on the ground. The word for this sort of massacre, Aaron had learned, was *pogrom*. It had been a pogrom. And the men on the horses were Cossacks. Hated word. Cossacks.

_____

_____

_____

_____

_____

"Aaron's Gift" by Myron Levoy (text page 116)
"Water" by Helen Keller (text page 122)

Literary Focus: Climax

The moment of high tension in a story is known as the **climax**, or turning point. It is the point at which the story could go one way or another. Writers who build up to climaxes shape their stories and accounts carefully. They present the events that lead up to this decisive moment in a part of a story known as the **rising action**. They also let readers know what happens after the climax; this part of the story is know as the **conclusion**.

DIRECTIONS: Use the diagrams below to record the events that lead up to the climaxes in "Aaron's Gift"" and "Water." Also note what happens in each work's climax and conclusion in the spaces indicated.

"Aaron's Gift"

Climax

_____ Event

_____ Event

Rising Action

_____ Event

Conclusion

"Water"

Climax

_____ Event

_____ Event

Rising Action

Event

Conclusion

In a sentence or two, identify the climax of each work.

"Aaron's Gift":

_____

_____

"Water":

_____

_____

"How to Write a Poem About the Sky" by Leslie Marmon Silko (text page 128)
"I'll tell you how the Sun rose—" by Emily Dickinson (text page 129)
"Wilderness Rivers" by Elizabeth Coatsworth (text page 130)

Build Vocabulary

Using the Suffix -*less*

The suffix -*less* means "without". For example, a *fearless* person is one who is without fear, or has no fear. A *clueless* person is someone who is without a clue or has no clue about what's going on.

A. DIRECTIONS: Use the suffix -*less* to form a word that fits each of the following definitions, and write it in the space provided. The first one has been done as an example.

1. without pain _____painless_____

2. without color_____

3. having no hair _____

4. without power_____

5. without a flaw_____

6. having no hope_____

Using the Word Bank

dense	horizons	membranes	amethyst
staid	relentless	exultant	

B. DIRECTIONS: In the following sentences, fill in the blanks with the correct word from the Word Bank.

1. Our hearts and brains are surrounded by tough protective _____membranes_____.

2. From the ship, our view of the _____ stretched as far as we could see.

3. The fog was too _____ to see through, so we had to drive very slowly.

4. The playful chimpanzees leaped from branch to branch, while the _____ older chimps sat quietly in the tree.

5. The _____ fans of the winning team raced onto the field, cheering.

6. The _____ wind howled all night, making it hard for us to sleep.

7. In the moonlight, the jewel in her ring shone with an _____ gleam.

"How to Write a Poem About the Sky" by Leslie Marmon Silko (text page 128)
"I'll tell you how the Sun rose—" by Emily Dickinson (text page 129)
"Wilderness Rivers" by Elizabeth Coatsworth (text page 130)

Build Spelling Skills: Using *y* to Spell the Short *i* Sound

Spelling Strategy Sometimes the letter *y* is used to spell the short *i* sound in a word, such as the *y* in *amethyst*. There is no rule to tell you when to use a *y* or an *i* to spell the short *i* sound. When you come across a word in which the short *i* sound is spelled with a *y*, try to remember it. If you are not sure whether to use *i* or *y* to spell the short *i* sound in a word, look up the word in a dictionary.

Examples:

amethyst	gymnasium	physical	symbol
crystal	gypsy	physician	syrup
cymbals	mystery	rhythm	system

A. Practice: In each of the following sentences, choose the *i* or *y* in parentheses to complete the italicized word. If you are not sure which letter to choose, look at the list of words above.

1. The music had a good *rh____thm* (i, y) for dancing.

2. Hanging in the window, the glass *cr____stal* (y, i) glittered in the sunlight.

3. It's important to know that library books are arranged according to a *s____stem.* (i, y)

4. It was a *m____stery* (y, i) to me how the magician made the piano disappear.

5. She played the *c____mbals* (i, y) in the school band.

B. Practice: Complete each of the following sentences with a word from the list above. Be sure to spell each word correctly.

1. I love waffles with butter and _____

2. They will play the basketball game in the _____

3. We went to see the doctor for a _____ examination.

4. A flag is a _____ of a country.

Challenge: In her poem, "I'll tell you how the Sun rose," Emily Dickinson mentions a bird called the *bobolink.* This bird got its name from its call, which some think sounds like "*bob-o-lee, bob-o-link.*" Many other words, such as those listed below, sound like the sounds that they describe. Choose from these words to complete the following sentences.

crunch   hoot   splash   thud

1. She jumped into the pool with a loud _____.

2. It is scary to hear an owl _____ at night.

3. The falling book hit the floor with a _____.

4. As she ate the celery, I could hear the _____ from across the room.

"How to Write a Poem About the Sky" by Leslie Marmon Silko (text page 128)

"I'll tell you how the Sun rose—" by Emily Dickinson (text page 129)

"Wilderness Rivers" by Elizabeth Coatsworth (text page 130)

Build Grammar Skills: Action Verbs and Linking Verbs

The two main kinds of verbs are **action verbs** and linking verbs. **Action verbs**, such as *walk* and *push*, express physical action; action verbs such as *decide* and *think* express mental action. **Linking verbs** express a state of being. They tell what the subject of a sentence is or is like by linking the subject with a word that identifies or describes it. Common linking verbs include *am, is, are, was, were, appear, feel, seem, look, become.* Here are some examples:

Action verbs: I'll <u>tell</u> you how the sun <u>rose</u>.   There are rivers that I <u>know</u>.

Linking verbs: Emily Dickinson <u>was</u> a poet.   The river <u>looks</u> cold.

A. Practice: In each of the following sentences, identify the italicized word as an action verb or a linking verb. In the space provided, write "A" for action or "L" for linking.

____ 1. The weather *became* hot later in the day.

____ 2. After lunch, we *washed* the dishes.

____ 3. My older sister *reads* a lot of books.

____ 4. It *seems* like a good idea to dress warmly.

____ 5. The baby *smiled* at me from his crib.

____ 6. The puppy *was* tired out from playing.

B. Writing Application: In most writing, it is best to use more action verbs than linking verbs. Action verbs make your writing sound livelier and stronger. Of course, when your meaning requires you to use a linking verb, do so. Just for practice, read the sentences below. Each one has a linking verb. If you think the sentence would sound better with an action verb, revise it on the line below. If you think the sentence should remain as is, write "no change." The first two sentences have been done as examples.

1. Emily Dickinson was a describer of the beauties of nature in many of her poems.
   Emily Dickinson described the beauties of nature in many of her poems.

2. She is one of our most outstanding poets.
   no change

3. Leslie Marmon Silko is a lover of the beauties of nature.

   _____

4. Elizabeth Coatsworth was a resident of Maine.

   _____

5. Emily Dickinson was not comfortable with people other than her family.

   _____

"How to Write a Poem About the Sky" by Leslie Marmon Silko (text page 128)
"I'll tell you how the Sun rose—" by Emily Dickinson (text page 129)
"Wilderness Rivers" by Elizabeth Coatsworth (text page 130)

Reading Strategy: Envision

Poets use words to create vivid visual images. For example, a poet may concentrate on a single detail of a scene, describing that detail in very precise words. When you read those words, your imagination converts them into a mental picture that you **envision** with your "mind's eye."

DIRECTIONS: In the chart below, the left column contains visual details from the poems. In the right column, describe the mental picture the detail leads you to envision. The first row of the chart has been filled in for you as an example. If you need more space, use an extra sheet of paper.

Detail	What You Envision
1. ...the frozen river / so dense and white / little birds / walk across it.	It's so cold, the river is frozen over, and pure white snow covers its icy surface. I envision small birds walking on the snow-covered river, leaving their little footprints in the smooth, drifting snow.
2. "You see the sky now / but the earth / is lost in it"	
3. "The Steeples swam in Amethyst"	
4. "only paddles, / swift and light, / flick that current / in their flight."	

Unit 2: Reaching Out

"How to Write a Poem About the Sky" by Leslie Marmon Silko (text page 128)
"I'll tell you how the Sun rose—" by Emily Dickinson (text page 129)
"Wilderness Rivers" by Elizabeth Coatsworth (text page 130)

Literary Focus: Sensory Language

Sensory language describes sensory details. It is the language a poet uses to make you almost experience the way things in a poem look, sound, taste, smell, and feel. When you recognize sensory language in a poem, you can use it as a cue to bring your own senses into action.

DIRECTIONS: Choose two of the poems in this grouping, and for each one use a sensory language "sun" below to note the details that help you see, hear, taste, smell, or feel what the poet describes.

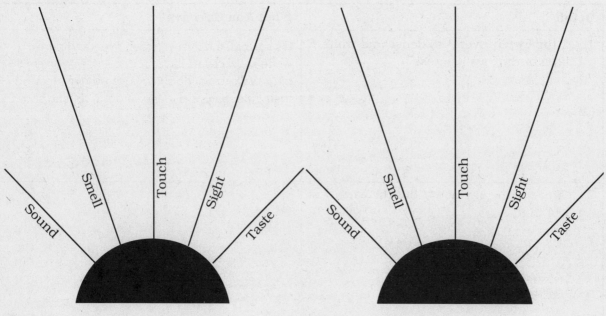

Poem: _____   **Poem:** _____

© Prentice-Hall, Inc.

"The Great Flood" Retold by Geraldine McCaughrean (text page 135)

Build Vocabulary

Using Words From the Selection

provisions: supplies	sordid: unclean	abuse: bad treatment
jeered: made fun of, insulted	pelting: throwing at	daub: smear, paint

A. DIRECTIONS: Complete each of the following sentences by writing one of the words above in the space provided.

1. The children were yelling and _____ each other with snowballs.

2. The group protects animals from _____.

3. We need to bring our own _____ on the camping trip.

4. I used to love to _____ finger paints on big sheets of paper.

5. The angry fans _____ at the umpire.

6. Before it was cleaned up, the area near the railroad tracks looked _____.

B. DIRECTIONS: Use the following clues to fill in the crossword puzzle below with words from the box above.

ACROSS

3. The audience was _____ the villain in the play with tomatoes.

5. The explorers took enough _____ to last six months.

6. Circus clowns _____ makeup on their faces.

Down

1. A few people were rude and _____ the speaker.

2. Causing pollution is a form of land _____.

4. The opposite of "clean and pure" is _____ .

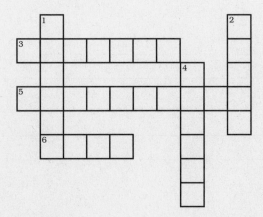

"The Great Flood" Retold by Geraldine McCaughrean (text page 135)

Connecting a Story From the Bible to Social Studies

Mount Ararat, where Noah's ark is said to have landed, is near an area known as **ancient Mesopotamia**, where the world's earliest civilization developed. Ancient Mesopotamia was a crescent-shaped area between the Mediterranean Sea and the Persian Gulf. Most of this region is now occupied by the modern country Iraq.

Because of the region's fertile soil and its two rivers, the Tigris and the Euphrates, farming communities began to develop there more than six thousand years ago. Archaeologists have found that, about the year 4000 B.C., farmers had begun to dig ditches to control the flooding of the two rivers and used the water in the ditches for their crops. Gradually, some of the communities grew into villages and larger towns. The towns became trade centers to which farmers from the surrounding areas brought their crops.

Sometime before 3500 B.C., new settlers arrived, although it is not sure from where they came. They took control over a large part of the region and formed the kingdom of Sumer. Sumerian control of ancient Mesopotamia lasted more than a thousand years, reaching a peak of power under a strong ruler named Sargon. Town grew into cities. The Sumerians developed the first schools we know of, the first system of laws, and the first known written language. Modern scholars have learned from translating their writings that the Sumerians were familiar with the sciences of astronomy and medicine. They were also skilled in metalworking, stone carving, and weaving. Able sailors and boat builders, the Sumerians traveled to neighboring countries and traded with them.

In the 1700's B.C., a ruler named Hammurabi conquered Sumer. He developed a legal system that we now call the "Code of Hammurabi." The code of laws stated that "the strong should not abuse the weak," and that the rights and traditions of conquered nations should be respected.

Ancient Mesopotamia deserves to be known as the birthplace of civilization because it was the first place in which many people lived together in permanent, organized communities under a widely accepted system of laws.

DIRECTIONS: On the lines, explain why each of the following contributions to civilization are important:

Schools:

_____

_____

Laws:

_____

_____

Written language:

_____

_____

"Zlateh the Goat" by Isaac Bashevis Singer (text page 146)

Build Vocabulary

Unit 2: Reaching Out

Using the Prefix *ex-*

The prefix *ex-* means "out" or "away from." For example, the word *exhale* means "breathe out."

A. DIRECTIONS: In the space provided, write the word that fits the definition by combining the word part *ex-* with the main part of the word in parentheses. The first one has been done as an example.

_____expel_____   1. (-pel): to force out

_____   2. (-tract) to take out

_____   3. (-plode) to burst out or blow apart

_____   4. (-tend) to reach out or away from

_____   5. (-ile) to send away

_____   6. (-clude) to leave out

Using the Word Bank

bound	conclusion	trace	rapidly	exuded

B. DIRECTIONS: Answer each of the following riddles by filling in the blank space with a word from the Word Bank.

1. What is the best way to escape from a hungry lion? _____

2. Why did the farmer tie up his cows? So that they were _____ to give milk.

3. Why did the children turn on the lamp after dark? Because the lamp _____ light.

4. How did the student finish the arithmetic problem? She reached a _____ .

5. Why couldn't the graffiti artist be found? He left without a _____ .

Recognizing Antonyms

C. DIRECTIONS: Circle the letter of the word or phrase most nearly *opposite* in meaning of the word in CAPITAL LETTERS.

1. CONCLUSION
   a. suspicion   c. reason
   b. introduction   d. question

2. BOUND
   a. free   c. curious
   b. eager   d. happy

3. RAPIDLY
   a. hopefully   c. slowly
   b. carefully   d. angrily

4. EXUDED
   a. broke   c. explored
   b. soaked up   d. welcomed

"Zlateh the Goat" by Isaac Bashevis Singer (text page 146)

Build Spelling Skills: Spelling the Final *s* Sound With *ce*

Spelling Strategy Sometimes the *s* sound at the end of a word is spelled with *ce*, as in the following words: *force, ice, since.* Since there is no rule to tell you when to use *ce* to spell the *s* sound, look a word up in a dictionary if you are not sure of its spelling.

A. Practice: In each of the following sentences, choose the letter or letters from the ones in parentheses to spell the italicized word, and write the correctly spelled word in the space provided. The first one has been done as an example.

1. We liked the movie so much that we saw it *twi*(s, ce) _____ twice _____ .

2. You can have your *choi*(s, ce) _____ of chocolate or vanilla ice cream.

3. We must learn to *expre*(ss, ce) _____ ourselves clearly.

4. I drink a glass of orange *jui*(s, ce) _____ every morning.

5. There was a *fen*(ce, s) _____ around the yard to keep the dog in.

6. Can you tell the difference between a duck and a *goo*(se, ce) _____ ?

7. The students decorated the room for their school *dan*(s, ce) _____ .

B. Practice: Complete each of the following sentences with one of the words below. Use each word only once.

price   choice   space   source   chance

1. Aaron did not want to take Zlateh to the butcher, but he knew that he had no _____.

2. If Aaron and Zlateh had not found shelter from the snow, they would have had little _____ of survival.

3. There was just enough _____ n the haystack for Aaron and Zlateh.

4. After Zlateh saved Aaron's life, the family would not sell the goat for any _____.

5. Zlateh was the _____ of the milk that Aaron drank.

Challenge: "Zlateh the Goat" mentions the Jewish holiday Hanukkah. The word *Hanukkah* means "dedication" in Hebrew, one of the oldest languages still in use. The Jewish new year is called *Rosh Hashanah* (Rohsh Hah-SHAH-nah), Hebrew for "beginning of the year."

Some English words come from Hebrew words. For example, the word "Sabbath," meaning "day of rest," comes from the Hebrew word *Shabat* (shah-BAHT). Have you ever heard the word *kosher* used to mean "acceptable"? *Kosher* (KOH-shuhr), means "proper" and applies to food that is acceptable for religious Jews to eat. Use the information above to fill in the blanks below.

1. The Jewish year begins on the holiday called _____ .

2. _____ food has been prepared according to special religious laws.

3. Many people do not work on the _____ , the day of rest.

"Zlateh the Goat" by Isaac Bashevis Singer (text page 146)

Build Grammar Skills: Principal Parts of Verbs

Every verb, or word that expresses an action or state of being, has four main forms, or **principal parts**. These parts show a verb's tense, letting you know when an action took place. Most verbs are **regular**, meaning that they all form their principal parts in the same way. Some verbs, however, are **irregular**, meaning that the forms of their principal parts do not conform to general rules. The principal parts of irregular verbs must be learned. See some examples in the chart below.

Principal Part	Regular Verbs	Irregular Verbs
Present tense	talk, jump, finish, expect	am/is/are, have/has, sing, become/becomes, bring, write
Past tense	Add *ed*: talk*ed*, jump*ed*, finish*ed*, expect*ed*	was/were, had, sang, became, brought, wrote
Present participle	Add *ing*: (am/is/are) talk*ing*, jump*ing*, finish*ing*, expect*ing*	(am/is/are) being, having, singing, becoming, bringing, writing
Past participle	Add *ed*:(has/have/had) talked, jumped, finished, expected	(has/have/had) been, had, sung, become, brought, written

A. Practice: For each of the following sentences, identify which principal part of the underlined verb is being used. The first one has been done as an example.

_____past_____ 1. The sun <u>shone</u> most of the time.

_____ 2. Reuven *is* <u>having</u> a bad year.

_____ 3. Aaron <u>knows</u> the way to Feivel's house.

_____ 4. He *has* <u>agreed</u> to take Zlateh there.

_____ 5. Aaron <u>placed</u> the rope around Zlateh's neck.

_____ 6. He *is* <u>feeling</u> sad.

_____ 7. Aaron and Zlateh *have* <u>gotten</u> lost in a storm.

_____ 8. The story <u>has</u> a happy ending.

B. Writing Application: On the lines provided, complete each of the following sentences, using the correct principal part of the verb in parentheses.

1. Reuven the furrier had _____decided_____ to sell the goat. (decide)

2. Feivel had _____ eight gulden for her. (offer)

3. While they were walking, Zlateh _____ Aaron's hand. (lick)

4. The snow had _____ Aaron's knees. (reach)

5. When the story ends, Aaron and Zlateh are _____ home. (return)

6. This is a story that _____ happily. (end)

"Zlateh the Goat" by Isaac Bashevis Singer (text page 146)

Reading Strategy: Summarize

While you are reading, pause now and then. Go over in your mind the events that have taken place so far and think about why they happened. When you pause and think about a story in this way, you are **summarizing**, or reviewing the story up to that point.

A **summary** contains only the most important information about the events in the story. For example, read the passage below and the summary that follows it:

> The sun was shining when Aaron left the village. Suddenly the weather changed. A large black cloud with a bluish center appeared in the east and spread itself rapidly over the sky. A cold wind blew in with it. The crows flew low, croaking. At first it looked as if it would rain, but instead it began to hail as in summer. It was early in the day, but it became dark as dusk. After a while the hail turned to snow.
>
> **Summary:** When Aaron left the village, the sun was shining, but it suddenly grew cold, windy, and dark, and began to snow.

A. DIRECTIONS: One way of summarizing is to make a timeline on a sheet of paper and add to it each time you pause. Use the diagram below as a timeline for "Zlateh the Goat." In the spaces on the timeline, write the letters of the following events from the story in the order in which they occur. Start at the left end of the timeline and finish at the right.

a. Aaron digs a hole in the haystack so that he and Zlateh can take shelter from the blizzard.
b. Reuven the furrier decides to sell Zlateh to the butcher.
c. Aaron hears the ringing of sleigh bells.
d. A neighbor runs to tell Aaron's family that Aaron and Zlateh are on their way home.
e. It begins to snow heavily.

BEGINNING ├────────┼────────┼────────┼────────┤ **ENDING**
　　　　1. _____　　　2. _____　　　3. _____　　　4. _____　　　5. _____

B. DIRECTIONS: On the lines provided, write a one-sentence summary of each of the following passages from "Zlateh the Goat."

1. In his twelve years Aaron had seen all kinds of weather, but he had never experienced a snow like this one. It was so dense it shut out the light of day. In a short time their path was completely covered. The wind became as cold as ice. The road to town was narrow and winding. Aaron no longer knew where he was. He could not see through the snow. The cold soon penetrated his quilted jacket.

_____

_____

2. For three days Aaron and Zlateh stayed in the haystack. Aaron had always loved Zlateh, but in these three days he loved her more and more. She fed him with her milk and helped keep him warm. She comforted him with her patience. He told her many stories and she always cocked her ears and listened. When he patted her she always licked his hands and face. Then she said, "Maaaa," and he knew it meant, I love you too.

_____

_____

Name _____ Date _____

Literary Focus: Conflict With Nature

A **conflict** is a struggle between two forces. The struggle may be between two people, a person and herself or himself, or between a person and something in nature. Often, part of the enjoyment of reading a story is waiting to find out who will win the conflict. In "Zlateh the Goat," the conflict is between Aaron and the snowstorm. Aaron, a character in the story, has to battle a blizzard, one of nature's most powerful and dangerous forces. The battle between Aaron and the blizzard creates tension and suspense, and Aaron's fight for survival tells readers a great deal about his bravery and resourcefulness.

DIRECTIONS: In the chart below, the left column contains passages from "Zlateh the Goat." For each passage, complete the second and third columns. In the second column, write the problem that Aaron faces. In the third column, write how Aaron solves the problem. The first row has been filled in as an example.

Passage	Danger	Solution
1. "He could not see through the snow."	Aaron is lost.	He finds the haystack.
2. "His hands were numb and he could no longer feel his toes."		
3. Aaron ate his bread and cheese, but after the difficult journey he was still hungry."		
4. "The snow had blocked up his window."		

"Door Number Four" by Charlotte Pomerantz (text page 156)
"Count That Day Lost" by George Eliot (text page 156)
"The World Is Not a Pleasant Place to Be" by Nikki Giovanni (text page 157)
"The Children's Hour" by Henry Wadsworth Longfellow (text page 158)

Build Vocabulary

Using the Prefix *de-*

The prefix *de-* often means "down," as it does in the Word Bank word *descending*. A person who is descending a flight of stairs, a ramp, or a ladder is going down.

A. DIRECTIONS: Complete each sentence by adding the prefix *de-* to each word part in parentheses. Write the words on the lines provided.

1. When you (de- + crease) _____ the volume on your radio, you turn the volume down.

2. If there is a (de- + cline) _____ in the popularity of a best-selling soft drink, the soft drink's popularity is going down.

3. If a boss decides to (de- + mote) _____ an employee, he or she decides to move the employee down in position or rank.

4. If you (de- + press) _____ a key on a keyboard, you push it down.

5. If a driver makes his or her car (de- + celerate) _____ , he or she makes the car slow down.

Using the Word Bank

eased	descending	fortress

B. DIRECTIONS: For each word in the Word Bank, write an original sentence that demonstrates the word's meaning.

1. (eased) _____

2. (fortress)_____

3. (descending) _____

Analogies

C. DIRECTIONS: Each item consists of a related pair of words in CAPITAL LETTERS, followed by four lettered pairs of words. Circle the letter of the pair that best expresses a relationship similar to that expressed in the pair in capital letters.

1. FORTRESS : STRENGTH
   a. chair : legs
   b. honey : sweetness
   c. paper : color
   d. tunnel : concrete

2. EASED : SOOTHED
   a. fixed : repaired
   b. built : destroyed
   c. answered : silenced
   d. walked : sailed

3. ASCENDING : DESCENDING
   a. disregard : ignore
   b. consider : reconsider
   c. move : transport
   d. increase : decrease

"Door Number Four" by Charlotte Pomerantz (text page 156)
"Count That Day Lost" by George Eliot (text page 156)
"The World Is Not a Pleasant Place to Be" by Nikki Giovanni (text page 157)
"The Children's Hour" by Henry Wadsworth Longfellow (text page 158)

Build Spelling Skills: Spelling the s Sound With the Letters *sc*

Spelling Strategy Sometimes the s sound is spelled with the letters *sc*. Look at the Word Bank word *descending*, for example. Notice that the s sound in the middle is spelled *sc*.

Each of the following words also contains an *s* sound that is spelled *sc*. Read the words and then pronounce each one quietly to yourself: *science, scenery, susceptible, ascending*.

A. Practice: Choose the correctly spelled word to complete each sentence.

1. For this year's class play, Bill is helping to design the (senery, scenery) _____.

2. Pam wears a warm hat because she is (susceptible, suseptible) _____ to colds.

3. My sister's favorite subjects are math and (science, sience) _____ .

4. The two climbers passed each other as one was (asending, ascending) _____ the mountain and the other was (desending, descending) _____ .

B. Practice: Write each of the following words once to complete the sentences below.

scissors   reminiscent   scene   scented

1. The girls were using red construction paper and _____ to make valentines.

2. They were also making a _____ candle to give as a gift.

3. The _____ was warm and touching.

4. It was _____ of the situation in "The Children's Hour."

Challenge: The word *fortress* from the Word Bank contains the word *fort*, which means "an enclosed place used for defense" or "an army post." Both *fortress* and *fort* come from the Latin word *fortis*, meaning "strong." Many place names contain the word "fort." As you might guess, that is because they were once the site of military forts. Here are a few examples.

Fort Knox: a military reservation in Kentucky where gold belonging to the U.S. government is kept

Fort Lauderdale: a city on Florida's Atlantic coast

Fort Worth: a city in northern Texas

DIRECTIONS: Answer the following questions using the place names listed above. Write your answers on the lines.

1. Which place might you visit if you were touring Texas? _____

2. Which place is used to store gold? _____

3. Where might you go if you wanted to spend some time at the beach? _____

"Door Number Four" by Charlotte Pomerantz (text page 156)
"Count That Day Lost" by George Eliot (text page 156)
"The World Is Not a Pleasant Place to Be" by Nikki Giovanni (text page 157)
"The Children's Hour" by Henry Wadsworth Longfellow (text page 158)

Build Grammar Skills: Verb Tenses

You use verbs such as *deliver, play, be,* and *become* to express actions and states of being. To show when the actions and the states of being occur, you use forms of the verbs called **verb tenses**. For example, when you say, "I *played* a new computer game," "I *deliver* the newspapers every day," or "I *will* be at my friend's house," you are using verb tenses that tell when.

The three simple, or basic, tenses are the past, the present, and the future. The chart below shows three different verbs in each of these tenses.

TENSES			
Present	I listen	I speak	I become
Past	I listened	I spoke	I became
Future	I will listen	I will speak	I will become

The verb *listen* is known as a regular verb. Notice that the past tense of this verb is formed by adding *-ed.* Now notice that the past tense forms of *speak* and *become* are formed in a different way. These are irregular verbs. One of the most common irregular verbs is *be;* note these forms:

Present—*am, is, are;* Past—*was, were;* Future—*will be.*

Finally, look at the future tense of all three verbs. Notice that they all use the helping verb *will.*

A. Practice: Above each italicized verb in the following sentences, write *PR* if it is in the present tense, *PA* if it is in the past tense, and *F* if it is in the future tense.

1. George Eliot *was* the pen name of Mary Ann Evans.

2. This famous English writer *lived* during the 1800's.

3. Henry Wadsworth Longfellow *is* another writer who *became* famous during the last century.

4. When you *read* his poems, you *will understand* why he *was* so popular.

5. Nikki Giovanni *writes* poems that *appeal* to readers of all ages.

B. Writing Application: Write a sentence about each topic provided below, using the verb and verb tense given.

1. Write a sentence about friendship, using the verb *be* in the present tense.

_____

2. Write a sentence about one of the poems, using the verb *make* in the past tense.

_____

3. Write a sentence about one of your friends using a verb of your choice in the future tense.

_____

"Door Number Four" by Charlotte Pomerantz (text page 156)
"Count That Day Lost" by George Eliot (text page 156)
"The World Is Not a Pleasant Place to Be" by Nikki Giovanni (text page 157)
"The Children's Hour" by Henry Wadsworth Longfellow (text page 158)

Reading Strategy: Paraphrase

When you **paraphrase** a difficult phrase, sentence, or passage that appears in a poem, you "translate" it into your own words. Restating the poet's words in this way can help you clarify the poem's meaning. For example, here is one way you might paraphrase lines 5–8 of "The Children's Hour."

I heard in the chamber above me   The sound of a door that is opened,
   The patter of little feet,   And voices soft and sweet.

Paraphrase: I heard the footsteps of children, a door opening, and soft, sweet voices coming from upstairs.

Notice that when you paraphrase lines like these, you can change the poet's words into simpler, more everyday words. You can also change the order of words or ideas, if doing so helps you to clarify the meaning.

A. DIRECTIONS: Paraphrase each of the following excerpts from "The Children's Hour." Write your paraphrases on the lines provided.

1. From my study I see in the lamplight, / Descending the broad hall stair, / Grave Alice, and laughing Allegra, / And Edith with golden hair.

_____

_____

2. Do you think, O blue-eyed banditti, / Because you have scaled the wall, / Such an old mustache as I am / Is not a match for you all!

_____

_____

B. DIRECTIONS: Paraphrase "The World Is Not a Pleasant Place to Be" by Nikki Giovanni. Write your paraphrase, one section at a time, on the lines provided. Remember to convey the poet's message about friendship as you restate her ideas in your own words.

1. the world is not a pleasant place / to be without / someone to hold and be held by

_____

_____

2. a river would stop / its flow if only / a stream were there / to receive it

_____

_____

3. an ocean would never laugh / if clouds weren't there / to kiss her tears

_____

_____

"Door Number Four" by Charlotte Pomerantz (text page 156)
"Count That Day Lost" by George Eliot (text page 156)
"The World Is Not a Pleasant Place to Be" by Nikki Giovanni (text page 157)
"The Children's Hour" by Henry Wadsworth Longfellow (text page 158)

Literary Focus: Speaker

Who do you think is saying the following words from "Door Number Four" by Charlotte Pomerantz?

Above my uncle's grocery store / is a pintu, / is a door. / On the pintu / is a number, / nomer empat, / number four.

The imaginary person who says the words of a poem is known as the poem's **speaker**. Based on the words above, you can gather that speaker of "Door Number Four" has an uncle and enjoys using and sharing words from another language. These facts, together with the simple and playful quality of the lines might suggest to you that the speaker is a child.

Sometimes the speaker of a poem may be very much like the poet, and sometimes there are important differences. For example, an adult such as Charlotte Pomerantz may write a poem in which the speaker is a child. Or, a female poet might write a poem in which the speaker is a man, and vice versa. In other cases, the one who is speaking may not have a definite identity as a man, woman, or child. Instead, the speaker can be described as "a voice of wisdom" or "a voice of the heart."

DIRECTIONS: Answer the following questions based on the excerpts given.

1. How do the following lines from "Door Number Four" further suggest that the speaker is a child?

   In the door / there is a key. / Turn it, / enter quietly. / Hush hush, diam-diam, / quietly.
   There, in lamplight / you will see / a friend, / teman, / a friend, / who's me.

   _____

   _____

   _____

2. Based on the following lines from "Count That Day Lost," who do you think the poem's speaker is? What words or ideas in the lines make you think so?

   If you sit down at set of sun / And count the acts that you have done, / And, counting, find / One self-denying deed, one word / That eased the heart of him who heard, / One glance most kind / That fell like sunshine where it went— / Then you may count that day well spent. /

   _____

   _____

   _____

"Old Ben" by Jesse Stuart (text page 164)
"Feathered Friend" by Arthur C. Clarke (text page 168)
"Childhood and Poetry" by Pablo Neruda (text page 172)

Build Vocabulary

Forms of *regulate*

Many words are forms of other words. For example, *regulate* means "to govern according to a rule." The following words are related in form and meaning to the verb *regulate*: the noun *regulation* means "a rule"; the noun *regulator* means "a person who regulates"; and the adjective *regulatory* means "having to do with regulations."

A. DIRECTIONS: Complete each of the following sentences by filling in the blank space with the correct form of *regulate*. Choose from the forms above.

1. There is a _____ that requires drivers to drive slowly near a school.

2. The factory employs a _____ to see that workers follow the rules.

3. Without umpires, there would be no one to _____ baseball games.

4. The government has a _____ agency that makes sure food is packaged according to strict health rules.

Using the Word Bank

scarce	regulation	fusing	ceased
minuscule	furtively	persecution	

B. DIRECTIONS: In the space provided next to each Word Bank word, write the letter of the word or phrase that is closest in meaning.

____ 1. FUSING: a. breaking b. hitting c. joining d. cutting

____ 2. REGULATION: a. goal b. question c. problem d. rule

____ 3. SCARCE: a. tricky b. frightening c. rare d. useful

____ 4. PERSECUTION: a. unfair treatment b. wishful thinking c. careful planning
d. lack of interest

____ 5. CEASED: a. fastened b. folded c. stopped d. arranged

____ 6. FURTIVELY: a. eagerly b. angrily c. slowly d. secretly

____ 7. MINUSCULE: a. powerful b. complicated c. ridiculous d. tiny

Recognizing Antonyms

C. DIRECTIONS: For each of the following Word Bank words, circle the letter of the word or phrase that is most nearly *opposite* in meaning. The first one has been done as an example.

_a_ 1. SCARCE: a. plentiful b. useful c. funny d. dull

____ 2. MINUSCULE: a. heavy b. thin c. huge d. clean

____ 3. CEASED: a. cleaned b. covered c. asked d. began

____ 4. FURTIVELY: a. wisely b. openly c. sadly d. willingly

"Old Ben" by Jesse Stuart (text page 164)
"Feathered Friend" by Arthur C. Clarke (text page 168)
"Childhood and Poetry" by Pablo Neruda (text page 172)

Build Spelling Skills: Adding Suffixes to Words Ending in Silent *e*

Spelling Strategy When a word ends in silent *e*, drop the final *e* when you add a suffix that begins with a vowel. Keep the silent *e*, however, when you add a suffix beginning with a consonant.   ventilat**e** + -ing = ventilating   precis**e** + -ly = precis**e**ly

A. Practice: Add the suffix to each word. Write the new word on the line. Remember to use the rules above for adding suffixes that begin with vowels or consonants to words ending in silent *e*.

1. amaze + -*ing*   =   _____
2. rude + -*ly*   =   _____
3. brave + -*ly*   =   _____
4. hope + -*ful*   =   _____
5. write + -*ing*   =   _____

6. skate + -*ing*   =   _____
7. polite + -*ly*   =   _____
8. drive + -*ing*   =   _____
9. spite + -*ful*   =   _____
10. shake + -*ing*   =   _____

B. Practice: Complete the paragraph by adding the indicated suffix to each given word and writing each new word on the space provided.

While (take + -ing) _____ Old Ben home, the boy was not sure that his father would let him keep the snake. The boy thought that Old Ben would be (use + -ful) _____ on the farm, and eat the mice that were always (nibble + -ing) _____ the corn in the corncrib. However, his father had no (like + -ing) _____ for snakes. At first, his parents watched the snake (close + -ly) _____, because they did not know whether they could trust Old Ben. But, as time went by, the boy saw that his father was (come + -ing) _____ to like the snake. He even began (place + -ing) _____ bowls of water in the corncrib for Old Ben to drink.

Challenge: The author of "Old Ben" mentions two kinds of snake: the blacksnake and the copperhead. Both their names describe their appearance. The blacksnake is all black, and the copperhead has a copper-colored head. Below are some descriptions of other animals and a list of animal names. Write the letter of the animal name that matches each description.

a. yellow-bellied sapsucker   c. hammerhead shark   e. walking stick
b. praying mantis   d. calico cat   f. bottle-nosed dolphin

____ 1. a three-colored, brightly marked cat

____ 2. an insect that is protected by looking like a twig or stick

____ 3. a sea animal with a long, narrow snout

____ 4. a fish with a flat, wide head

____ 5. a bird with a belly the color of an egg yolk

____ 6. an insect that folds its front legs to look like a pair of praying hands

"Old Ben" by Jesse Stuart (text page 164)
"Feathered Friend" by Arthur C. Clarke (text page 168)
"Childhood and Poetry" by Pablo Neruda (text page 172)

Build Grammar Skills: The Perfect Tenses

The perfect tenses of verbs give narrative writers three ways of relating an event to what came before it. The perfect tenses include a form of the verb to *have* plus the past participle of the main verb.

- The **present perfect tense** shows that an event **began in the past** and continues into the present. The present perfect includes a **present-tense** form of *have* plus the **past participle** of the main verb: I <u>have been</u> a lucky man.

- The **past perfect tense** shows that an event took place before another past event or time. It includes a **past-tense** form of *have* plus the **past participle** of the main verb: He <u>had cleaned</u> the corncrib of mice.

- The **future perfect tense** shows that an event will be completed before another future event or time. It includes a **future-tense** form of *have* plus the **past participle** of the main verb: You <u>will have learned</u> who committed the crime before you finish the book.

A. Practice: In the space provided, identify the tense of the italicized words as either present perfect, past perfect, or future perfect. The first one has been done as an example.

past perfect   1. The boy's father *had hated* snakes before he met Old Ben.

_____   2. I *have had* many pets, but never as good a pet as that snake.

_____   3. The Spacers *had adopted* the canary as their pet before she saved their lives.

_____   4. By the time the new stadium is built, the team *will have played* for thirty years in the old one.

_____   5. We *have enjoyed* many evenings in the park.

_____   6. By noon tomorrow, we *will have finished* our homework.

B. Writing Application: Rewrite each of the following sentences on the lines provided, filling in the specified perfect tense of the verb in parentheses. The first one has been done as an example.

1. We _____ the test before the bell rang. (past perfect, *finish*)
   We had finished the test before the bell rang.
   _____

2. The players _____ the locker room to start the game. (present perfect, *leave*)
   _____

3. By the end of the year, they _____ the whole book. (future perfect, *read*)
   _____

4. Before going to the store, we _____ to the bank. (past perfect, *go*)
   _____

5. The club _____ not to meet next week. (present perfect, *decide*)
   _____

"Old Ben" by Jesse Stuart (text page 164)
"Feathered Friend" by Arthur C. Clarke (text page 168)
"Childhood and Poetry" by Pablo Neruda (text page 172)

Reading Strategy: Context Clues

Sometimes, you can figure out the meaning of an unfamiliar word by finding clues in the word's **context**—the words, phrases, and sentences around the new word. For example, in "Childhood and Poetry," the author writes about "the *tiny* objects and *minuscule* beings of my world." Even if there were no definition available, you could use the word *tiny* as a context clue to tell you that *minuscule*, like *tiny*, means "very small." When you come across a new word in your reading, look for context clues before you reach for a dictionary. After you try to figure out the meaning of the word from the clues you find, compare your conclusion with the dictionary definition.

DIRECTIONS: In each of the following passages from the selections, there is an italicized word. Look for context clues in the passage that may give you a hint about the word's meaning. Then, write the context clue and the meaning of the word on the line provided. The first one has been done as an example.

1. There he lay coiled like heavy *strands* of black rope. He was a big bull blacksnake.

   Context clue: _____"of black rope"_____ Meaning: _____cords or ropes_____

2. The more I petted him, the more *affectionate* he became. He was so friendly I decided to trust him.

   Context clue: _____ Meaning: _____

3. . . . it was a difficult job, for a space suit is not the most convenient of *garbs* in which to work.

   Context clue: _____ Meaning: _____

4. . . . you will picture Sven at once as a six foot-six inch Nordic giant. . . . Actually he was a *wiry* little fellow. . .

   Context clue: _____ Meaning: _____

5. Though of course there is no "day" and "night" when you are floating in *permanent* sunlight . . .

   Context clue: _____ Meaning: _____

6. My mind seemed to be very *sluggish* that morning, as if I was still unable to cast off the burden of sleep.

   Context clue: _____ Meaning: _____

"Old Ben" by Jesse Stuart (text page 164)

"Feathered Friend" by Arthur C. Clarke (text page 168)

"Childhood and Poetry" by Pablo Neruda (text page 172)

Literary Focus: Narratives

A **narrative** is a story made up of events linked together. The events may be nonfiction (true) like "Old Ben" and "Friends All of Us." They might be fiction (made up) like "Feathered Friend." One way in which many narrative events are linked is that one event causes, or leads to, another. When you read a narrative, you may find it useful to keep track of the events and how one leads to another by using a graphic organizer like the one below.

A. DIRECTIONS: The following events all occur in "Feathered Friends," but in a different order. In the graphic organizer below, write the number of each event in the order in which it occurs in the story. The first and last events have been filled in as examples.

1. Sven finds Claribel motionless and thinks the canary is dead.

2. Sven smuggles a canary on board a space station.

3. The narrator realizes that there is something wrong with the air in the space station.

4. Claribel revives after being given oxygen, but passes out again.

5. The narrator is startled to hear a bird song just behind his head while he is working.

6. Jim, the engineer, discovers that the air purifying system has not been working properly.

7. The crew make Claribel a company pet.

8. The narrator wakes up with a headache and feeling tired.

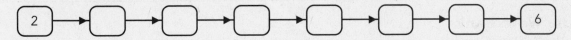

B. DIRECTIONS: On the lines below, write the events, thoughts, and statements of the narrator's father that show how his attitude toward Old Ben changes from the beginning of the narrative to the end. Write the events, thoughts, and statements in the order in which they occur in the narrative.

1. _____

2. _____

3. _____

4. _____

5. _____

6. _____

7. _____

from *The Pigman & Me* by Paul Zindel (text page 189)

Build Vocabulary

Using the Suffix *-tion*

The suffix *-tion*, meaning "the act, result, or condition of," generally changes a verb into a noun.

Examples: construct (to build); construction (the act or result of building)
imitate (to copy or ape); imitation (the act or result of copying or aping)

A. DIRECTIONS: In the first column of the following chart is a list of words. In the third column, each word has had the suffix *-tion* added to it. Fill in the blanks with the meanings of the words. (Hint: Each meaning in the last column will begin with "the act of . . . ," "the result of . . . ," or "the condition of . . . "). One example is provided.

Word	Meaning	Word with *-tion*	Meaning
1. educate	teach	education	the result of teaching
2. select		selection	
3. invite		invitation	
4. connect		connection	
5. subtract		subtraction	

Using the Word Bank

exact	tactics	undulating	goading
distorted	groveled	condemnation	

B. DIRECTIONS: All the Word Bank words below have been scrambled. Unscramble the words, and write the letter of the correct Word Bank word next to the word's definition.

    a. dgvrleoe   c. xtace   e. duntigunal   g. scatsic
    b. dmancotnonie d. isdtroedt   f. gnaigod

____ 1. pushing someone into action   ____ 5. methods used to achieve a goal

____ 2. harsh judgment or disapproval   ____ 6. crawled on the ground hoping
                                                             for mercy

____ 3. take by force

____ 4. moving in waves   ____ 7. twisted out of normal shape

C. DIRECTIONS: Circle the letter of the word that means the same as the word in CAPITAL LETTERS.

1. CREATION: a. the act of creating b. to create c. creativity d. imagination

2. INSTRUCTION: a. to teach b. the act of learning c. the act of teaching d. learned

3. PROTECTION: a. to protect b. protecting c. desire to protect d. result of protecting

from *The Pigman & Me* by Paul Zindel (text page 189)

Build Spelling Skills: Spelling the Sound *shun* at the End of a Word

Spelling Strategy When the base form of a word ends with a *t* sound, usually use *-tion* to spell the sound *shun* as a suffix. Other words spell the final *shun* sound *sion*.

    Examples: promote + *shun* = promo**tion**

                       express + *shun* = expres**sion**.

Note that you need to change the spelling of most words before adding *-tion*. For example, the final e is dropped from *promote* to form *promotion*; the final *s* is dropped from *express* to form *expression*.

  Exceptions: For many words, there is no clear rule for when to use *-tion* and when to use *-sion*. It is a good idea to check the spelling of such words in a dictionary if you're not sure of which spelling to use.

A. Practice: In the space provided, write the word formed by adding the *-tion* or *-sion* to the following words. Follow the instructions for how to change the spelling of each word before adding *-tion* or *-sion*. The first word has been done as an example.

1. prevent + shun = _____prevention_____ (Drop the final *t*.)

2. confess + shun = _____ (Drop the final *s*.)

3. elevate + shun = _____ (Drop the final *te*.)

4. protect + shun = _____ (Drop the final *t*.)

5. interrupt + shun = _____ (Drop the final *t*.)

6. profess + shun = _____ (Drop the final *s*.)

7. provide + shun = _____ (Drop the final *de*.)

8. condemn + shun = _____ (Add a final *a*.)

B. Practice: Proofread the following paragraph. After each underlined word, write the letter "C" if the word is spelled correctly; if the word is spelled incorrectly, write the correct spelling on the line in parentheses. The first one has been done as an example.

    Paul did not know how to handle the new <u>complicasion</u> (_____complication_____) in his life. Because of some <u>confution</u> (_____) about playground rules, he had to choose between fighting another boy or getting the <u>reputation</u> (_____) of being a coward. He did not want to ask his friend for <u>protection</u> (_____), but he could not think of any way out of his <u>situasion</u> (_____). In <u>desperasion</u> (_____), he spoke to Nonno Frankie, but their <u>discussion</u> (_____) was not very helpful. Paul came to the sad <u>conclution</u> (_____) that he would probably have to fight John Quinn on Monday afternoon.

Name _____ Date _____

Build Grammar Skills: Adjectives

An **adjective** is a word that describes a noun by telling more about the person, place, or thing. An adjective answers questions such as, *What kind? Which one? How many?* or *How much?* In the following sentences, all the underlined words are adjectives.

Examples: He repeated the <u>weird</u> sentence.
Weird answers the question, "**What kind** of sentence?"

He once killed <u>two million</u> enemies in <u>one</u> hour.
Two million answers the question, "**How many** enemies were killed?" *One* answers the question "**How many** hours did it take?"

This happened on the <u>first</u> Friday, during gym period . . .
First answers the question, "**Which** Friday?"

A. Practice: Underline the adjective in each of the following sentences. On the line following each sentence write the question the adjective answers: *What kind? Which one?* or *How many?* The first sentence has been done as an example.

1. Paul was a <u>new</u> student in school. ___What kind?_____

2. Paul did not know that fifteen minutes was the limit for using a paddle. _____

3. It was only Paul's first week of school. _____

4. A huge crowd was waiting to see the fight. _____

5. Paul tried to kick John's left shin, but missed. _____

6. Paul's brave sister saved him from being attacked. _____

B. Writing Application: On each of the lines provided, write a sentence using the word in parentheses as an adjective, describing a person, place, or thing. The first one has been done as an example.

1. (energetic) ___An energetic person will take on many projects._____

2. (dangerous) _____

3. (eighteen) _____

4. (chocolate) _____

5. (exciting) _____

6. (angry) _____

7. (difficult) _____

Reading for Success: Interactive Reading Strategies

Interactive Reading is a process through which you get involved with what you are reading. Use the following reading strategies to get involved with the ideas images, and information presented in the text.

- **Set a Purpose for Reading.** Before you begin, determine your reason for reading. Are you reading for enjoyment or to obtain factual information? The details to which you pay attention will change, depending on the purpose you set.

- **Ask Questions.** Make the reading an active experience by asking questions and trying to answer them as you read. Ask why characters behave as they do, what causes events to happen, and why the writer includes certain information.

- **Relate to Your Own Experience.** Stories and poems are great inventions for letting you see things through the eyes of others. You can tune in a better picture, however, by relating what you read to experiences in your own life.

- **Predict.** Don't just wait to find out what happens next. Make a prediction based on what you have read. Then check to see if your predictions were right and make new predictions as you gain new information.

DIRECTIONS: Read the following passage from "The Sneaker Crisis" by Shirley Jackson, and apply the reading strategies to interact with the text. In the margin, note where you set a purpose, ask questions, relate your experience. Finally, respond briefly to the selection on the lines provided.

from *"The Sneaker Crisis"* by Shirley Jackson

The following passage describes the beginning of a strange family emergency.

Day after day I went around the house picking things up. I picked up books and shoes and toys and socks and shirts and gloves and boots and hats and handkerchiefs and puzzle pieces and pennies and pencils and stuffed rabbits and bones the dog had left under the living-room chairs. I also picked up tin soldiers and plastic cars and baseball gloves and sweaters and children's pocketbooks with nickels inside and little pieces of lint off the floor.

Every time I picked up something I put it back down again somewhere else where it belonged better that it did in the place where I found it. Nine times out of ten, I did not notice what I was pickling up or where I put it until sometime later when someone in the family needed it. Then, when Sally said where were her crayons I could answer at once: kitchen windowsill, left. If Barry wanted his cowboy hat I could reply: playroom, far end of bookcase. If Jannie wanted her arithmetic homework, I could tell her it was under the ashtray on the dining-room buffet.

I could locate the little nut that came off Laurie's bike wheel, and the directions for winding the living room clock. I could find the recipe for the turkey cutlets Sally admired and the top to my husband's fountain pen. I could even find, ordinarily, the little plastic strips which went inside the collar of his nylon shirt.

If I could not respond at once, identifying object and location in unhesitating answer to the question, the article was very apt to remain permanently lost. Like Jannie's pink Easter-egg hat, which disappeared—let me see—it was the day Laurie got into the fight with the Haynes boys, and the porch rocker got broken—make it the end of October.

(continued next page)

We had many small places in our big house where an Easter-egg hat could get itself hopelessly hidden, so when Jannie asked one night at dinner, the end of October, "Who took my Easter-egg hat?" and I found myself without an immediate answer, it was clear that the hat had taken itself off, and although we searched half-heartedly, Jannie had to wear a scarf around her head until the weather got cold enough to wear her long-tailed knitted cap.

Laurie's sneaker was of considerably more moment, since, of course, he could not play basketball with a scarf tied around his left foot. He came to the top of the back stairs on a Saturday morning and inquired gently who had stolen his sneaker.

I opened my mouth to answer, found my mind blank, and closed my mouth again. Laurie came halfway down the stairs and bawled, "Moooooom, where'd my sneaker get to?" and I still could not answer. "I neeeeeed my sneaker," Laurie howled. "I got to play baaaaaaasketball."

He crashed down the stairs and into the study, where I sat reading the morning paper and drinking a cup of coffee. "I got to play basketball. I can't play on the basketball court without sneakers. So I need—"

"Have you looked? In your room? Under your bed?"

"Yeah, sure." He thought. "It's not there, though."

"Outdoors?"

"Now what would my sneaker be doing outdoors, I ask you? You think I get dressed and undressed on the lawn?"

"Well," I said helplessly, "you had it last Saturday."

"I know I had it last Saturday."

"Wait." I went and stood at the foot of the back stairs and called, "Jannie?"

There was a pause. Then Jannie said, sniffling, "Yes?"

"Good heavens," I said, " Are you reading Little Women again?"

Jannie sniffled. "Just the part where Beth dies."

"Look," I said, "the sun is shining, the sky is blue and—"

"You seen my sneaker?" Laurie yelled from in back of me.

"No."

"You sure?"

Jannie came to the top of the stairs, wiping her eyes. "Hey," she said, "maybe some girl took it. For a keepsake."

"Wha?" said Laurie, incredulously. "Took my sneaker?"

"Like Mr. Brook did Meg's glove, in Little Women, because he was in love with her and they got married."

"Wha?" For a minute Laurie stared at her. Then he turned deliberately and went back to the study. "My sister," he announced formally to his father, "has snapped her twigs."

_____

_____

_____

_____

_____

_____

_____

_____

_____

Name _____ Date _____

from *The Pigman & Me* by Paul Zindel (text page 189)

Literary Focus: Internal Conflict

In a story, a **conflict** is a struggle that take place between opposing characters or forces. An **internal conflict** takes place inside a person or character. For example, in *The Pigman and Me*, the narrator has a conflict within himself after John Quinn challenges him to a fight. On the one hand, he is a new student at school and does not want to look like he is a coward. On the other hand, he does not want to fight. His struggle is internal.

A. DIRECTIONS: Answer the following questions on the lines provided.

1. What would happen if Paul simply chose to look courageous and not cowardly? _____

    _____

    Why would this outcome be undesirable for Paul? _____

2. What would happen if Paul simply decided to avoid a fight? _____

    _____

    Why would this outcome be undesirable for Paul? _____

B. DIRECTIONS: The following quotations from *The Pigman and Me* demonstrate how Paul's internal conflict makes him feel. Choose one of these quotations, and use the lines provided to explain why Paul's conflict makes him feel the way he does.

1. By the time Monday morning came, I was a nervous wreck.

2. Nevertheless, my mind was numb with fear all day at school.

3. . . . I thought I was going to pass out.

    _____

    _____

    _____

    _____

    _____

    _____

    _____

"**Thunder Butte**" by Virginia Driving Hawk Sneve (text page 201)

Build Vocabulary

Using Related Words: Forms of *vary*

The Word Bank word *variegated* is related to the familiar word *vary*, which means "to differ." Like all words related to *vary*, *variegated* includes the idea of "difference" in its meaning. Something that is variegated is marked with different colors, just like the agates that Norman finds on the butte. Here are some other words related to *vary*.

variety: a collection of different things
varied: of different kinds; many-sided
various: of different kinds; many or several
variable: tending to change or become different

A. DIRECTIONS: Use the correct word to complete each sentence.

1. I don't know what kind of tape to get for Mark because his taste in music is so (variegated, variable) _____; one week all he listens to is classical music, and the next week he won't listen to anything but jazz.

2. I think I'll go to Music World to shop for something, because they have the greatest (variety, various) _____ of tapes to choose from.

3. After looking in (various, variable) _____ sections of the store, I decided to get something by the Beatles.

4. I thought that Mark would be sure to find something that he likes in their music, since their songs are so (variety, varied) _____.

Using the Word Bank

meanderings	diminutive	variegated	heathen	adamant

B. DIRECTIONS Match each word in the left column with its definition in the right column. Write the letter of the definition on the line next to the word it defines.

____ 1. variegated   a. not willing to give in

____ 2. adamant   b. not civilized

____ 3. meanderings   c. wanderings

____ 4. heathen   d. very small

____ 5. diminutive   e. marked with different colors

"Thunder Butte" by Virginia Driving Hawk Sneve (text page 201)

Build Spelling Skills: Syllables

Spelling Strategy A word is made up of one or more units of sound called **syllables**. For example, if you say the following words out loud and slowly, you will hear each syllable.

rock (one syllable); **summit** (two syllables); **thunderbolt** (three syllables); **meanderings** (four syllables)

Noticing the syllables in these and other words will help you include all the sounds when you spell them.

A. Practice: Pronounce each of the following words to yourself. Then indicate the number of syllables in each on the lines provided.

1. diminutive	_____	7. grandfather	_____
2. rocky	_____	8. agate	_____
3. rattlesnake	_____	9. overhanging	_____
4. warrior	_____	10. stick	_____
5. morning	_____	11. laboriously	_____
6. sun	_____	12. top	_____

B. Practice: Complete the following paragraph. Using the clues in parentheses for help, choose six words from Practice A to fill in the blanks.

Early one (two-syllable word) _____, Norman leaves to see his (three-syllable word) _____, who lives on the west side of Thunder Butte. The journey is demanding and dangerous, because he must follow a steep, (two-syllable word) _____ trail in order to get to the other side of the hill. Along the way, Norman climbs an (four-syllable word) _____ ledge, avoids a (three-syllable word) _____, and jumps down a twenty-foot gap. He also finds an old coup (one-syllable word) _____, which becomes a source of conflict within his family.

Challenge: The Word Bank word *diminutive*, meaning "very small," might remind you of other words such as *minimum* and *miniature*, which contain the syllable *min* and have meanings related to the idea of smallness. Also related are the words *miniskirt*, *minibus*, and *minivan*, since the prefix *mini-* is a short form of miniature. All these words come to us from the Latin word *minor*, which means "small."

On the lines below, write three sentences using the following words: *diminutive*, *miniature*, and *minimum*. Use a different word in each sentence.

_____

_____

_____

Name _____ Date _____

Build Grammar Skills: Possessives as Adjectives

Adjectives are words that modify nouns or pronouns. They can answer the questions *what kind?* and *how many?* They can also answer the question *whose?* Look at these sentences.

The sun's rays heated the rocky landscape.

<u>Norman's</u> mother told him to be careful.

The boy found a Sioux <u>warrior's</u> *coup* stick on the butte.

In these sentences, the words *sun's*, *Norman's*, and *warrior's* are possessive nouns—nouns that show possession or ownership. These possessives function as adjectives because they answer the question *whose?* Now look at these sentences.

Norman examines the stick and *its* markings.   He showed the stick to *his* grandfather.

In these sentences, the words *its* and *his* are possessive pronouns—pronouns that show possession or ownership. Other possessive pronouns function as adjectives include *my, your, her, our, their*. All can answer the question *whose?*

A. Practice: Circle the possessives that function as adjectives in the each of the following sentences. Remember that these words answer the question *whose?*

1. Norman dressed in his oldest clothes and pulled on worn boots to protect his feet.

2. "Guess I'll go," Norman said to his mother, who was pouring hot water into her dish pan.

3. Norman whistled, trying to echo the meadowlarks' happy song, as he left on his journey.

4. The boy's heart pounded as he realized that the stick had once belonged to the old ones.

5. Norman's grandfather explained the thunderbolt's meaning.

6. Grandfather said, "The Thunders favored a certain few of the young men who sought their vision on the butte."

B. Writing Application: Write a sentence about each topic provided below, using possessives as adjectives as suggested. When you are finished, reread your sentences and underline any additional possessives that you used as adjectives.

1. Write a sentence about a challenge that you have faced, using the possessive my as an adjective.

   _____

2. Write a sentence that tells something about a member of your family. Use the person's name in a possessive form.

   _____

3. Write a sentence about your school. Use the possessive school's as an adjective.

   _____

4. Write a question that you might ask someone whom you recently met. Use the possessive your as an adjective.

   _____

"**Thunder Butte**" by Virginia Driving Hawk Sneve (text page 201)

Reading Strategy: Ask Questions

Why is he going there? What is she thinking? Where did that object come from? If you **ask questions** and search for answers as you read, you will be more fully aware of what's going on in a story. You will have a better understanding of the relationships between characters, events, and ideas.

For example, suppose that you arrived at this passage from the beginning "Thunder Butte." What questions might you ask?

> Norman reluctantly rose. Last night he had accepted his grandfather's command to go to Thunder Butte without too many doubts. Yet now in the morning's chill light the boy wondered if his grandfather's dreams were the meaningless meanderings of an old mind, or if his grandfather was really worthy of the tribe's respect as one of the few remaining wise elders who understood the ancient ways.

Two questions a reader like you might ask are: "Why did Norman's grandfather command him to go to Thunder Butte?" and "What did the grandfather see in his dreams?" You might also wonder along with Norman: "Are the grandfather's dream signs of ancient wisdom, or are they just "meaningless meanderings?" As you read on, you would search for information in the text that would answer your questions directly or for details that would help you form answers.

DIRECTIONS: Read the following passages from "Thunder Butte." After each one, jot down at least one question that you asked yourself as you read. Note that the events in the first passage take place after Norman finds the coup stick. The events in the second passage take place just after he returns home.

1. "But why should I have been the one to find it?" Norman questioned.

His grandfather shrugged. "Perhaps to help you understand the ways—the values of the old ones.

"But nobody believes in that kind of thing anymore," Norman scoffed. "And even if people did, I couldn't run out and hit my enemy with the stick and get away with it." He smiled, thinking of Mr. Brannon. "No one would think I was brave. I'd probably just get thrown in jail."

Suddenly Norman felt compelled to stop talking. In the distance he hear a gentle rumble which seemed to come from the butte. He glanced up at the hill looming high above and saw that it was capped with dark, low-hanging clouds.

Matt Two Bull looked too and smiled. "The Thunders are displeased with your thoughts," he said to Norman. "Listen to their message."

_____

_____

2. His mother was standing at the stove. "Oh, Norman," she greeted him, smiling. "I'm glad you're back. I was beginning to worry." Her welcoming smile turned to a frown as she saw the coup stick in Norman's hand. "What is that?"

"Grandpa say it's a coup stick. Here," Norman handed it to her, "take a look at it. It's interesting the way it is made and the decor—"

"No," Sarah interrupted and backed away from him. "I won't touch that heathen thing no matter what it is! Get it out of the house!"

_____

_____

"Thunder Butte" by Virginia Driving Hawk Sneve (text page 201)

Literary Focus: Atmosphere

Atmosphere is the feeling or mood of a work of literature. Through a careful choice of details, phrases, and images, a writer can create an atmosphere that is light-hearted or serious, cheerful or threatening, silly or mysterious.

A. DIRECTIONS: Read the following passage, and circle the images, phrases, or details that help to create a certain atmosphere. One the lines below, write a sentence describing the atmosphere that the details convey.

1. He was afraid that the cane may have plunged into a rattlesnake den. Carefully he pulled at the stout branch, wiggling it this way and that with one hand while he dug with the other. It came loose, sending a shower of rocks down the hill, and Norman saw that something else was sticking up in the hole he had uncovered.

_____

2. "Sarah," John said as he put the tools away, "think of the stick as an object that could be in a museum, a part of history. It's not like we were going to fall down on our knees and pray to it." His voice was light and teasing as he tried to make peace.

But Sarah stood stiffly at the stove preparing supper and would not answer. Norman felt sick. His appetite was gone. When his mother set a plat of food before him he excused himself saying, "I guess I'm too tired to eat," and went to his room.

_____

B. DIRECTIONS: Use the organizer below to record other details in the story that help to create atmosphere. Use the space in the center to name the mood or feeling you sense. Jot down the details that contribute to this atmosphere.

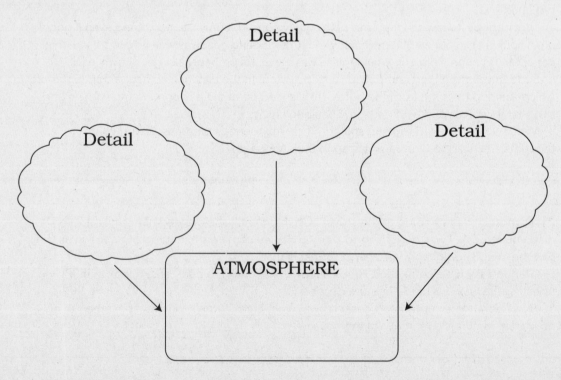

"Be Like the Bird" by Victor Hugo (text page 214)
"Dream Dust" by Langston Hughes (text page 214)
"Stage Fright" by Mark Twain (text page 215)
"Alone in the Nets" by Arnold Adoff (text page 216)

Build Vocabulary

Using Related Words: Forms of *oppose*

In "Alone in the Field," the speaker describes what it is like to be alone, defending your team's nets, as "half the opposition is pounding down the field." The *opposition* that the speaker refers to is the other, or *opposing*, team. Both *opposition* and *opposing* are forms of the word *oppose*, which means "to be against or in contrast."

A. DIRECTIONS: Use one of these forms of *oppose* to complete each question: *oppose, opposition, opposing, opposite*. Write your answers on the lines.

1. Sheila and Ted are the captains of the two debate teams that will _____, each other in the state championship.

2. Each team leader knows that the _____ is highly skilled and well prepared.

3. As experienced debaters, they know that it is important to listen carefully to catch all the details of the _____ argument.

4. You might think that Sheila and Ted have bad things to say about each other, but in fact the _____ is true.

Using the Word Bank

slight	compulsion	opposition	evaporate

B. DIRECTIONS: Answer each of the following questions to demonstrate your understanding of the Word Bank words. Circle the letter of your choice.

1. Which of the following would evaporate on a hot, sunny day?

    a. a puddle of water   b. a flower bud

2. Which of the following would you describe as the opposition during a tennis match?

    a. yourself   b. the person you are playing against

3. Which of the following might you describe as being slight?

    a. a jet plane   b. a fragile, hand-made kite

4. Which of the following situations involves some sort of compulsion?

    a. You take your little brother and his friends to the park because you promised

       to do so.

    b. You finally buy the bicycle that you've been saving for all year.

Unit 3: Proving Yourself

Name _____ Date _____

"Be Like the Bird" by Victor Hugo (text page 214)
"Dream Dust" by Langston Hughes (text page 214)
"Stage Fright" by Mark Twain (text page 215)
"Alone in the Nets" by Arnold Adoff (text page 216)

Build Spelling Skills: Spelling the Long *i* Sound With *igh*

Spelling Strategy The long *i* sound is sometimes spelled *igh*, as it is in the Word Bank word *slight*. For example, here are two words that rhyme with *slight* and that are spelled with *igh*:

    right, sight

Here are two other words in which the long *i* sound is spelled with *igh*: high, sigh

A. Practice: Write a word in which the long *i* sound is spelled *igh*, according to each clue given below. Write your answers on the lines.

1. This word rhymes with slight and means "the opposite of day." _____

2. This word rhymes with high and can complete the following sentence: The knee bone is connected to the _____ bone.

3. This word rhymes with right and means "the opposite of dull." _____

4. This word rhymes with sight. It can mean "strength," or it can mean "will possibly," as in "I _____ go to the movies this weekend."

5. This word rhymes with high and means "to breathe out in a way that expresses relief or sorrow." _____

6. This word rhymes with slight and means "the opposite of loose." _____

7. This word rhymes with sigh and means "the opposite of low." _____

8. This word rhymes with sight. It can means "the opposite of wrong." It can also mean "the opposite of left." _____

B. Practice: Use the following words to complete the paragraph below. Use one of the words twice.

    high   night   bright   flight   might

Writers and artists often use birds to represent ideas, feelings, and qualities, as Victor Hugo does in "Be Like the Bird." A bird that is in _____, soaring _____ above the ground, is a common symbol for freedom and creativity. A bluebird represents a _____] and cheerful outlook, as you might guess from the expression "the blue-bird of happiness." Owls are usually associated with wisdom, but because they are nocturnal birds, they _____ also be used to represent the _____. In fact, people who function at their best after dark are often call _____ owls.

"Be Like the Bird" by Victor Hugo (text page 214)
"Dream Dust" by Langston Hughes (text page 214)
"Stage Fright" by Mark Twain (text page 215)
"Alone in the Nets" by Arnold Adoff (text page 216)

Build Grammar Skills: Articles

The words *a*, *an*, and the belong to a special group of adjectives called **articles**. Articles are the most frequently used of all adjectives.

The is called a **definite article** because it points out a particular person, place, thing, or idea. *A* and *an* are called **indefinite articles** because each of these words does not point out a particular person, place, thing, or idea.

Examples:

Indefinite Article	**Definite Article**
We asked Ms. Leung to give <u>a</u> speech.	<u>The</u> speech lasted thirty minutes.
I gave my ticket to <u>an</u> usher.	<u>The</u> usher who took my ticket is over there.

When should you use the indefinite article *a* and when should you use *an*? If you look at the examples above, you'll notice that *a* is used before a word that begins with a consonant sound: *a speech. An* is used before a word that begins with a vowel sound: *an usher.*

A. Practice: Underline all of the articles in the following sentences. Then above each one, write *D* if it is a definite article or *I* if it is an indefinite article.

1. In "Alone in the Nets," Arnold Adoff describes a tense and exciting sporting event.

2. The sport that the poem focuses on is soccer.

3. The poem takes place on a cold and rainy afternoon.

4. The poem's speaker defends the nets from the opposition.

5. A player who does this job on a soccer team is known as a "goalie."

6. At one point, the speaker feels caught in a frozen moment and asks, "Why am I here?"

7. Things brighten when the speaker intercepts a shot made by the other team's forward.

8. The entire poem is told from the point of the view of the goalie.

B. Writing Application: As you read the following paragraph, cross out each incorrect use of a, an, or the, and write the correct word above the line. One example is given.

an
In "Stage Fright," Mark Twain describes ~~the~~ experience that many people have had in one

form or another. As he puts it, he was making a appearance before a audience of human be-

ings, and he came down with the terrible case of stage fright. He compares stage fright to sea-

sickness, proclaiming that the two are the pair. In both cases, an person's knees shake so

badly that he or she can hardly stand up. Fortunate, according to Twain, a dreadful case of

stage fright left him after a first five minutes of the speech he was giving, never to return.

"Be Like the Bird" by Victor Hugo (text page 214)
"Dream Dust" by Langston Hughes (text page 214)
"Stage Fright" by Mark Twain (text page 215)
"Alone in the Nets" by Arnold Adoff (text page 216)

Reading Strategy: Relate to Your Own Experience

When you make connections between the events, feelings, and ideas in a work of literature and your own memories, feelings, and thoughts, you **relate** the work of literature to your own experience. Connecting ideas and experiences in this way will make the works you read more meaningful for you.

A. DIRECTIONS: Use the chart to relate the works in this grouping to your own experiences. First, identify the main experiences and feelings described within a work by filling in the first two columns. Then, in the third column, write a sentence or two explaining how these relate to your own experience. Note that part of the entry for "Stage Fright" has been filled in for you.

	Topic of Work	Feelings Described	My Experience
"Be Like the Bird"			
"Dream Dust"			
"Stage Fright"	speaking before a large audience for the first time in your life	fear, nervousness	
"Alone in the Nets"			

B. DIRECTIONS: Did you find that one of the works related to your experiences more than any of the others in the group? Identify the work that you felt came closest to capturing feelings and experiences that you have had. Then write a few sentences explaining why you chose it.

_____

_____

_____

_____

"Be Like the Bird" by Victor Hugo (text page 214)
"Dream Dust" by Langston Hughes (text page 214)
"Stage Fright" by Mark Twain (text page 215)
"Alone in the Nets" by Arnold Adoff (text page 216)

Literary Focus: Levels of Meaning

Poems and other works of literature often have two or more **levels of meaning**. One level that is always there for you to understand is made up of the literal meaning—what the words actually say. On the level or levels beyond you can grasp deeper meanings that relate to ideas about life in general.

For example, think about the different levels of meaning within "Be Like the Bird" as you reread the poem. What is the poem's literal meaning? What deeper meaning does it contain?

Be like the bird who / Halting in his flight / On limb too slight / Feels it give way beneath him.
/ Yet sings / Knowing he has wings.

On a literal level, the poem describes a bird who is able to use his wings to lift off from a branch that is too light to hold him. On a deeper level, it is about life. The poet advises us to use our "wings," or special abilities, to rise above our mistakes and misfortunes.

DIRECTIONS: Reread "Dream Dust" and "Alone in the Nets." Summarize the literal meaning of each work. Then jot down your ideas about the deeper meaning.

1. **"Dream Dust"**

Literal meaning: _____

_____

_____

_____

Deeper meaning: _____

_____

_____

_____

2. **"Alone in the Nets"**

Literal meaning: _____

_____

_____

_____

Deeper meaning: _____

_____

_____

_____

Unit 3: Proving Yourself

"The Dog of Pompeii" by Louis Untermeyer (text page 221)

Build Vocabulary

A. DIRECTIONS: For each of the definitions below, write the appropriate word from the following box. Write one letter of the word in each space. Then, on the bottom write the letters from the circled spaces. The word you write will describe Bimbo, the dog of Pompeii.

sham	villa	barometer	proverb	vapors

1. an instrument to forecast changes in weather (_) _ _ _ _ _ _ _ _

2. fumes _ _ _ (_) _

3. fake _ _ (_) _

4. large house (_) _ _ _ _

5. short saying that expresses an obvious truth _ _ _ _ (_) _

The word that describes Bimbo: _ _ _ _ _

B. DIRECTIONS: Complete each of the following sentences by writing one word from the list of words above in the blank space.

1. The family lived in a huge _____ surrounded by beautiful gardens.

2. "Early to bed, early to rise . . . " is the beginning of a _____.

3. The cover of the book was _____ leather, but it looked just like the real thing.

4. On a cold day, thick _____ hung above the lake, making it impossible to see the far side.

5. We made a _____ in science class that let us know when the weather was going to change.

"The Dog of Pompeii" by Louis Untermeyer (text page 221)

Connect a Short Story to Social Studies

"The Dog of Pompeii" describes the destruction of Pompeii in A.D. 79 by an eruption of the Mount Vesuvius volcano. Because the molten ash from the volcano preserved the city, scientists and historians have been able to learn much about life and culture in that ancient time. Louis Untermeyer took advantage of that knowledge and included many details about Roman life in "The Dog of Pompeii."

DIRECTIONS: Complete the chart Ancient Roman life and culture, based on details in the story.

Life and Culture in Ancient Rome	
1. Economy	
2. Professions	
3. Religious beliefs	
4. Food	
5. Entertainment	

Unit 3: Proving Yourself

"Mowgli's Brothers" by Rudyard Kipling (text page 238)

Build Vocabulary

Using the Prefix mono-

The prefix *mono-* means "one," as you can see in the meaning the Word Bank word *monotonous*. Something that is monotonous is tiresome because it has one sound or quality that does not vary. Here are some other words that contain the prefix *mono-*.

monograph: a scholarly book or article focusing on one specific subject
monologue: a long speech made by one speaker or one character in a play
monopoly: the control of an entire business by one company
monorail: a railway with a single track
monosyllables: words of one syllable

A. DIRECTIONS: Complete each sentence using one of the words listed above.

1. Paul is rehearsing his _____ for the school play.

2. Now there are two gas stations in town, and no one has a _____.

3. Professor Dawes is writing a _____ about ancient Egyptian mummies.

4. My little brother was mad and barely speaking to me, and whenever I tried to ask him questions, he answered in _____.

5. In only five minutes, the _____ will take you to the airport terminal.

Using the Word Bank

scuttled	quarry	fostering	veterans	monotonous	dispute	clamor

B. DIRECTIONS: Write the Word Bank word that you would use to describe each of the following.

1. an animal being hunted or pursued: _____

2. the noise made by six-year-old twins who loudly refuse to go to bed: _____

3. a tiresome task that you had to do over and over: _____

4. committee members who have worked on the same project year after year: _____

5. the way a chipmunk moved: _____

6. another way to say "taking care of": _____

7. another word for "argument": _____

C. DIRECTIONS: Each item consists of a related pair of words in CAPITAL LETTERS, followed by four lettered pairs of words. Choose a pair that best expresses a relationship similar to that expressed in the pair in capital letters. Circle the letter of your choice.

1. HUNTER: QUARRY
   a. contestant : prize
   b. tiger: lion
   c. chase : pursue
   d. farmer : weather

2. MONOTONOUS : LIVELY
   a. loud : noisy
   b. top : bottom
   c. smooth : bumpy
   d. pleased : joyful

"Mowgli's Brothers" by Rudyard Kipling (text page 238)

Build Spelling Skills: Three Vowels in a Row

Spelling Strategy If you remember that the word *monotonous* has three *o's* in a row—one in each of the first three syllables—you will more easily remember how to spell this long word. Here are some other long words that are spelled with the same vowel in three or more syllables in a row. Remembering that the vowel repeats itself will help you remember the spelling of these words, too.

asp<u>a</u>r<u>a</u>gus   <u>e</u>m<u>e</u>rg<u>e</u>ncy   <u>i</u>nqu<u>i</u>s<u>i</u>tive   m<u>o</u>n<u>o</u>l<u>o</u>gue   <u>u</u>n<u>u</u>s<u>u</u>al

A. Practice: One word in each pair below is spelled with the same vowel in three syllables in a row; the other is not. Use the clues to help you fill in the blanks. You can use a dictionary if you are not sure of the spellings of any of the words.

1. a. a fruit with a thick yellow peel: b __ n __ n __

   b. a large, round fruit that grows on palm trees and has a hard, brown husk: c __ c __ n __ t

2. a. a person or animal in a story: ch __ r __ ct __ r

   b. an indented group of sentences: p __ r __ gr __ ph

3. a. politeness: c __ v __ l __ ty

   b. fame: c __ l __ br __ ty

4. a. a southern state: A __ rk __ ns __ s

   b. a northern state: M __ ch __ g __ n

B. Practice: Some place names, such as *Mississippi*, have the same vowel in three or more syllables in a row. Complete the following crossword puzzle to discover six more of these names. The first letter of each is given.

Clues

1. The state capital of _____ is Juneau.

2. Little Rock is the capital of _____.

3. _____ is our neighbor to the north.

4. _____ is a country, a canal, and a hat.

5. The capital of _____ is Nashville.

6. The capital and largest city of Georgia is _____.

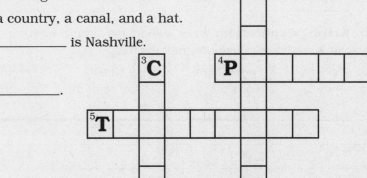

Build Grammar Skills: Adverbs

Adverbs modify verbs, adjectives, and other adverbs. They answer the questions *how? when? where?* and *to what extent?*

Adverb	Word it modifies	Question it answers
We waited <u>patiently</u>.	waited (verb)	How did we wait?
He <u>often</u> travels by train.	travels (verb)	When does he travel by train?
She goes there on foot.	goes (verb)	Where does she go on foot?
Were you <u>very</u> tired from your trip?	tired (adjective)	To what extent were you tired?

A. Practice: Underline the adverb in each of the following sentences and draw an arrow to the word that it modifies. Then, on the line below the sentence, write the question that the adverb answers. One example is given

1. Father Wolf awoke <u>early</u> one morning.

   When did Father Wolf awaken? _____

2. He scratched himself, stretched out his paws, and yawned loudly.

   _____

3. He looked at the moonlit sky and declared that he must now hunt.

   _____

4. Before he could leave, the voice of the jackal Tabaqui greeted him softly.

   _____

5. Father Wolf allowed him to enter, but he also told him that he would find no food there.

   _____

6. Tabaqui declared that his needs were extremely modest.

   _____

7. A dry bone would make a perfectly adequate meal for a poor, lowly jackal.

   _____

B. Writing Application: Write a short paragraph about a tiger catching and eating its dinner. Use at least five of the following adverbs.

silently	here and there	suddenly	rapidly	hungrily	very
later	afterward	contentedly	happily		

_____

_____

_____

_____

"Mowgli's Brothers" by Rudyard Kipling (text page 238)

Reading Strategy: Predict

As you read an exciting story like "Mowgli's Brothers," you will probably find yourself predicting what characters will do or what events will occur next. The **predictions** you make are logical guesses based on information you encounter in the story.

As an active reader, you will also find yourself revising your predictions at times. For example, suppose that at one point in your reading, you predicted that Mother and Father Wolf would hurt the human child. What effect would these words, spoken by Mother Wolf, have on your prediction?

> "The man's cub is mine, Lungri—mine to me! He shall not be killed. He shall live to run with the Pack and to hunt with the Pack. . . . "

Based on this new information, you would revise, or change, your prediction. You would conclude that just because Mother and Father Wolf are capable of killing the "man's cub," it doesn't necessarily mean that they will choose to do so.

DIRECTIONS: Use the chart below to make and check predictions as your read "Mowgli's Brother's." Use the first and second columns to jot down your predictions and the details that helped you make them. In the third column, note the evidence from the story that helped you to confirm or revise your prediction. One entry has been modeled for you, based on the example given above.

Prediction	Reasons	Was I Right or Wrong?
Mother and Father Wolf will hurt the child.	Father Wolf says: "I could kill him with a touch of my foot" and "The man's cub is ours—to kill if we choose."	Wrong—Mother Wolf decides to protect the child because she wants to defy Shere Khan.

"Mowgli's Brothers" by Rudyard Kipling (text page 238)

Literary Focus: Animal Characters

Most of the characters in "Mowgli's Brothers" are animals. **Animal characters** behave according to their animal characteristics, but they also have human traits. Reread the opening passage from the story. What animal characteristics do you see in the characters being introduced? What are their human characteristics?

You probably noticed that Mother and Father Wolf do several things that are consistent with the behavior of wolves: they sleep, yawn, stretch, and keep an eye on their cubs. However, Father Wolf also displays one trait that is definitely human: he speaks, expressing his thoughts in words. As the story unfolds, Mother and Father Wolf will reveal more animal and human traits, as will other animal characters.

A. DIRECTIONS: Read the following passage. Then write a sentence or two to answer the questions below.

> It was the jackal—Tabaqui the Dishlicker—and the wolves of India despise Tabaqui because he runs about making mischief, and telling tales, and eating rags and pieces of leather from the village rubbish-heaps....
> "Enter, then, and look," said Father Wolf, stiffly; "but there is no food here."
> "For a wolf, no," said Tabaqui; "but for so mean a person as myself a dry bone is a good feast. Who are we, the Gidur-log [the jackal-people], to pick and choose?" He scuttled to the back of the cave, where he found the bone of a buck with some meat on it, and sat cracking the end merrily.
> All thanks for this good meal," he said, licking his lips. "How beautiful are the noble children! How large are their eyes! And so young too! Indeed, indeed, I might have remembered that the children of Kings are men from the beginning!"
> Now, Tabaqui knew as well as anyone else that there is nothing so unlucky as to compliment children to their faces; and it pleased him to see Mother and Father Wolf look uncomfortable.

1. What characteristics does Tabaqui show that reflect the way real jackals behave?

_____

_____

_____

_____

2. What characteristics does he show that normally belong only to humans?

_____

_____

3. Identify two human characteristics that Mother and Father Wolf display in this passage.

_____

_____

Names/Nombres" by Julia Alvarez (text page 250)
"The Southpaw" by Judith Viorst (text page 254)

Build Vocabulary

Using the Prefix *trans-*

The prefix *trans-* means "over," "through," or "across." Knowing the meaning of this prefix can help you remember that the Word Bank word *transport* means "to carry over or across a distance." It can also help you figure out the meanings of the following words:

transplant   transform   transparent   transcontinental   transmitter   translate

A. DIRECTIONS: Complete each sentence by writing one of the words listed above. Look in a dictionary if you are not sure of the meaning of any of the words.

1. Our _____ railroad trip started in Atlanta, Georgia, and ended in Seattle, Washington.

2. It is fascinating to see a thick, fuzzy caterpillar _____ into a beautiful butterfly.

3. The _____ plastic wrap lets you see exactly what is in the bowl.

4. A radio _____ is a device that sends radio signals though the air.

5. Early spring and late fall are the best times to _____ these shrubs.

6. Can you help me _____ these words from French into English?

Using the Word Bank

transport	initial	inevitably	chaotic	inscribed

B. DIRECTIONS: Match each word in the left column with its definition in the right column. Write the letter of the definition on the line next to the word it defines.

____ 1. chaotic   a. original; first

____ 2. inevitably   b. written on

____ 3. initial   c. confused; messy

____ 4. inscribed   d. carry from one place to another

____ 5. transport   e. unavoidably

Recognizing Antonyms

C. DIRECTIONS: Circle the letter of the word or phrase that is most nearly opposite in meaning to the word in CAPITAL LETTERS.

1. INEVITABLY: a. finally   b. avoidably   c. never   d. invisibly

2. CHAOTIC: a. attractive   b. noiseless   c. tiny   d. orderly

Name _____ Date _____

Build Spelling Skills: Spelling the *k* Sound With the Letters *ch*

Spelling Strategy In some words, the *k* or "hard c" sound is spelled with the letters *ch*. The word *chaotic* is one example. Here are some others:

character   chemistry   mechanic

A. Practice: Quietly pronounce the underlined word in each of the following sentences. Then write the word in the appropriate column in the chart below.

ch pronounced k as in chaotic	ch pronounced ch as in chair

1. A <u>chorus</u> is a singing group.

2. <u>Chocolate</u> is a popular treat.

3. <u>Chrome</u> is a shiny metal.

4. A <u>chameleon</u> is a reptile that can change its color.

5. <u>Chimneys</u> vent smoke and fumes from fireplaces and furnaces.

6. A <u>choreographer</u> is a person who creates dances.

7. A <u>chapter</u> is part of a book.

8. An act of <u>charity</u> is an act of kindness.

9. When you <u>cherish</u> something, you treasure it.

10. A <u>characteristic</u> is a trait or quality.

B. Practice: Read the following sentences, and to correct the errors in the spelling of words that have the *k* sound. If you are not sure of a spelling, look in a dictionary. The first one has been done as an example.

                              chronicles
1. Julia Alvarez ~~cronicles~~ what it was like to grow up with a "foreign-sounding" name.

2. She usually did not correct people at school when they mispronounced her name.

3. She describes the Dominican custom of having a long and chomplicated names.

4. "The Southpaw" looks at a conflict from the point of view of two different caracters.

5. The story is told through a series of letters, presented in cronological order.

6. The boy is the chaptain of a baseball team, and the girl campaigns to play for the team.

Names/Nombres" by Julia Alvarez (text page 250)
"The Southpaw" by Judith Viorst (text page 254)

Build Grammar Skills: Adverbs Modifying Adjectives and Adverbs

In addition to modifying verbs, **adverbs** can modify adjectives and other adverbs.

Adverb *eagerly* modifies the verb *read*:
Julia Alvarez <u>eagerly</u> read books, stories, and poems when she was in high school.

Adverb *sometimes* modifies the verb *read*:
Judith Viorst's children <u>sometimes</u> appear as characters in her books.

Adverb *very* modifies the adverb *touchingly* and answers the question *how*?:
Julia Alvarez writes <u>very</u> touchingly about her family.

Adverb *rather* modifies the adjective *unusual* and answers the question *to what extent*?:
Judith Viorst tells the story of two friends in a <u>rather</u> unusual way.

Here are some adverbs commonly used to modify adjectives and other adverbs:

almost   too   so   very   quite   rather   usually   much   more

A. Practice: Look at the underlined adverb or adverbs in each sentence. Draw an arrow to the word that each one modifies, and write whether it is an adjective or another adverb. One example is given.

1. Julia Alvarez's family names changed <u>almost</u> immediately. _____ adverb _____

2. Julia was <u>too</u> shy to correct people who mispronounced her name. _____

3. By the time she got to high school, she was <u>more</u> confident. _____

4. She became <u>quite</u> popular and <u>very</u> outgoing. _____

5. "Southpaw" presents a <u>rather</u> different kind of situation. _____

6. Two <u>usually</u> close friends exchange a series of angry letters. _____

7. They disagree <u>strongly</u> with one another. _____

B. Writing Application: Revise the paragraph below so that it contains adverbs that modify adjectives and other adverbs. Choose from the following adverbs.

extremely   very   so   quite

Julia Alvarez loved literature and knew that she wanted to become a writer. When she was in high school, she read _____ much that her parents called any famous author her "friend," as in "your friend Shakespeare." Their teasing was not meant to embarrass her, however. On the contrary, it was _____ gentle and loving. When Julia graduated from high school, her parents gave her a(n) _____ thoughtful gift. It was a typewriter for writing her stories and poems. Some day, they told her, her name would be _____ well-known throughout the United States.

Unit 3: Proving Yourself

Names/Nombres" by Julia Alvarez (text page 250)
"The Southpaw" by Judith Viorst (text page 254)

Reading Strategy: Set a Purpose for Reading

Setting a purpose for reading means giving yourself a focus for your thoughts and reactions as you read. Often, special features and qualities of the work you are reading will help you set a particular purpose. For example, a story that is full of suspenseful clues and details will encourage you to keep making predictions about what will happen next or how a mystery will be solved. Works such as "Names/Nombres" and "Southpaw," which present interesting situations from distinctive viewpoints, encourage you to look at events through other people's eyes.

DIRECTIONS: Jot down notes on the lines below to keep track of characters' viewpoints and your reactions "Names/Nombres" and "Southpaw." One set of notes, based on the beginning of "Southpaw," has been modeled for you.

What Happened

Richard did not allow Janet to play on the Mapes Street baseball team.

_____

_____

_____

_____

How Character Reacts

Janet gets mad. She tells Richard that she doesn't want to be friends anymore. Richard defends his decision.

_____

_____

_____

_____

Character's Point of View (Reason for His or Her Reaction)

Janet thinks the decision is unfair. Richard says that girls have never been allowed on the team and that

things should continue that way

_____

_____

_____

Do I Sympathize With Character's Point of View?

I agree (disagree) with Janet

_____

_____

_____

_____

Names/Nombres" by Julia Alvarez (text page 250)
"The Southpaw" by Judith Viorst (text page 254)

Literary Focus: Narrator's Perspective

The narrator—or person who tells a story—presents his or her own **perspective** on the events that he or she is describing. For example, in "Names/Nombres," Julia Alvarez writes from her own perspective about experiences that she had as a recent immigrant to the United States. The two "former friends" who are the narrators of "Southpaw" present two different perspectives on a disagreement about who should and should not play on a certain baseball team.

A. DIRECTIONS: Read the following passage from "Names/Nombres." One the lines below, use your own words to identify the situation or event that the narrator is describing. Then identify two different feelings or reactions that she reveals as part of her perspective.

> These relatives had such complicated names and there were so many of them, and their relationships to myself were so convoluted. There was my Tía Josefina, who was not really an aunt but a much older cousin. And her daughter, Aida Margarita, who was adopted, una hija de crianza. My uncle of affection, Tío José, brought my madrina Tía Amelia and her co-madre Tía Pilar. My friends rarely had more than a "Mom and Dad" to introduce.

_____

_____

_____

_____

B. DIRECTIONS: Read the following passage from "The Southpaw." Then answer the questions below.

Dear Janet,
    Ronnie caught the chicken pox and Leo broke his toe and Elwood had these stupid violin lessons. I'll give you first base, and that's my final offer.
    Richard

Dear Richard,
    Susan Reilly plays first base, Marilyn Jackson catches, Ethel Kahn plays center field, I pitch. It's a package deal.
    Janet
    P.S. Sorry about your 12-game losing streak.

1. What specific issue or situation do Richard and Janet disagree about?

_____

_____

2. What is Richard's position on this issue?

_____

_____

3. What is Janet's position?

_____

_____

© Prentice-Hall, Inc.

Unit 3: Proving Yourself

"Adventures of Isabel" by Ogden Nash (text page 262)

"I'll Stay" by Gwendolyn Brooks (text page 263)

"Wilbur Wright and Orville Wright"
by Rosemary and Stephen Vincent Benét (text page 264)

Build Vocabulary

Using the Suffix *-ous*

The suffix *-ous* means "having the qualities of" or "full of." For example, *virtuous* means "full of virtue," and *famous* means "having the quality of fame."

A. DIRECTIONS: In the space next to each of the following definitions in the left column, write the letter of the word from the right column that best fits the definition.

____ 1. angry, full of fury	a. miraculous
____ 2. risky, full of danger	b. disastrous
____ 3. terrible, like a catastrophe	c. furious
____ 4. wonderful, delightful	d. dangerous
____ 5. amazing, like a miracle	e. glorious

Using the Word Bank

cavernous	ravenous	rancor	grant

B. DIRECTIONS: Complete crossword puzzle below. Hint: The Across list contains the answers for the clues in the Down list; the Down list contains the answers for the clues in the Across list.

Across
3. admit
4. hungry
6. big and empty
8. hate

Down
1. cavernous
2. rancor
5. ravenous
7. admit

Sentence Completions

C. DIRECTIONS: Fill in the blanks with the word that best completes each sentence.

grant   ravenous   rancor   cavernous

1. After their long hike, the campers were _____.

2. The kids had to _____ that the clever magician had fooled them

3. The fans' voices echoed in the _____ arena.

"Adventures of Isabel" by Ogden Nash (text page 262)
"I'll Stay" by Gwendolyn Brooks (text page 263)
"Wilbur Wright and Orville Wright"
by Rosemary and Stephen Vincent Benét (text page 264)

Build Spelling Skills: Spelling Words That Use the Suffix *-ous*

Even though you do not hear the *o* sound in the suffix *-ous*, be sure to use an *o* when you spell any words ending in that suffix.

ravenous   delicious   poisonous

A. Practice: Write the word ending in *-ous* that fits each of the following definitions in the space provided. The first one has been done as an example.

1. evil, having the qualities of a villain _____villainous_____

2. happy, full of joy_____

3. large and empty, having the qualities of a cavern_____

4. very loud, having the quality of thunder _____

5. funny, full of humor _____

6. stylish, having the quality of glamour_____

B. Practice: Complete each of the following sentences by filling in the blank with a word formed by adding the suffix *-ous* to the word in parentheses. Hint: If you are not sure of a word is spelled, look it up in a dictionary. The first one has been done as an example.

1. Ogden Nash wrote many (humor) _____humorous_____ poems, such as "Adventures of Isabel."

2. Isabel seems like a very (adventure) _____ girl.

3. She finds herself in some (ridicule) _____ situations.

4. Wilbur and Orville Wright realized that flying can be (danger) _____.

5. The people who flew the first airplanes were (courage) _____.

Challenge: In "Adventures of Isabel," Isabel eats zwieback, a kind of biscuit that is first baked and then toasted. The fact that it is cooked twice gives it its name, which is German for "twice baked." In fact the word *biscuit* comes from the French—*bis* (twice) *cuit* (cooked). Many other foods get their names from the ways in which they are prepared or how they look. Below is a list of some tasty foreign dishes. Can you match each with its description? If you're unsure of the meaning of a word, look in a dictionary.

____ 1. French: croissant   a. spicy dish made with chili

____ 2. Chinese: lo mein   b. long thin pasta, whose name means "worms"

____ 3. Italian: vermicelli   c. chopped cabbage that has been pickled in sour vinegar

____ 4. Spanish: enchilada   d. crescent-shaped roll

____ 5. German: sauerkraut   e. noodles mixed with various other foods

"Adventures of Isabel" by Ogden Nash (text page 262)

"I'll Stay" by Gwendolyn Brooks (text page 263)

"Wilbur Wright and Orville Wright"
by Rosemary and Stephen Vincent Benét (text page 264)

Build Grammar Skills: Adjective or Adverb?

Adjectives describe nouns and pronouns; they answer questions such as *Which? What kind?* and *How many?* **Adverbs** describe verbs, adjectives, or other adverbs; they answer questions such as *How? When? Where?* and *To what extent?*

Adjectives:

The <u>first</u> real airplane really flew . . . (**Which** airplane?)

Isabel met a <u>hideous</u> giant. (**What kind of** giant?)

There never were <u>two</u> brothers more devoted . . . (**How many** brothers?)

Adverbs:

Isabel <u>calmly</u> cured the doctor. (**How** did she cure the doctor?)

They <u>sometimes</u> skinned their noses. (**When** did they skin their noses?)

They glided <u>here</u>, they glided <u>there</u>. (**Where** did they glide?)

<u>Here</u> and <u>there</u> describe the verb "glided." (Both adverbs answer the question, **Where?**)

Wilbur and Orville were <u>completely</u> loyal to each other. (**To what extent** were they loyal?)

Keep in mind that some words can be adjectives *or* adverbs, depending on how they are used in a sentence. In "She is a *fast* runner," *fast* is an adjective that describes the noun "runner," and answers the question, **What kind** of runner. But in "She runs *fast*," *fast* is an adverb that describes the verb "runs," and answers the question **How** does she run?

A. Practice: In each of the following sentences, you will find an italicized adjective or adverb. If it is an adjective, write *adj* in the space provided. If it is an adverb, write *adv.*

_____ 1. We worked *tirelessly* to finish our project on time.

_____ 2. Ramon is a very *capable* student.

_____ 3. We were *really* glad when vacation time came.

_____ 4. My sister is an *excellent* tennis player.

_____ 5. My bicycle is still *fairly* new.

B. Writing Application: On the lines provided, write sentences using each of the following adjectives or adverbs. In each sentence, underline the word the adjective or adverb modifies. The first two have been done as examples.

1. beautiful (adjective) ___She grew beautiful <u>flowers</u> in her garden_____

2. carefully (adverb) ___The boy carefully <u>set</u> the model ship on its stand._____

3. slightly (adverb)_____

4. several (adjective) _____

5. anywhere (adverb) _____

6. gentle (adjective) _____

"Adventures of Isabel" by Ogden Nash (text page 262)

"I'll Stay" by Gwendolyn Brooks (text page 263)

"Wilbur Wright and Orville Wright"
by Rosemary and Stephen Vincent Benét (text page 264)

Reading Strategy: Use Prior Knowledge

Your prior knowledge includes everything you know—what you have learned at school, at home, and from any activities or experiences that have been part of your life. For example, if you've ever learned to ride a bicycle, you probably know what it is to fall and skin your knees or your nose. Therefore, even though you may know nothing about building or flying airplanes, you can appreciate how Wilbur and Orville Wright felt when they "sometimes skinned their noses" during their glider flights. Choose one of the poems in the group, and fill in the graphic organizer below. In the top half, write the prior knowledge you brought to the poem. In the bottom half, explain what you got out of the poem.

WHAT I BROUGHT TO THE POEM

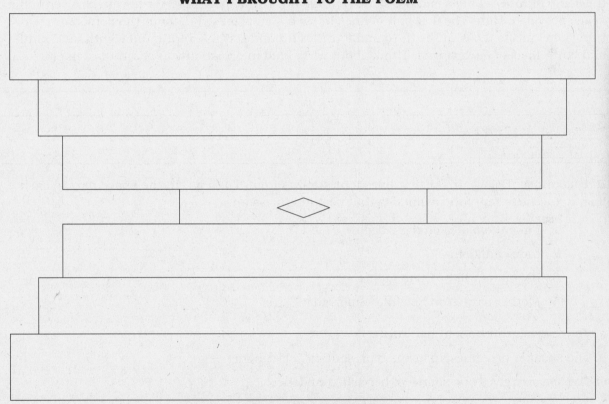

WHAT I GOT FROM THE POEM

Unit 3: Proving Yourself

"Adventures of Isabel" by Ogden Nash (text page 262)

"I'll Stay" by Gwendolyn Brooks (text page 263)

"Wilbur Wright and Orville Wright"
by Rosemary and Stephen Vincent Benét (text page 264)

Literary Focus: Stanzas

A prose paragraph focuses on a single main idea, and is separated by indenting or spacing from other paragraphs. **Stanzas** in poetry are similar to paragraphs in prose. They are groups of lines that usually focus on one main idea and are separated by spaces from other groups of lines. The stanzas in many poems are regular; they have the same number of lines and the same rhythm and rhyme pattern. In this grouping of poems, both "Adventures of Isabel" and "Wilbur Wright and Orville Wright" are written in regular stanzas. Stanzas can be irregular, which is true of "I'll Stay." The stanzas in this poem do not follow a regular pattern. Each one, however, focuses on a central idea.

A. DIRECTIONS: In what ways are the stanzas of "Adventures of Isabel" alike, other than having the same number of lines and the same rhythm and rhyme patterns? Write your answer in the space provided. Hint: The first pair of lines in each stanza tells you about the person or creature Isabel meets. Look at the third and fourth, fifth and sixth, seventh and eighth, and ninth and tenth lines of each stanza. Think about what kind information you get from each pair.

_____

_____

_____

_____

B. DIRECTIONS: Below are the first lines four stanzas from "I'll Stay." In the space next to each line, write the letter of the main idea that best fits that stanza.

____ 1. I like the plates on the ledge

____ 2. I am confident

____ 3. My name will be Up in Lights

____ 4. Mother says "You rise in the morning—"

a. The speaker talks about her future.

b. The speaker describes an image representing self-confidence.

c. The speaker gives one source of her self-confidence.

d. The speaker talks about the way she sees herself.

from "Lou Gehrig: The Iron Horse" by Bob Considine (text page 283)

Build Vocabulary

Using the Word Root -chron-

The word root -chron- means "time." For example, a *chronometer* is a very accurate watch or clock, used to make precise measurements of time. If you tell the events of a in *chronological* order, you tell them in time order—the order in which they took place.

A. DIRECTIONS: Complete each of the following sentences by filling in the blank with the correct word from the list below. Look in a dictionary if you need help.

synchronize   chronicler   chronic   chronological   chronicle

1. Columbus kept a detailed _____ of his voyage to America, writing everything that happened along the way.

2. Some illnesses are _____ and can last for many years.

3. The timeline of the Civil War shows the events in _____ order.

4. We have to _____ our watches so they all show the same time.

5. A careful _____, Thomas Edison kept an accurate record of all of his work.

Using the Word Bank

renowned	contemptuous	consecutive	eminent
concluded	chronic	irrepressible	

B. DIRECTIONS: Read the clues below and fill in the crossword puzzle with words from the Word Bank. Each word is used once and only once.

Across
2. following in order
5. famous
6. enthusiastic, unrestrained
7. ended

Down
1. disrespectful, scornful
3. standing above
4. lasting a long time, constant

Unit 4: Seeing It Through

from "Lou Gehrig: The Iron Horse" by Bob Considine (text page 283)

Build Spelling Skills: Adding Endings to Words Ending in *ic*

When you add the ending -*al* or -*ally* to a word ending in *ic*, simply add the ending to the word without adding any other letters. When adding the ending -*ing*, -*ed*, or -*y* to a word ending in *ic*, put a *k* between the word and the ending.

Examples: music + al = mus<u>ic</u>al (simply add -*al*)

                chronic + ally = chron<u>ic</u>ally (simply add -*ally*)

                frolic + ing = frolic<u>k</u>ing (add *k* + -*ing*)

                mimic + ed = mimic<u>ked</u> (add *k* + -*ed*)

                panic + y = panic<u>ky</u> (add *k* + -*y*)

A. Practice: Add the indicated endings to each word. Write the new word on the line.

1. physic + ally = _____

2. garlic + y + _____

3. magic + al = _____

4. frantic + ally = _____

5. mimic + ed = _____

6. panic + ed = _____

B. Practice: In the blanks, write the correct spelling of the word in italics. If the italicized word is spelled correctly, write C in the blank.

Lou Gehrig was a remarkable person, not only *athletically* _____, but in

other ways as well. Gehrig was a man of great *physical* _____ strength

who played every game for the New York Yankees for many seasons. His *statistickal*

_____ record for playing in the most consecutive games was not broken

for almost sixty years. When Gehrig realized that he could no longer play baseball at his usual

level, he never *paniced* _____. He calmly told his manager, Joe McCarthy,

to remove him from the Yankee lineup. His amazing consecutive-game record ended quietly,

rather than *dramatically* _____. The Yankees, for whom Gehrig had

played so *heroickally* _____ for so long, recognized his contribution to the

team by honoring him shortly after he had played his last game. *Tragically*

_____, Gehrig's disease took his life two years later.

from "Lou Gehrig: The Iron Horse" by Bob Considine (text page 283)

Build Grammar Skills: Prepositions

A preposition is a word or group of words that shows a relationship between two or more persons, places, events, or things; for example, "I kept my head <u>above</u> water," and "The dog sat <u>between</u> Sam and me." The following is a list of commonly used prepositions:

Prepositions:

about	at	down	like	to
above	because of	during	near	toward
according to	before	except	of	through
across	behind	for	off	under
after	below	from	on	until
against	between	in, into	outside	up, upon
among	by	in spite of	over	with, within, without

A. Practice: Underline <u>all</u> of the prepositions in each of the following sentences.

1. The pitch went between his wrists.

2. On the morning of the first game against Detroit, Lou called McCarthy.

3. Lou checked into the Mayo Clinic.

4. Lou returned to the team for the remainder of the season.

5. He delivered the lineups to the umpires before the games.

6. I consider myself the luckiest man on the face of the Earth.

B. Writing Application: On the lines provided, rewrite each of the following sentences, filling in the spaces with prepositions that make sense. *Note:* There may be more than one way to fill in some spaces.

1. Gehrig played _____ the New York Yankees _____ 1923 _____ 1939.

   _____

2. Gehrig played more consecutive games than any other player _____ his record was broken _____ Cal Ripken, Jr. in 1995.

   _____

3. Though he won his battles _____ the ballfield, he could not win his battle _____ illness.

   _____

4. _____ 1939, Lou Gehrig was elected _____ the Baseball Hall of Fame.

   _____

5. The Yankees showed their gratitude _____ Gehrig's accomplishments.

   _____

© Prentice-Hall, Inc.

Unit 4: Seeing It Through

Reading for Success: Strategies for Constructing Meaning

To understand a work of literature fully, you must go beyond a simple scan of the page to put the writer's ideas together in your own mind. Use these strategies to help you construct meaning.

- **Make inferences.** It's a reader's job to fill in details the author doesn't provide. You can do so by making inferences, or drawing conclusions, based on the details that are provided, combined with your own knowledge and experience.
- **Interpret what you read.** Interpret or explain the meaning or significance of what you read.
- **Identify important ideas.** Ask the question, "What is the author's main point in this paragraph?" and identify the supporting details for each main idea.
- **Compare and contrast characters and ideas.** By comparing and contrasting characters or ideas, you can find out more about how they fit together.

DIRECTIONS: Read the following excerpt from "Thirteen," a story by Jessamyn West, and use the reading strategies to increase your comprehension. In the margins, note where you make inferences, interpret what you read, identify important ideas, and compare and contrast characters and ideas.

from "*Thirteen*" by Jessamyn West

In the following passage, Cress Delahanty is waiting for a friend.

Then suddenly the first hour was gone by; it was past three and already the wind seemed a little sharper, the sun less bright, the boardwalk less crowded. More of her hair had come uncurled; her hat took more righting to keep it straight; her neck ached from holding her head high enough to see out from under the hat's brim; occasional stabs of pain shot up the calves of legs unaccustomed to the pull of high heels. A thought, with the swiftness of a stone dropping through water, settled in her mind; he isn't coming. It was a possibility she had not even thought about before. She had thought he would have to come. The hat was for him. The day was for him. How could she possibly, without seeing him, meet her father and mother, say yes, say no, eat ice cream, get in the car, go home, take off her hat, go to bed, sleep?

It was fifteen after three. At first she had been willing that Edwin see her first. Now, she searched every figure, every slight, short man or boy's figure, for as great a distance as she could make them out, saying, "Be Edwin." So strongly did she will it that she thought she might, by determination alone, transform a stranger into Edwin.

It was three-thirty. It was fifteen of four. Her hat was on one side, her mouth weary from practicing her smile on strangers, the pleat out of her freshly starched skirt, her feet mere stumps of pain. Still, she would not give up. "Edwin, appear, Edwin appear," she willed.

Edwin did appear, crossing the street a block away, small and neat and thin in white duck pants and a white shirt. He crossed and turned toward Cress, walking steadily toward her. In two minutes or three he would see her, and see the hat and notice her new gentleness. All tiredness and pain left Cress. She could very easily have flown, or played a piece she had never seen before on the piano, or kissed a mad dog and not been bitten. She had just time to arrange herself, resettle her hat, give her now completely uncurled hair a quick comb upward. To do this she took her hat off, stood on tiptoe, and with fingers which trembled with excitement managed to get it up onto the top of one of the rectangular glass aquariums which by chance stood conveniently before her in the middle of the sidewalk. Before she, herself, understood what had happened someone was jovially yelling, "Hey, sis, bread crumbs is what you feed them," and there was her hat, slowly, gracefully settling among the startled fish of the aquarium.

The man who had yelled was a short fat man, wearing pants, but no shirt or undershirt. He had sand in the hair on his chest; like dandruff, Cress thought wildly, unable for shame to raise her eyes to his face. "What's the idea, sis?" he asked.

Forcing her eyes away from the sandy dandruff, Cress saw that her hat, still gradually, gracefully floundering, was bleeding flamingo red into the aquarium, so that the amazed fish now swam in sunset waters.

"I thought it had a top," she whispered to no one in particular.

"The hat, sis?" asked the shirtless man.

"The glass place for the fish," Cress whispered. "I thought it had a top."

"It didn't, sis."

"I was resting my hat on it," Cress whispered, "while I fixed my hair."

"You was resting your hat on air, sis."

"It dropped," said Cress. "It fell right out of my hands."

"Gravity, sis," said the fat man. "It was gravity."

"Will it make the fish sick?" asked Cress.

"Make 'em die, sis, in my opinion."

"What'll I do?" asked Cress.

"Watch 'em die," said the fat man comfortably. "That one's a goner already."

Cress wanted to die herself. She willed it very hard, but she couldn't. She couldn't even faint, though she held her breath and willed her heart to stop beating. But a sort of numbness did come over her, making all the voices blurred and indistinct, making all the people, and there were dozens, hundreds it seemed to Cress, now pressed about the aquarium, distant and hazy.

It was a field day for fish and humans. It was a great occasion for the fish, who had nothing more exciting to look forward to than death in the frying pan: a big blunt-nosed fish swam at the hat as if to ram it; smaller fish circled it curiously; nervous fish parted the darkening waters in a fishy frenzy. It was a glorious moment for humans, too, a sight they had never expected to see.

_____

_____

_____

_____

_____

_____

_____

_____

_____

_____

© Prentice-Hall, Inc.

from "Lou Gehrig: The Iron Horse" by Bob Considine (text page 283)

Literary Focus: Biographical Narrative

The difference between a **biography** and a **biographical narrative**, such as this selection, is that a biography provides only actual facts, while a biographical narrative may also include details invented by the writer in order to make the writing more vivid or effective. The writer of a biographical narrative, for example, might describe a character's thoughts and feelings and include dialogue, even though the writer has no way of knowing exactly what that character was thinking, feeling, and saying at the time. The writer may also create dialogue to fill out a scene at which he or she was not present. Read the following passages from the selection. On the lines below each passage, write down the details that you believe were created by the author, and explain why you think that they are imaginary and not factual. The first one has been done as an example.

1. Lou returned to the team for the remainder of the 1939 season, slowly suiting up each day, taking McCarthy's lineups to home plate to deliver to the umpires before each game. It was his only duty as captain. It was another winning season for the Yankees, but hardly for Lou. The short walk from the dugout to home plate and back exhausted him.

    "slowly suiting up"—The author would not actually know how quickly

    Gehrig got into his uniform.

2. For Lou, now beginning to hollow out from his disease, one basic ingredient was missing. Babe Ruth wasn't there. Babe, the one he wanted to be there more than he wanted any of his old buddies, had not answered the invitations or the management's phone calls.

    Then, with little warning, a great commotion and rustle and rattle in the stadium. The Babe was entering. He magnetized every eye, activated every tongue.

    _____

    _____

    _____

    _____

"Lob's Girl" by Joan Aiken (text page 293)
"The Tiger Who Would Be King" by James Thurber (text page 302)
"The Lion and the Bulls" by Aesop (text page 303)

Build Vocabulary

Using Forms of *decide*

To *decide* means "to make up one's mind," or "to reach a conclusion about a question." Other words that are related to *decide* are *decision*," the act of making up one's mind" or "a conclusion that a person reaches," and *decisive*, meaning "positive" or "firm."

A. DIRECTIONS: Fill in the blank in each of the following sentences with one of the words below.

decisive	decide	indecision	decisively	decision

1. It was a difficult _____, but we finally chose apple pie for dessert.

2. The home team scored a _____ victory over the visiting team.

3. Once you _____ which book you want to read, get it from the library.

4. The officer stated _____ that there was no cause for alarm.

5. We have no time for your _____. Either come along, or stay at home.

Using the Word Bank

decisively	atone	resolutions	melancholy	intimated
aggrieved	prowled	repulse	slanderous	

B. DIRECTIONS: In each flower petal, write the Word Bank word whose definition matches the number of the petal.

1. hinted, made known

2. offended, wronged

3. untrue and damaging

4. with determination

5. intentions, things decided

6. crawled quietly and secretly

7. repel at attack, drive back

8. make up for a wrong

9. sad, gloomy

Selection Support **111**

"Lob's Girl" by Joan Aiken (text page 293)
"The Tiger Who Would Be King" by James Thurber (text page 302)
"The Lion and the Bulls" by Aesop (text page 303)

Build Spelling Skills: *ie* or *ei*?

To spell words in which the letters *i* and *e* appear together, remember this rule:

Spell *i* before *e*: relieve, grief, piece

Except after *c*: receive, conceited, deceit

Or when the sound is *ay* as in: neighbor, weigh

Notable exceptions: weird, seize, seizure, leisure, height, either, neither, forfeit

A. Practice: Use the rules above to work out the spelling of the following incomplete words. Write the complete words on the lines provided.

1. A person who steals is a th____ ____f. _____

2. A room usually has a floor, four walls, and a c____ ____ling. _____

3. It is hard to bel____ ____ve that people have actually walked on the moon. _____

4. The h____ ____ght of the skyscraper was awesome. _____

5. Tigers and bears can be very f____ ____rce animals at times. _____

6. He has a very w____ ____d sense of humor. _____

7. Have you ever taken a sl____ ____gh ride on a winter evening? _____

8. The lion dec____ ____ed the bulls. _____

B. Practice: Fill in the blanks in each of the following sentences with the correctly spelled version of the word in parentheses.

1. Mr. Dodsworth travels hundreds of miles to (retrieve, retreive) _____ his dog.

2. Finally, he (percieves, perceives) _____ that Lob wants to stay with Sandy.

3. Sandy's family is (seized, siezed)_____ with (greif, grief) _____.

4. The tiger (beleives, believes) _____ that he ought to be the king of the beasts.

5. The lion does not want to (yield, yeild) _____ his place as king.

"**Lob's Girl**" by Joan Aiken (text page 293)
"**The Tiger Who Would Be King**" by James Thurber (text page 302)
"**The Lion and the Bulls**" by Aesop (text page 303)

Build Grammar Skills: Prepositional Phrases

A **prepositional phrase** is a group of words that begins with a preposition and ends with a noun or pronoun. The noun or pronoun at the end of the phrase is called the **object of the preposition**. For example, in "The Tiger Who Would Be King," Thurber writes that "the tiger prowled through the jungle...." *Through the jungle* is a prepositional phrase, in which *through* is the preposition, and *jungle* is the object of the preposition.

A. Practice: Draw a circle around the prepositional phrase in each sentence. Then underline the preposition once and the object of the preposition twice. The first one has been done as an example.

1. Everyone helped to clean up (after the party).

2. The cat escaped by running up a tree.

3. Yesterday, I got a postcard from my sister.

4. No one is allowed to talk during the test.

5. The train reached the end of the line.

6. The tired campers crawled into their tents.

7. Among Aesop's fables, "The Fox and the Grapes" is my favorite.

8. She squeezed between her parents to watch the parade.

9. The acrobat balanced herself on one hand.

10. I saved my dessert for my brother.

B. Writing Application: Complete each sentence with a prepositional phrase.

1. The sun was hidden _____

2. She threw the litter _____

3. When he had finished reading, he replaced the book _____

4. Ferdinand Magellan led the first expedition to sail_____

5. We brought the flowers especially _____

6. The painters leaned the ladder _____

7. We hung our coats_____

8. After school, she played _____

9. The dog ran _____

10. We do not go to school _____

Unit 4: Seeing It Through

"Lob's Girl" by Joan Aiken (text page 293)
"The Tiger Who Would Be King" by James Thurber (text page 302)
"The Lion and the Bulls" by Aesop (text page 303)

Reading Strategy: Compare and Contrast Characters

Like real people, fictional characters are alike in some ways and different in others. When you study the ways in which they resemble each other in behavior, thought, and feelings, you **compare** characters. When you concentrate on differences between characters, you **contrast** them. A Venn diagram can help you sort out the details for your comparison/contrast. The diagram consists of two overlapping circles, one for each character you are examining. Write the qualities both characters share in the area where the circles overlap. In the part of each circle that does not overlap, write those qualities that are true only of the character represented by that circle.

DIRECTIONS: Fill in the Venn diagram to compare and contrast Mr. Dodsworth and Sandy from "Lob's Girl." Use the results to answer the questions below.

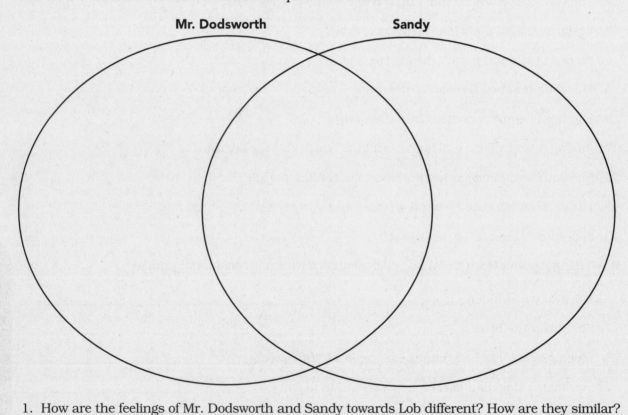

1. How are the feelings of Mr. Dodsworth and Sandy towards Lob different? How are they similar?

_____

_____

_____

2. What qualities in Sandy might make her a more suitable owner for Lob than Mr. Dodsworth is?

_____

_____

"Lob's Girl" by Joan Aiken (text page 293)
"The Tiger Who Would Be King" by James Thurber (text page 302)
"The Lion and the Bulls" by Aesop (text page 303)

Literary Focus: Foreshadowing

When an author makes hints that suggest what may take place later in a story, he or she is using a technique called **foreshadowing**. You might find such hints in dialogue, description, narrative, or even in a title. The purpose of foreshadowing may be to create or heighten suspense, or to provide a warning to readers that the story may take a sudden turn in mood or action. If you have not yet read these stories, look for hints of things to come and think about what they foretell. If you have read them already, look through them again to find places where the authors used foreshadowing.

A. DIRECTIONS: On the lines provided, answer the following questions.

1. What does the title, "Lob's Girl," foreshadow in the story?

   _____

   _____

2. What does this paragraph from "Lob's Girl" lead readers to think might take place in the story?

   > Some people choose their dogs, and some dogs choose their people. The Pengelly family had no say in the choosing of Lob; he came to them in the second way, and very decisively.

   _____

   _____

B. DIRECTIONS: In each of the following details from "Lob's Girl," underline the passage that foreshadows events in the story. Write what the underlined passages foreshadow in the lines provided.

1. As usual, each member of the family was happily getting on with his or her own affairs. Little did they guess how soon this state of things would be changed by the large new member who was going to erupt into their midst.

   _____

   _____

2. Suddenly, history repeating itself, there was a crash from the kitchen. Mrs. Pengelly leaped up, crying, "My blackberry jelly!"

   _____

   _____

Unit 4: Seeing It Through

"Life Doesn't Frighten Me" by Maya Angelou (text page 308)
"Arithmetic" by Carl Sandburg (text page 309)
"Was Worm" by May Swenson (text page 310)

Build Vocabulary

Using Color Words

Many words that name colors come from plants, minerals, and other things in nature. For example, the word *saffron* from the Word Bank comes from the saffron flower, which has a bright yellow-orange center. Parts of this bright yellow-orange center are dried to make a spice that is also called *saffron*.

A. DIRECTIONS: You'll find more color words that come from things in nature. On the lines provided, write the color that matches each description. Use a dictionary if you need help.

aquamarine	amethyst	coral	cranberry	daffodil
ebony	jade	lavender	plum	salmon

1. a soft yellow spring flower _____

2. a bright red sour berry that grows in bogs _____

3. a pinkish orange large fish _____

4. the purple birthstone for February _____

5. a soft medium green stone that is often used in carvings and jewelry _____

6. a light purple flower with a sweet, spicy scent _____

7. a reddish purple fruit that has a large pit _____

8. the greenish blue birthstone for March _____

9. the deep black wood of a tree that grows in tropical rainforests? _____

Using the Word Bank

mosaic	saffron	weaned	metamorphosis

B. DIRECTIONS: Match each word in the left column with its definition in the right column. Write the letter of the definition on the line next to the word it defines.

____ 1. metamorphosis   a. outgrown

____ 2. mosaic   b. picture made from small pieces of glass, stone, or tile

____ 3. saffron   c. change in form

____ 4. weaned   d. orange-yellow color

"Life Doesn't Frighten Me" by Maya Angelou (text page 308)
"Arithmetic" by Carl Sandburg (text page 309)
"Was Worm" by May Swenson (text page 310)

Build Spelling Skills: Consonant Blends

Spelling Strategy A consonant blend is a combination of consonants in which each sound is pronounced. For example, the word *saffron* from the Word Bank contains a blend of the consonants *f* and *r*. These words from "Was Worm" also contain consonant blends:

<u>fl</u>oating   <u>br</u>ight   <u>sw</u>addled   <u>dr</u>inks

When you spell words that contain consonant blends, pronounce the word to yourself to make sure you include all the letters in the blend. Also note that one of the letters in the blend might be doubled, as the *f* in *saffron* is.

A. Practice: Use the clues to fill in the puzzle with words containing consonant blends. *Hint:* All of the words appear in the poem "Life Doesn't Frighten Me."

Across

2. screech, shriek

3. scare

5. mythical creatures that sometimes breathe fire

7. the part of a sweater that fits around each of your arms

8. flickering fire at the end of a candle

9. taking air in and letting it out, respirating

Down

1. amphibians that begin life as tadpoles

2. people not known to you

4. a slithering creature

5. mental images during sleep

6. where you put a rug

B. Practice: Fill in the blanks in these sentences, using the clues in parentheses for help. Note that each word you write appears in "Arithmetic," and each one contains a consonant blend.

1. In "Arithmetic," Carl Sandburg suggests that it is a good idea to memorize the _____ table. (an arithmetic operation)

2. He also creates that humorous image of a zebra who eats animal _____ (cookies)

3. He describes the zebra as being a _____ animal. (appearance)

"Life Doesn't Frighten Me" by Maya Angelou (text page 308)
"Arithmetic" by Carl Sandburg (text page 309)
"Was Worm" by May Swenson (text page 310)

Build Grammar Skills: Adjective and Adverb Phrases

There are two types of prepositional phrases: **Adjective phrases** tell more about nouns or pronouns and answer the question *which one?* **Adverb phrases** tell more about verbs, adjectives and other adverbs and answer the questions *in what way? when?* and *where?* Look at the following sentences.

Adjective phrase modifies the noun *butterfly* and answers the question *Which one?*
Do you see the butterfly **with** orange and black wings?

Adverb phrase modifies the verb *landed* and answers the question *Where?*
It just landed **on** the flower.

A. Practice: Underline the prepositional phrase in each of the following sentences and draw an arrow to the word it modifies. Then, on the line below the sentence, identify the phrase that you underlined as an *adjective phrase* or an *adverb phrase*. Also write the question that it answers. The first one is done as an example.

1. Large flocks of orange and black monarch butterflies are a spectacular sight.
   adjective phrase answering which flocks? _____

2. People who live in the eastern and western United States can see them each fall.
   _____

3. The butterflies migrate to Mexico each year.
   _____

4. The flocks spend the winter there and then return north in the spring.
   _____

5. Then nectar of many different flowers provides them with food.
   _____

B. Writing Application: Write a sentence about each topic provided below, using adjective and adverb phrases as suggested.

1. Write a sentence about a shadow or shadows, using an adjective phrase.
   _____

2. Write a sentence about a dragon or dragons, using an adjective phrase.
   _____

3. Write a sentence about how long it takes you to get to school, using an adverb phrase.
   _____

4. Write a sentence about a place where you like to swim, walk, or run, using an adverb phrase.
   _____

"Life Doesn't Frighten Me" by Maya Angelou (text page 308)
"Arithmetic" by Carl Sandburg (text page 309)
"Was Worm" by May Swenson (text page 310)

Reading Strategy: Interpret Poetry

When you **interpret poetry**, you explain the meaning or significance of the poem. Pausing to question and interpret images, lines, and phrases will help you unlock meaning as you read. For example, as you read "Life Doesn't Frighten Me," you might stop to think about the following lines:

Bad dogs barking loud / Big ghosts in a cloud / Life doesn't frighten me at all.

From reading these lines, you might conclude that the speaker is frightened neither by everyday sights like big, barking dogs nor by imaginings of her mind, such as "big ghosts in a cloud."

DIRECTIONS: Answer the questions posed in the graphic organizer below to interpret one of the poems in this grouping. Ask yourself the same questions to help interpret the other poems.

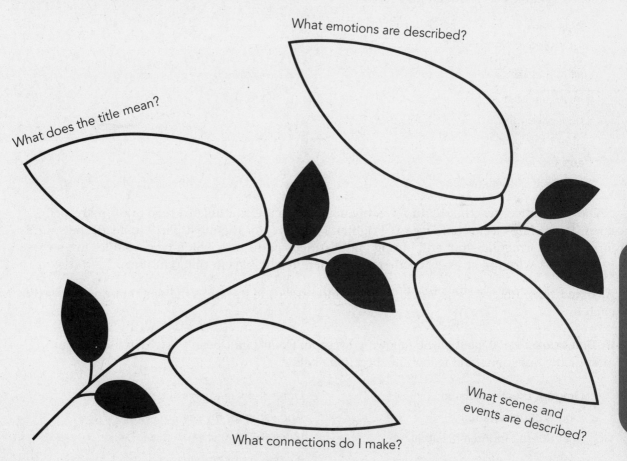

What does the title mean?

What emotions are described?

What scenes and events are described?

What connections do I make?

Unit 4: Seeing It Through

"Life Doesn't Frighten Me" by Maya Angelou (text page 308)
"Arithmetic" by Carl Sandburg (text page 309)
"Was Worm" by May Swenson (text page 310)

Literary Focus: Rhythm

In poetry, **rhythm** is the sound pattern created by stressed and unstressed syllables. Stressed syllables receive more emphasis than unstressed syllables. For example, read the following lines from "Life Doesn't Frighten Me" several times. Tap out the rhythm of the stressed and unstressed syllables as you read. Note that the stressed syllables are underlined.

> <u>Sha</u>dows <u>on</u> the <u>wall</u>
>
> <u>Noi</u>ses <u>down</u> the <u>hall</u>
>
> <u>Life</u> <u>does</u>n't <u>fright</u>en <u>me</u> at <u>all</u>

Now read these lines from "Was Worm." Again, tap out the rhythm of stressed and unstressed syllables as you read and reread.

> Was worm
> swaddled in white
>
> Now tiny queen
> In sequin coat
> peacockbright
> drinks the wind
> and feeds
> on sweat of the leaves

Did you notice that the rhythm was *not* made up of alternating stressed and unstressed lines, as the lines from "Life Doesn't Frighten Me" were, for the most part? Instead, the sounds form a more irregular—but still strong and distinct—pattern in which two syllables are stressed in each line, with the stresses occurring on different syllables in different lines.

A. DIRECTIONS: Reread "Was Worm," above, and underline the two syllables that are stressed in each line.

B. DIRECTIONS: Read each of the following excerpts from "Life Doesn't Frighten Me." Then answer the questions and follow the directions below.

> Dragons breathing flame   Don't show me frogs and snakes
> On my counterpane   And listen for my scream,
> That doesn't frighten me at all.   If I'm afraid at all,
>   It's only in my dreams.

1. Which of the two excerpts sounds the same as the excerpt at the top of the page?

   _____

2. Show the rhythm of each excerpt by underlining the stressed syllables in each line.

"The Friends of Kwan Ming" by Paul Yee (text page 315)

Build Vocabulary

Using the Word Bank

meager	retorted	warily	stingiest

A. DIRECTIONS: Answer each of the following questions to demonstrate your understanding of the Word Bank words. Circle the letter of your choice.

1. Which of the following describes something that the stingiest person in town might do on Halloween?

   a. throw a party for all the children in the neighborhood

   b. pretend not to be home in order to avoid handing out treats

2. Which of the following would you consider warily?

   a. an offer for a free prize that seems too good to be true

   b. a back-to-school sale at a local department store

3. Which of the following describes a child who retorted when she was asked how old she was.

   a. a child who answered, "That's for me to know and you to find out."

   b. a child who was too shy to answer

4. How would you feel if, like Kwan Ming, you were offered a job that paid meager wages?

   a. lucky

   b. disappointed

Recognizing Synonyms

B. DIRECTIONS: Circle the letter of the word that is closest in meaning to the word in CAPITAL LETTERS.

1. RETORTED
   a. returned
   b. hid
   c. answered
   d. fixed

2. WARILY
   a. peacefully
   b. cautiously
   c loudly
   d. regretfully

3. STINGIEST
   a. cheapest
   b. richest
   c. poorest
   d. narrowest

4. MEAGER
   a. limited
   b. foreign
   c. abundant
   d. heavy

"The Friends of Kwan Ming" by Paul Yee (text page 315)

Connecting a Short Story to Social Studies

The difficulties that Kwan Ming experiences as he tries to find work and build a new life for himself in a new country reflect the difficulties faced by the thousands of Chinese immigrants who arrived in the United States in the mid-1800's. Like those real-life immigrants, Kwan Ming makes the six-week voyage across the Pacific Ocean in uncomfortable conditions on an over-crowded ship. Although he had heard that jobs were plentiful, he finds doors slamming in his face as he looks for work. There was, according to the story, "not a job to be found anywhere, for there were too many men looking for work in a country that was still too young." Also, be-cause he has little money, he finds himself living in a humble inn, together with others who are unsuccessfully searching for work, and living on meager meals.

Kwan Ming did not encounter only obstacles and disappointments, however. The story also reflects one of the bright sides of the immigrant experience. Chinese Americans and other im-migrant groups have traditionally lent a helping hand to fellow immigrants in several important ways. These include giving jobs to newcomers, lending them money to start new businesses, and forming associations to help others obtain educational opportunities in their new country.

A. DIRECTIONS: On the lines below, write down details from "The Friends of Kwan Ming" that show how the characters who are Chinese immigrants helped each other survive and get along in the United States.

_____

_____

_____

_____

_____

_____

B. DIRECTIONS: Using the information in the story and your own knowledge, compare and con-trast the experiences of Chinese immigrants in the mid-1800's with the experiences of early English, Dutch, or French settlers in North America. Consider such questions as what kind of expectations the newcomers brought with them, what kinds of opportunities they actually found, and whether they met with discrimination. Use the space below to identify the group you chose and list one similarity and one difference. You can use an encyclopedia or other ref-erence source to add to the information you already have.

_____

_____

_____

_____

_____

_____

Name _____ Date _____

Build Vocabulary

Using Related Words: Forms of *grief*

The Word Bank word *grief* is a noun that means "deep sadness or distress." In this story, the fisherman keeps his grief, or deep sadness, to himself, instead of burdening his wife with it. Other words related to the word *grief* convey the same meaning of deep sadness. For example, the word *grieve* is a verb that means "to feel deep sadness or to mourn."

People may *grieve* when they lose someone they love.

Grievous is an adjective that means "serious enough to cause sadness or distress."

The boy's *grievous* actions caused his friends to feel great distress.

A. DIRECTIONS: Use one of the following words to complete each of the sentences below: *grief*, *grievous*, and *grieve*.

1. Spreading unkind rumors about a person is a _____ act.

2. Kyla was filled with _____ when her dog Dakota died.

3. The fisherman and his wife _____ because they do not have a child.

Using the Word Bank

sheared	slough	wallowed	grief

B. DIRECTIONS: Using context clues, fill in the blank in each sentence with the correct word from the Word Bank.

1. When we studied reptiles in science class, we saw a snake _____ off its old skin.

2. At the zoo, a mother hippopotamus and her baby _____ in the mud.

3. With several strong strokes of the razor, the rancher _____ off the sheep's woolly coat.

4. The fisherman brought the seal pup home, hoping it would end his wife's _____.

Recognizing Synonyms

C. DIRECTIONS: Circle the letter of the word or words that that are closest in meaning to the word in CAPITAL LETTERS.

1. SLOUGH   a. shed   b. energetic   c. put on   d. swamp

2. SHEARED   a. saw through   b. tilted   c. cut   d. thought about

3. WALLOWED   a. digested   b. permitted   c. rolled around   d. wandered around

4. GRIEF   a. extreme happiness   b. deep feeling   c. intense anger   d. deep sadness

"Greyling" by Jane Yolen (text page 328)

Build Spelling Skills: The Sound *uff* Spelled *ough*

Spelling Strategy The Word Bank word *slough*, meaning "to cast off," or "get rid of," is one of a few English words that spell the *uff* sound with *ough*. Here are some others:

rough   not gentle
tough   very strong or sturdy
enough   plenty

The *uff* sound may also be spelled *-uff*, as in *stuff* and *fluff*. Use a dictionary if you are not sure which way to spell the *uff* sound.

A. Practice: On the lines provided, write four sentences using each of the following words in each: *slough, rough, tough,* and *enough*.

1. _____
2. _____
3. _____
4. _____

B. Practice: Proofread the following paragraph. Look for words in which the *uff* sound is spelled incorrectly. Cross out each incorrectly spelled word and write the correct spelling above it.

Just as the fisherman's wife thought no one would risk entering the ruff sea to save her

huband, Greyling decided he'd had enuff. Though it was a steep drop to the water below, the

boy plunged from the cliffs into the churning sea and fought his way to his father's floundering

boat. The waves made the going tuff. The water pushed against him, pulling off his clothes and

shoes. Finally, the boy seemed to sluff off his skin, and he swam swiftly towards his father.

Challenge: In the story, *Greyling*, the word for the color of the boy's hair and eyes is spelled *grey*. Most dictionaries, however, list *gray* as the preferred spelling for this word, and *grey* as a second spelling that is also considered correct. Several words in English have more than one acceptable spelling. Dictionaries usually list the preferred spelling of the word first. In your own writing, it is usually best to use the first spelling of these words. Here are some other examples of words with two acceptable spellings. In each pair, the preferred spelling is listed first:

theater, theatre   glamour, glamor   dialogue, dialog

Use each word in the above list in a sentence. Use the preferred spelling of each word.

1. _____
2. _____
3. _____

"Greyling" by Jane Yolen (text page 328)

Build Grammar Skills: Interjections

An interjection is a word or group of words that expresses emotion. Interjections are most often placed at the beginning of sentences and followed by a comma or exclamation point. For example, the interjections *oh* and *wow* are placed at the beginning of the sentences below. Notice that *oh* is followed by a comma, and *wow* is followed by an exclamation point:

> *Oh*, how I wish Greyling had stayed with his mother!
> *Wow!* Who'd have thought he'd turn back into a selchie?

Some interjections are placed in the middle of sentences. The interjection *oh* is found in the middle of the following sentence. Notice that the word *oh* is set off by commas:

> It was a terrible storm, but, *oh*, I wish one of the townspeople would have helped out.

Interjections can also stand alone. as in the following examples: *Hooray!* and *Oh, dear.*

A. Practice: Three of the following sentences have interjections. If there is an interjection in a sentence, write the interjection in the blank. If there is no interjection in the sentence, write the letter N in the blank.

1. Now, I told you to wear a jacket. _____

2. Gosh! I didn't mean to do that. _____

3. Now Greyling had finally gone back to the sea. _____

4. What did you do that for? _____

5. Oh, that storm was scary. _____

B. Writing Application: Rewrite each of the following sentences, adding an interjection to each one. Choose from the interjections in the list below. Add the necessary punctuation. (You don't have to use all the interjections in the list. You may use some of them more than once.) The first example has been done for you.

| *Oh no* | *Please* | *Unbelievable* | *Absolutely* | *Oh, dear* | *Help* | *No way* |

1. I'm going to be late. _____ Oh dear, I'm going to be late. _____

2. You don't really think I'd do that, do you?

_____

3. How could you say that?

_____

4. I agree with you completely.

_____

5. I'm not going to be there.

_____

6. It's dark and scary in here.

Name _____ Date _____

Reading Strategy: Predict

Predict means "make a logical guess." As you read, details in a story will help you predict what might happen next. As you continue to read, new details, such as events, descriptions of characters, or something a character says, may cause you to revise, or change, your original predictions. Making predictions as you read makes you want to read on to see if your predictions will come true. In the following passage from *Greyling*, for example, you are given some details that help you predict what Greyling will do next.

> As Greyling disappeared beneath the waves, little fingers of foam tore at his clothes. They snatched his shirt and his pants and his shoes and sent them bubbling away to the shore. And as Greyling went deeper beneath the waves, even his skin seemed to slough off till he swam, free at last, in the sleek grey coat of a great grey seal.
> The selchie had returned to the sea.

You have learned a new detail, that Greyling has become a seal again, at home in the stormy sea. When you add this to the details you've already gathered from the story — that Greyling is a devoted son and that he's willing to risk his life to help his family — you might make the prediction that Greyling will swim to the boat and rescue his father. Or is it be possible that the call of the sea will prove stronger than Greyling's loyalty to his father? Perhaps Greyling will disappear under the waves and leave the fisherman to his fate. The possibility that your prediction could be wrong provides suspense. You want to read on to find out what will happen next. Making predictions and revising them actively involves you in a story as you read.

A. DIRECTIONS: Use the chart below to keep track of details and make predictions as you read. The first row has been filled in as an example.

Detail	New Detail	My Prediction
The fisherman's wife is lonely	The fisherman brings home a seal pup	They will keep the seal pup.

"Greyling" by Jane Yolen (text page 328)

Literary Focus: Conflict

Characters in stories often struggle with each other, with nature, or with their own feelings or problems. It is usually such a struggle, or **conflict**, that makes a story exciting to read. You want to read on to find out how the conflict turns out. A character who struggles with feelings within himself or herself has an inner, or **internal** conflict. For example, at the beginning of *Greyling*, we read about an inner conflict the fisherman experiences as he struggles to keep an outward show of cheerfulness even as he suffers inside. A character who struggles with other characters or with a force of nature such as the storm in *Greyling* has an outer, or **external**, conflict.

A. DIRECTIONS: Read each of the following sentences and decide whether it is an example of internal or external conflict. In the blank, write **I** for *internal* or **E** for *external*.

1. With waves crashing over him, the fisherman fought to hold onto the mast of his sinking ship. _____

2. Greyling felt torn, not knowing whether to stay with his mother or dive into the beckoning sea. _____

3. It was difficult for Greyling to swim because the heavy winds and rain made enormous waves that pushed against him as he tried to move forward. _____

4. After Greyling disappears into the sea, the fisherman's wife has mixed feelings: she sighs, cries, then finally accepts what happened. _____

B. DIRECTIONS: For each of the following quotations from *Greyling*, explain the conflict that is going on. The first example has been done for you.

1. "She would weep and wail and rock the cradle that stood by the hearth."
   The fisherman's wife wants a baby, but she does not have one.

2. "But he kept his sorrow to himself so that his wife would not know his grief and thus double her own."
   _____
   _____

3. ". . . he knew how his wife had wanted a child. And in his secret heart, he wanted one, too, yet he felt, somehow, it was wrong."
   _____
   _____

4. "But though he often stood by the shore, . . . looking and longing and griefing his heart for what he did not really know, he never went into the sea."
   _____
   _____

5. "Let the boy go," said one old man. . . . But the fisherman's wife clasped Greyling in her arms. She did not want him to go into the sea. She was afraid he would never return."
   _____
   _____

Unit 4: Seeing It Through

"Abuelito Who" by Sandra Cisneros (text page 336)
"who knows if the moon's" by E. E. Cummings (text page 338)
"The Open Road" by Walt Whitman (text page 339)

Build Vocabulary

Compound Connecting Words

Compound words are two or more words joined together. When they are used to connect one thought, idea, or event to the next, they are called **compound connecting words**. Examples include *however*, *meanwhile*, and *moreover*. Generally compound connecting words are set off by commas from the rest of the sentence. Look at these examples:

The compound connecting word *however* means "yet," or "in spite of that."
My grandparents left late for the airport. However, they still made their flight.
The compound connecting word *meanwhile* means "at the same time."
Lisa watched the moon through her telescope. Meanwhile, Leon looked at a photograph of the moon in a science magazine.
The compound connecting word *moreover* means "in addition to what has been said; also."
The road was narrow and winding; moreover, it was covered with stones.

A. DIRECTIONS: Use *however, meanwhile,* or *moreover* to complete each sentence.

1. The day was hot and humid, and _____ there wasn't a cloud in the sky.

2. The wind was cold. _____, Sheila was warm in her parka.

3. I prepared the meal. _____, my brother set the table.

4. The dessert looked delicious. _____ I was too full to eat it.

5. I have tons of homework tonight. _____ I have band practice, too.

Using the Word Bank

henceforth	whimper	querulous

B. DIRECTIONS: Use one word from the Word Bank to replace the underlined word or words in each sentence below. Rewrite your new sentences on the lines provided.

1. My dog used to make a low whining sound when he wanted to go out. _____

2. Today I missed the bus. From now on, I'll wear my watch. _____

3. The team members were in a complaining mood after losing the game on a bad call from the umpire. _____

Recognizing Antonyms

C. DIRECTIONS: Circle the letter of the word or words that is most nearly opposite in meaning to the word in capital letters.

1. HENCEFORTH   a. because   b. in addition   c. never again   d. from this time on
2. WHIMPER   a. whine   b. giggle   c. beat up   d. listen to
3. QUERULOUS   a. complaining   b. not careful   c. talented   d. approving

"**Abuelito Who**" by Sandra Cisneros (text page 336)
"**who knows if the moon's**" by E. E. Cummings (text page 338)
"**The Open Road**" by Walt Whitman (text page 339)

Build Spelling Skills: Compound Connecting Words

Spelling Strategy When combining words to form a compound connecting word, the spelling of each word in the compound usually remains the same. This is true whether the compound connecting word is formed from two or more words.

For example: hence + forth = henceforth   never + the + less = nevertheless

A. Practice: In each sentence, below, join the words in parentheses to spell a compound connecting word. Write the compound connecting word on the line next to each sentence.

1. One day our dog ran away. (There, after), we kept her on a leash. _____

2. Today was (some, what) warmer than yesterday. _____

3. The theater was crowded. (None, the, less), we all got seats. _____

4. You vacuum the living room. (Mean, while), I'll make the beds. _____

5. We finished our jobs; (there, fore), we had time to play. _____

6. You did a good job, (not, with, standing) a few mistakes. _____

7. Speak loudly when you give a speech; (how, ever), don't shout. _____

8. I was late for school again. (Hence, forth), I will get up earlier. _____

B. Practice: Complete the following short passages with compound connecting words. Choose six of the compound connecting words that you wrote on the lines above. Some compound connecting words have similar meanings, so try not to use a connecting word more than once. If you are not sure of the meaning of a compound connecting word, use your dictionary.

1. Sandra Cisneros grew up in a poor neighborhood in Chicago, Illinois. _____, the difficult times in her early life did not deter her from developing her talents as a writer who feels deeply about her family and her Mexican heritage. In "Abuelito Who," she lovingly describes her grandfather's habits. _____, she expresses her love for him and the great sense of loss she feels after his death.

2. E. E. Cummings ("e. e. cummings") was a painter, a playwright, a poet. He actually painted more than he wrote. _____, it is through his poetry that he is best known. His lyrical but _____ quirky poems are unique. He experimented with form, phrasing, and punctuation (or lack of it), sometimes splashing lines across, down, and diagonally on a page.

3. Walt Whitman is considered one of the greatest American poets. He had strong feelings about freedom, democracy, and America. He wanted others to celebrate individual freedom and dignity and the brotherhood of people. He _____ wrote of his beliefs in his poetry. His choice of subject matter and his use of rhythmical free verse in his most famous volume of poems, *Leaves of Grass*, set a new standard for other writers. His poem, "The Open Road," expresses his feelings about taking new paths.

Unit 4: Seeing It Through

"Abuelito Who" by Sandra Cisneros (text page 336)
"who knows if the moon's" by E. E. Cummings (text page 338)
"The Open Road" by Walt Whitman (text page 339)

Build Grammar Skills: Conjunctions

Conjunctions are words that connect other words, groups of words (phrases and clauses), and whole sentences. When conjunctions join words or groups of words of the same type, they are called **coordinating conjunctions**; they link noun with noun, verb with verb, phrase with phrase, and so on. The coordinating conjunctions are *and, but, for, or, nor,* and *yet.* Look at the following examples:

Abuelito is a watch <u>and</u> glass of water.

How wonderful to think of skipping <u>or</u> floating through the air.

I waited inside the building <u>but</u> outside the auditorium.

I know the moon really has no face, <u>yet</u> sometimes I think I see one.

A. Practice: Circle the coordinating conjunction in each sentence and underline the words or word groups it connects.

1. Poets compose poems in rhyme or create poems in free verse.

2. Abuelito sleeps in his room all night and day.

3. He used to laugh with me and tell me *you are my sky.*

4. Abuelito doesn't live here anymore, but he talks to me inside my head.

5. The moon could be a balloon, for it floats in the sky.

6. She is a strong yet shy person.

7. I don't expect to receive good fortune from others, nor will I expect to receive it from others in the future.

8. Strong and content, I travel the open road.

B. Writing Application: Join each pair of sentences with a comma followed by a coordinating conjunction. Write each complete sentence on the line.

1. I can write poems in rhyme. I can write poems in free verse.

_____

2. I took good care of the garden. My flowers never bloomed.

_____

3. You can ride the bus. You can travel by train.

_____

4. Do not ask help of others. You can do this yourself.

_____

"Abuelito Who" by Sandra Cisneros (text page 336)
"who knows if the moon's" by E. E. Cummings (text page 338)
"The Open Road" by Walt Whitman (text page 339)

Reading Strategy: Make Inferences

To understand what you read, you need to **make inferences**, or educated guesses, based on the information you are given and your own knowledge and experience. In poetry, especially, meanings are not always obvious. You have to use the images and other details the poem provides to infer the underlying meaning of the poem. For example, in the poem "Abuelito Who," you read that Abuelito "is dough and feathers." What does that really mean?

The poet wants you to think about the kind of person Abuelito is. First, you need to think of the qualities of dough and feathers: Dough is a somewhat soft and pliable; feathers are light, airy, warm, often colorful, and feel gentle against the skin. You can infer from the qualities of dough that Abuelito is a yielding and giving person. You can infer from the qualities of feathers that Abuelito is a warm, uplifting, and kind person.

When you read poetry, you will often make inferences based on the images the poet creates. Remember to use the stated words and your own knowledge and experience to decide what the poet wants you to figure out about a person, event, or idea.

DIRECTIONS: In the left-hand column of the chart below, you will find details from the poems you read. Complete the chart by filling in the right-hand column with your inferences. Go back and reread the poems to find the details listed so that you can make inferences.

Details	Inferences
1. Abuelito doesn't live here anymore.	
2. Abuelito talks to me inside my head.	
3. Abuelito is blankets and spoons and big brown shoes.	
4. we'd go up higher with all the pretty people than houses and steeples and clouds:	
5. Strong and content, I travel the open road.	

Unit 4: Seeing It Through

"Abuelito Who" by Sandra Cisneros (text page 336)
"who knows if the moon's" by E. E. Cummings (text page 338)
"The Open Road" by Walt Whitman (text page 339)

Literary Focus: Free Verse

Free verse is a form of poetry in which there is no formal pattern of lines that rhyme or regular rhythmic pattern. A free-verse poem may take any shape and be any length to express the poet's ideas. What makes the poem effective is the sound, sense, and rhythm created by the following:

- choice and position of words

- use of repeated words or use of rhyming words close together

- varied length of lines

- special use of, or lack of, punctuation

The three poems in this group are free verse. They have their own shape and length, as well as the other qualities listed above. Each expresses very different ideas and emotions. For example, in "Abuelito Who," Cisneros repeats the word *who* numerous times, at the beginning of lines and within lines. This repetition gives the poem a sense of sound and creates a rhythm of its own.

A. DIRECTIONS: Read the excerpt from each poem. On the lines provided, write the rhyming and/or repeated words used by the poets.

from **"Abuelito Who"**

is tired shut the door
doesn't live here anymore
is hiding underneath the bed
who talks to me inside my head
is blankets and spoons and big brown shoes
who snores up and down up and down up
    and down again

1. Rhyming Words:

    _____

2. Repeated Words:

    _____

from **"who knows if the moon's"**

who knows if the moon's
a balloon, coming out of a keen city . . .
. . .
go sailing
away and away sailing into a keen
city which nobody's ever visited.

3. Rhyming Words:

    _____

4. Repeated Words:

    _____

from **"The Open Road"**

Henceforth I ask not good-fortune, I myself
am good-fortune.
Henceforth I whimper no more, postpone
no more, need nothing.

5. Repeated Words:

    _____

    _____

"A Backwoods Boy" by Russell Freedman (text page 344)
"Jackie Robinson: Justice at Last"
by Geoffrey C. Ward and Ken Burns (text page 353)

Build Vocabulary

Using the Prefix: *re-*

The Word Bank word *retaliated* contains the prefix *re-*, which means "back." The word means "got revenge" or "paid back." Like many other prefixes, *re-* can have additional meanings, such as "again." Here are some other words using the prefix *re-*. Notice the way in which each one is used in the example sentence.

return: go back or give back
We *return* to school in the fall.   Will you please *return* the book to the library?

renew: make new again, make like new
The sun and rain will *renew* the wilted plant and make it thrive again.

reflect: turn back or throw back
A mirror can *reflect* your image, making it seem that you are looking back at yourself.

A. DIRECTIONS: Combine the underlined words with the prefix *re-*. Write the new words on the lines provided.

1. After making it disappear, the magician <u>produced</u> _____ the egg.

2. The historian <u>traced</u> _____ the steps of Lewis and Clark.

3. We were eager to <u>unite</u> _____ with our friends after the summer.

4. Matt <u>placed</u> _____ the clothes in the closet after cleaning it out.

Using the Word Bank

aptitude	intrigued	treacherous	integrate	retaliated

B. DIRECTIONS: Match each word in the left-hand column with its definition in the right-hand column. Write the letter of the definition on the line next to the word it defines.

_____ 1. treacherous   a. fascinated

_____ 2. aptitude   b. remove barriers and allow access to all

_____ 3. retaliated   c. natural ability

_____ 4. intrigued   d. dangerous

_____ 5. integrate   e. harmed someone in return for an injury

Analogies

C. DIRECTIONS: Circle the letter of the pair of words that expresses the same relationship as the pair in CAPITAL LETTERS.

1. SUNSET : BEAUTIFUL
   a. heart : integrate
   b. mystery : intrigued
   c. flood : treacherous
   d. forgave : retaliated

2. MUSIC : TALENT
   a. math : aptitude
   b. curious : intrigued
   c. combine : integrate
   d. angry : retaliated

"A Backwoods Boy" by Russell Freedman (text page 344)
"Jackie Robinson: Justice at Last"
by Geoffrey C. Ward and Ken Burns (text page 353)

Build Spelling Skills: The Suffix *-tude*

Spelling Strategy Words that end in the suffix *-tude* are always spelled with one *t*, never a double *t*. Examples include the Word Bank word *aptitude* as well as *attitude*, *gratitude*, and *solitude*.

A. Practice: Write the word from the following list that best completes each sentence.

gratitude   solitude   altitude   fortitude   multitude   aptitude   attitude

1. The highest peak in the mountain had an _____ of 4,000 feet.

2. We expressed our _____ to our teacher by giving her a dozen roses.

3. Max has a poor _____ in class and rarely completes his homework.

4. The soldier showed his _____ when he carried his wounded comrade to safety.

5. Martha has a great _____ for music and was playing the piano by age six.

6. We pushed our way through the great _____ of people in the shopping mall.

7. All alone in the library, Henry enjoyed the _____ as he read his book.

B. Practice: Complete the following paragraph. Choose six words from the list above to fill in the blanks.

   Abraham Lincoln and Jackie Robinson shared some of the same character traits. Both men had a positive _____ that helped them struggle against great obstacles. They also showed great _____ and courage in fighting slavery and racism in their times. Both were rewarded with the _____ of a nation for their achievements, although both were criticized during their lifetime. Men of action, Lincoln and Robinson were also thoughtful and enjoyed _____ to escape the demands of the _____ of people who often surrounded them. Of course, they had their differences, too. Lincoln's _____ lay in politics and speech making, while Robinson's gift was his athletic ability.

Challenge: In the first syllable of the Word Bank word *treacherous* the short *e* sound that you hear in the word *red* is spelled *ea*. That sound is spelled the same way in such words as *leather* and *ready*. Often, however, the *ea* combination is pronounced as a long *e*, as in *bead*. In the chart below, list the following words in the correct column, according to whether the short *e* sound is spelled with an *e* or with *ea*, or whether the *ea* combination is pronounced as a long *e*.

health   stream   seven   cream   fear   level   head   dear   steady
neat   intend   instead   treat   tread   deaf   never   kept   wedding

Short *e* sound spelled *e*	Short *e* sound spelled *ea*	Long *e* sound spelled *ea*

"A Backwoods Boy" by Russell Freedman (text page 344)
"Jackie Robinson: Justice at Last"
by Geoffrey C. Ward and Ken Burns (text page 353)

Build Grammar Skills: Conjunctions Joining Sentences

Conjunctions are words that link single words or groups of words. Conjunctions can also indicate the relationships between the ideas they join together in sentences. For example, the conjunction *and* indicates that a word or group of words is linked to another by *addition*. In the sentence below, the conjunction *and* indicates "in addition to."

He supported his family by living off his own land, *and* he watched for a chance to better himself.

In other words, Lincoln supported his family; *and in addition to that*, he planned to better himself.

The conjunction *but* indicates a *contrast* between two ideas. The conjunction *so* indicates a *cause-and-effect* relationship.

He stayed with his family through this first prairie winter, *but* he was getting restless.

There wasn't much business at Offutt's store, *so* he could spend long hours reading as he sat behind the counter.

In the first sentence, the two ideas are in contrast with each other. Lincoln stays with his family, *in spite of the fact* that he felt restless. In the second sentence, the two ideas are related by cause-and-effect. Lincoln had time to read *because* there was little business at the store.

A. Practice: Underline the conjunction in each of the following sentences. On the line, identify the relationship between the two parts of the sentence. Write A for addition, C for contrast, or CE for cause-and effect.

____ 1. Baseball was loved by America, but the major leagues were for white men only.

____ 2. The invasion began, and the governor called for volunteers.

____ 3. New Salem was still a small place, but it was growing.

____ 4. He knew nothing about surveying, so he bought couple of books on the subject.

____ 5. Thomas built a coffin, and nine-year-old Abraham whittled the pegs.

B. Writing Application: Write a two-part sentence about the topics below, using the conjunctions indicated to join the two parts together.

1. Write a sentence about something that happened to you when you were younger, using the conjunction <u>and</u>.

_____

2. Write a sentence about two of your favorite sports, using the conjunction <u>but</u>.

_____

3. Write a sentence about the life of a person you admire, using the conjunction <u>so</u>.

_____

"A Backwoods Boy" by Russell Freedman (text page 344)

"Jackie Robinson: Justice at Last"

by Geoffrey C. Ward and Ken Burns (text page 353)

Reading Strategy: Identify Main Ideas

Details make a piece of writing interesting to read. But good readers know that writers supply these details not only to capture your interest, but to lead up to or support their ideas. For example, in "Backwoods Boy," the main idea is that Abraham Lincoln went from being a poor backwoods farm boy to President of the United States. The following details lead you to identify that main idea:

- Lincoln was born in a log cabin with one window, one door, and a dirt floor.
- His parents couldn't read or write.
- Lincoln went to school only a few months a year.

DIRECTIONS: Use the following organizer to help you better understand the main ideas in "A Backwoods Boy" and "Jackie Robinson: Justice at Last." Read each passage below. In the first column of the organizer, fill in at least two details that help you identify the main idea of each passage. Then write in the main idea of the passage in the second column. The first two passages are about Abraham Lincoln and the third is about Jackie Robinson.

1. He would carry a book out to the field with him, so he could read at the end of each plowed furrow, while the horse was getting its breath. When noon came, he would sit under a tree and read while he ate. "I never saw Abe after he was twelve that he didn't have a book in his hand or in his pocket," Dennis Hanks remembered. "It didn't seem natural to see a feller read like that."

2. To support himself, he worked at all sorts of odd jobs. He split fence rails, hired himself out as a farmhand, helped at the local gristmill. With the help of friends, he was appointed postmaster of New Salem, a part-time job that paid about fifty dollars a year. Then he was offered a chance to become deputy to the local surveyor. He knew nothing about surveying, so he bought a compass, a chain, and a couple of textbooks on the subject. Within six weeks, he had taught himself enough to start work—laying out roads and townsites, and marking off property boundaries.

3. When Rickey met Jackie Robinson, he thought he'd found the right man. Robinson was 28 years old, and a superb athlete. In his first season in the Negro leagues, he hit .387. But just as importantly, he had great intelligence and sensitivity. Robinson was college-educated, and knew what joining the majors would mean for blacks. The grandson of a slave, he was proud of his race and wanted others to feel the same.

	Detail	Main Idea
Passage 1		
Passage 2		
Passage 3		

"A Backwoods Boy" by Russell Freedman (text page 344)
"Jackie Robinson: Justice at Last"
by Geoffrey C. Ward and Ken Burns (text page 353)

Literary Focus: Factual Accounts

In a **factual account**, an author tells you facts, or true information, about an event or a person. But just a list of facts would not be very interesting to read. By adding details, an author can interpret or explain facts. In other words, an author includes details to express what he or she thinks those facts really mean.

Read the following passage from "A Backwoods Boy."

> Yes, the law intrigued him. It would give him a chance to rise in the world, to earn a respected place in the community, to live by his wits instead of by hard physical labor.

In the passage, the author states a fact: **Abraham Lincoln was interested in the law**. He adds the following details to **explain** why Lincoln developed this interest:

1. Being a lawyer would give him a chance to rise in the world.

2. He would be respected by the community.

3. He would be able to earn a living without doing hard physical labor.

DIRECTIONS: Read the following two passages. The first is about Abraham Lincoln's journey to New Orleans with a friend. The second is the last paragraph of "Jackie Robinson: Justice at Last." On the lines below each passage write the fact stated in the passage and three details that explain or interpret that fact.

1. To support himself, he worked at all sorts of odd jobs. He split fence rails, hired himself out as a farmhand, helped at the local gristmill. With the help of friends, he was appointed postmaster of New Salem, a part-time job that paid about fifty dollars a year.

Fact:

_____

Details:

1. _____

2. _____

3. _____

2. Many fans and players were prejudiced—they didn't want the races to play together. Rickey knew the first black player would be cursed and booed. Pitchers would throw at him; runners would spike him. Even his own teammates might try to pick a fight.

Fact:

_____

Details:

1. _____

2. _____

3. _____

Unit 4: Seeing It Through

"The Strange Geometry of Stonehenge" by Katherine B. Shippen (text page 371)

Build Vocabulary

Using Forms of *orientation*

The word *orientation* means "finding the position or direction" of a person or object. Related words include the verb *orient*, meaning "to find the orientation of a person or object" and the adjective *disoriented*, meaning "lost" or "not knowing where one is, or in what direction one is going." There is an outdoor sport called *orienteering*, in which people find their way from a starting line to a finishing line through rugged, unknown country by using compasses and maps to *orient* themselves as they go.

A. DIRECTIONS: Fill in the blanks with the correct word from the following choices. A word may be used more than once.

orient	orientation	disoriented

1. He could see no familiar landmarks and felt _____.

2. The new students attended an _____ program before classes started.

3. I use a compass to _____ myself when I am hiking.

4. The _____ of the wall was from north to south.

5. After getting off the whirling ride, I felt _____ for a minute.

Using the Word Bank

immemorial	colossal	inscrutable	eradicate	orientation	successive

B. DIRECTIONS: For each of the following definitions, write the correct word bank word in the spaces provided. Then write the letters in the circled spaces on the line below, and you will find a word that describes the monuments at Stonehenge.

1. very old, extending back before memory __ _ _ _ _ _ _Ⓞ_

2. hard to understand _Ⓞ_ _ _ _ _ _ _ _ _

3. gigantic Ⓞ_ _ _ _ _ _ _

4. following one after another _ _ _ _ _ _ _Ⓞ_ _

5. position in relation to points of the compass _ _Ⓞ_ _ _ _ _ _ _Ⓞ

6. wipe out _ _ _ _ _ _ _Ⓞ_

A word that describes the Stonehenge monuments: _ _ _ _ _ _ _ _

C. DIRECTIONS: Circle the letter of the word or phrase that is closest in meaning to the word in CAPITAL LETTERS.

1. ERADICATE: a. clarify   b. destroy   c. arrange   d. fascinate

2. INSCRUTABLE: a. heavy   b. itchy   c. too high to climb   d. hard to understand

3. ORIENTATION: a. placement   b. rocking   c. treatment   d. taking apart

4. COLOSSAL: a. amusing   b. angry   c. huge   d. ugly

5. SUCCESSIVE: a. wealthy   b. in sequence   c. packed together   d. hot-tempered

"The Strange Geometry of Stonehenge" by Katherine B. Shippen (text page 371)

Build Spelling Skills: Using *cess* to Spell the Sound *ses*

Spelling Strategy Many words that contain the sound *ses*, such as *successive*, spell that sound *cess*. Other examples of words that spell the sound *ses* with the letters *cess* are *access*, *recess*, and *excess*.

A. Practice: In the spaces provided, complete each word by using the letters *cess* to spell the *ses* sound. Write each complete word.

1. suc + *ses* _____.

2. ex + *ses* + ive _____.

3. pro + *ses* + ion _____.

4. prin + *ses* _____.

5. ac+ *ses* _____.

6. suc + *ses* + ive _____.

7. inter + *ses* + ion _____.

8. ac + *ses* + ory _____.

B. Practice: Complete each of the following sentences by filling in the blank. Use the letters *cess* to spell the *ses* sound for each word in parentheses.

1. Stonehenge draws an (in- *ses* + ant) _____ stream of visitors.

2. One can imagine ancient (pro + *ses* + ions) _____ walking among the stones.

3. Only certain people get direct (ac +*sess*) _____ to the stones themselves.

4. Limiting access to the stones became a (ne + *ses* + ity) _____.

5. Scientists have not been (suc + *ses* + ful) _____ at solving the mysteries.

6. A (pro + *ses*) _____ called Carbon-14 dating was used.

Challenge: The formations found at Stonehenge are called *trilithons*. *Trilithon* is a word formed from two parts: the prefix *tri-*, meaning "three," and the word part *lith*, meaning "stone." The word *trilithon* refers to the three stones used to build the formation. The prefix *tri-* occurs in many English words, such as *triangle*. On the chart below, read the word parts in column 1 and their meanings in column 2. In column 3, form a new word by adding the prefix *tri-* to each word part. In column 4, complete the meaning of the new word. One row is completed for you.

Word	Meaning	New Word With *tri-*	Meaning
1. angle	angle	triangle	a shape with three angles
2. cycle	wheel or circle		a vehicle with
3. -athlon	athletic event		a race involving
4. monthly	every month		occurring every
5. weekly	every week		occurring every

"The Strange Geometry of Stonehenge" by Katherine B. Shippen (text page 371)

Build Grammar Skills: Complete Subjects and Predicates

A sentence is made up of two parts: a subject and a predicate. The **simple subject** is a noun or pronoun that tells what or who performs the action in the sentence. The **complete subject** includes the simple subject plus the other words around it.

┌─────── complete subject ───────┐
The <u>monument</u> called Stonehenge is located in England.
   simple subject

The **simple predicate** of a sentence is a verb that tells what the subject does or is. The **complete predicate** is that verb along with other words around it. Those words may be nouns that receive the action of the verb or further identify the subject; they may be words that describe the verb or the nouns.

┌─────────────── complete predicate ───────────────┐
Scientists <u>have had</u> many different opinions about the meaning of Stonehenge.
   simple predicate

A. Practice: For each of the following sentences, underline the complete subject *once*, and underline the complete predicate *twice*.

1. <u>The mysteries of Stonehenge</u> <u><u>have puzzled scientists and historians for hundreds of years.</u></u>

2. Somehow the enormous stones were moved and set upright by an ancient people.

3. An architect from the Eastern Mediterranean may have designed the ancient temple.

4. Tourists from all over the world come to view the ruins at Stonehenge.

5. The Druids did not actually build the structure.

6. Many cultures have contributed to the history and development of Great Britain.

7. One of the best-known theories about Stonehenge states that it was a solar observatory.

B. Writing Application: Finish each sentence by adding a complete subject or a complete predicate, as indicated in parentheses. The first sentence has been done for you.

1. (add complete predicate) The Romans _____ conquered Britain. _____

2. (add complete subject)_____attracts over a million tourists every year.

3. (add complete predicate) The architect Inigo Jones _____.

4. (add complete subject) _____ believed that the Druids built Stonehenge.

5. (add complete predicate) The sarsen stones at Stonehenge_____.

6. (add complete subject) _____ agree that there is still much to learn.

Reading for Success: Strategies for Reading Critically

As a critical reader, you must take the time to analyze carefully what you read, and consider how effectively an author has put together a piece of writing.

- **Recognize the writer's purpose.** Writers generally write to entertain, inform, call to action, or reflect on experiences. Notice the writer's choice of words and the details he or she includes. These clues will help you determine a writer's purpose. Then, judge whether the writer has achieved his or her purpose.

- **Distinguish fact from opinion.** It's important to distinguish facts from opinions.

    Fact: A statement that can be proven true or false by consulting a reliable source.

    Opinion: A belief that is based on a writer's attitude or values.

- **Evaluate the writer's message.** When you evaluate a writer's message, you make a judgment about how effectively a writer has proven his or her point. First, identify the writer's message. Then, look to see whether this message has been thoroughly supported by facts and details. Also, consider whether the writer is qualified to write on that subject.

DIRECTIONS: Read the following passage from "Paul Klee" by Hattie Clark, and use the reading strategies to increase your comprehension. In the margin, note where you recognize the writer's purpose, distinguish fact from opinion, and evaluate the writer's message. Finally, write a brief response to the selection on the lines provided.

from **"Paul Klee"** by Hattie Clark

The following passage is about the Swiss artist Paul Klee.

Klee was a master at line drawing and painting. Sometimes his lines were slender as a spider's web, sometimes as thick as a little finger. He made his lines slide, skitter, and squiggle across the canvas. But he never let them go too far. He never stopped them too soon. Nor did he let his lines stray. Klee made both his lines and his colors the servants of his ideas.

Many artists paint what they see around them, but Klee painted what he saw within his imagination. And his imagination was a castle filled with treasures . . . with clowns and gardens . . . with birds and beasts and make-believe creatures . . . with moons and funny machines, and even ghosts. These fantastic forms fill his paintings. And his paintings are sprinkled with humor, because humor was at the core of Klee's being.

At the same time he was deeply serious. He put into his paintings his intense feelings about human life and what was going on in the world.

Three-year-olds put their ideas and feelings into their artwork, too. But not in the same way as Klee. A young child usually works quite quickly. But Klee worked slowly. His paintings were built idea by idea, line by line. Sometimes he sat for hours without painting a stroke. And often he worked on several paintings at once. When he was finally finished, complex ideas had been carefully worked into his canvasses.

(continued next page)

In Klee's studio there was a table littered with what some would call clutter. But to him, they were objects of beauty, objects that triggered his imagination: a bird's egg, a pine cone, an odd-shaped root, coral, wire, wood, scraps of cloth.

Many such "finds" went into decorating the puppets that Klee made for his son, Felix. The first eight were given to Felix on his ninth birthday. In all, Klee created about fifty puppets from paper mache and plaster.

Among the puppets were a grandmother, a farmer, a policeman, a clown, a monk, and a ghost who was supposed to have escaped from an electrical outlet. Felix and his father spent many wonderful hours with these strange and wonderful "people."

Whether Klee made puppets or paintings, his imagination always turned cartwheels and played with clouds. Why not start your imagination working? Take a line for a walk as Klee did. Put your pencil on a paper. Draw a line. Make your line skip. Now run. Lead your line into an imaginary valley, over a mountain, and through a stream. Your line meets another line. Now you have two lines to work with. Together they meander through a forest. They hurry past a monster. Don't quit now. Keep going . . . going . . . going.

"The Strange Geometry of Stonehenge" by Katherine B. Shippen (text page 371)

Literary Focus: Analytical Essay

An analytical essay examines a large, complicated question by breaking it into smaller parts that are easier to understand and explain. This selection focuses on a big question: What are the answers to the mysteries surrounding Stonehenge? The author breaks down this big question into several smaller questions: Who built Stonehenge? When was it built? What was its purpose?

A. DIRECTIONS: Below are some of the parts into which Katherine Shippen has divided the over-all focus of her essay. For each of the following quotations from the selection, write the letter of the smaller question that the quotation addresses.

> a. Who built Stonehenge?
> b. When was Stonehenge built?
> c. What was the purpose of Stonehenge?

____ 1. Inigo Jones announced that without doubt it was a Roman Temple.

____ 2. Again it was said that this was a monument for Hengist and Horsa, who had come from Jutland to help fight off the Picts and Scots and had stayed to conquer the country for themselves.

____ 3. This artifact indicated that the builders had lived in the Bronze Age.

B. DIRECTIONS: Write a sentence from the selection that addresses each of the following questions on the lines provided. Do not repeat any of the sentences printed above.

1. What did Stonehenge look like originally?_____

_____

2. How old is Stonehenge? _____

_____

3. Who built Stonehenge? _____

_____

4. For what use was Stonehenge intended?_____

_____

"The Fun They Had" by Isaac Asimov (text page 383)

Build Vocabulary

Using the Prefix *non-*

The Word Bank word *nonchalantly* contains the prefix *non-*, which means "not" or "without." In the story, Tommy answers Margie's question *nonchalantly*, meaning "casually" or "without much interest." Because *non-* means "not" or "without," it gives the opposite meaning to a word to which it is attached. For instance, *non + sense = nonsense*, meaning, "without sense." *Non + stop = nonstop*, which means "not stopping" or "without stopping." *Non + fiction = not fiction*, or "fact." *Non + existent = nonexistent*, or "not existing."

A. DIRECTIONS: Complete each sentence by adding *non-* to the word in parentheses.

1. The concerned students held a (violent) _____ protest.

2. Dieters often choose (fat) _____ ice cream.

4. Because of the (stop) _____ arguments, the meeting was (productive) _____.

3. Most charities are (profit) _____ organizations.

Using the Word Bank

calculated	loftily	dispute	nonchalantly

B. DIRECTIONS: The underlined words in this paragraph don't make sense because they are not where they ought to be. Use clues in each sentence to decide which underlined word best fits the meaning of each sentence. Then rewrite the paragraph on the lines or on a separate sheet of paper. Write the underlined words where they will make sense.

Brian <u>dispute</u> boasted that he could finish the arithmetic quiz by the time the bell rang. He <u>loftily</u> picked up his pencil and began on the first problem. No one could <u>calculated</u> that he was good at math. He had <u>nonchalantly</u> all of the answers ten minutes ahead of schedule.

_____

_____

_____

_____

Recognizing Synonyms

C. DIRECTIONS: Circle the letter of the word that is closest in meaning to the word in CAPITAL LETTERS.

1. CALCULATED: a. guessed b. figured c. understood d. subtracted

2. NONCHALANTLY: a. without interest   c. without regret or sorrow

                 b. without anger or rage   d. without concern or excitement

3. LOFTILY: a. speedily b. proudly c. dreamily d. foolishly

4. DISPUTE: a. agree b. reason c. argue d. accept

"The Fun They Had" by Isaac Asimov (text page 383)

Build Spelling Skills: Using *ch* to Spell the *sh* Sound

Spelling Strategy *Ch* can be used to spell words that have the *sh* sound. This is the soft sound that is found in the Word Bank word *non*ch*alant*. Learn the spelling of these words as you come across them in your reading.

Examples: nonchalantly, chateau, chaperone, pistachio, chauffeur

Contrast hard *ch* sound: chair, chain, rich, much

A. Practice: The following words contain the soft *sh* sound spelled *ch* or *sh* or a hard *ch* sound spelled *ch*. Write each word in its proper column in the chart below. One example of each is given.

mustache shoe pistachio such dash choose chef crash nonchalant child shell
chauffeur approach shed champion wishes machine chandelier chateau charge

Soft *sh* Spelled *ch*	Soft *sh* Spelled *sh*	Hard *ch* Spelled *ch*
chandelier	crash	child

B. Practice: In the words below, the letters that spell the sound *sh* have been left out.

non___alantly *(ch)*   ma___ *(sh)*   ___auffeur *(ch)*   cra___ing *(sh)*   ma___ine *(ch)*

The letters in parentheses next to each word tell how the *sh* sound should be spelled in that word. Complete the paragraph below with the word from above that makes sense.

Margie and Tommy live in the age of the _____. A nonhuman robot can pre-

pare scrambled eggs or _____ potatoes. The family car can be operated by an

electronic _____, who can drive without _____. The people of

the future are not surprised by these developments and regard it all _____.

Challenge: In the Word Bank word *calculated* the *u* has a long $y\overline{oo}$ sound. You can find this sound spelled differently in other English words. On the lines below, write at least two words in which the long $y\overline{oo}$ sound is spelled with the letters indicated. Look in a dictionary for help if necessary.

1. **u** _____

2. **you** _____

3. **yu** _____

4. **eu** _____

Selection Support **145**

"The Fun They Had" by Isaac Asimov (text page 383)

Build Grammar Skills: Simple Subjects and Predicates

The **simple subject** of a sentence is the main word in the complete subject. The simple subject is a noun or a pronoun that shows the person, place, or thing the sentence is about. In the following examples the simple subject is underlined. Sometimes the simple subject is the complete subject, as *Margie* and *It* are in the examples below.

|—complete subject—|

Examples: Today's arithmetic <u>lesson</u> is on the addition of proper fractions.

<u>Margie</u> was disappointed. <u>It</u> was a very old book.

The **simple predicate** of a sentence is the main word or words in the complete predicate. The simple predicate is a verb that tells what the subject does or is.

In the following sentences, the complete predicate is in italics. The simple predicate is underlined twice.

Example: Tommy *<u>screamed</u> with laughter*. Today Tommy *<u>found</u> a real book*.

A. Practice: In the sentences below, underline the simple subject once and the simple predicate twice. The first exercise has been done for you.

1. The lucky <u>students</u> of long ago <u>had</u> human teachers.

2. The human teachers instructed groups of students.

3. They had a special building called a "school."

4. All the kids went there for classes.

5. They used a computer for a teacher.

6. This computer gave lessons and tests.

7. A real teacher was much more interesting.

8. Education was boring and lonesome.

B. Writing Application: Write three sentences telling why you would rather have a real teacher or a robot. Draw a line under the simple subject and two lines under the simple predicate in each sentence.

1. _____

_____

2. _____

_____

3. _____

_____

"The Fun They Had" by Isaac Asimov (text page 383)

Reading Strategy: Evaluate the Author's Message

   In many stories, as in "The Fun They Had," the author has a message to communicate to readers. Rather than directly stating that message, the author gets his or her point across by including certain details, such as things the characters do or say. Good readers use those details to figure out the author's points and then decide for themselves whether or not they agree. That is, they **evaluate** the author's message. For example, in "The Fun They Had," the author makes his main point, that computers do not make good teachers, by having the characters do and say things that let the reader know they are not enjoying or getting much out of their education.

DIRECTIONS: As you read "The Fun They Had," use the following chart to help you understand the author's message and express your own ideas about it. Fill in the chart with details the author includes and the points he makes by including those details. Write in whether you "agree" or "disagree" with each point, and then add your reasons. The first row in the chart has been filled in as an example.

Detail	Message	Agree/Disagree	Reason
Margie has to write out her homework in a punch code.	Doing homework on a computer is too hard and boring.	Disagree	We use computers, but we don't have to use punch codes.

"The Fun They Had" by Isaac Asimov (text page 383)

Literary Focus: Science Fiction

Science fiction is a special type of literature that usually focuses on the science and technology of the future. Because most science fiction stories take place in the future, authors have to combine what they know about technology at the time they are writing with how they imagine technology will advance at a later time. When Isaac Asimov wrote "The Fun They Had," he was sure that computers, which were in an early stage of use at that time, would be used for education. But he had to imagine exactly how they would be used. He predicted some details correctly, and others incorrectly.

DIRECTIONS: Look through "The Fun They Had." Look for details about computers that the author predicted correctly. Look for others that the author imagined, but predicted incorrectly. List the details you find on the chart below. The first two examples have been filled in for you.

Predicted Correctly	Predicted Incorrectly
Math problems on screen	No such thing as real books

"A Dream Within a Dream" by Edgar Allan Poe (text page 390)
"The Spring and the Fall" by Edna St. Vincent Millay (text page 391)
"Ankylosaurus" by Jack Prelutsky (text page 392)

Build Vocabulary: The Prefix *in-*

The prefix *in-* means *not.* When you add the prefix *in-* to most words, it changes the meaning of the word to its opposite. For example, if you add the prefix *in-* to the base word *capable*, which means *able*, the word becomes *incapable*, which means *not able.* Usually, you can figure out the meaning of a word that begins with the prefix *in-* if you know the meaning of the base word. Just add "not" to the base word.

Not all words starting with *in-* follow this rule, however. The word *indebted*, for example, means the condition of being *in debt,* of owing something, rather than *not* owing something. If you are not sure what a word starting with *in-* means, look it up in a dictionary.

A. DIRECTIONS: In the chart below, base words and their meanings are given in columns 1 and 2. In column 3, rewrite each base word, adding the prefix *in-*, and in column 4, write the new meaning. The first one has been done as an example.

Base Word	Meaning	Add *in-*	New Meaning
1. consolable	able to be comforted	inconsolable	not able to be comforted
2. edible	able to be eaten		
3. constant	staying the same		
4. compatible	able to get along		
5. credulous	believing		
6. humane	kind		

Using the Word Bank

deem	bough	raucous	inedible	cudgel

B. DIRECTIONS: In the blank, write the word that best replaces the word or phrase in parentheses.

1. The crowd at the game grew (rough and harsh-sounding) _____.

2. The tough meat was (not capable of being eaten) _____.

3. He looked frightening, waving his (thick club) _____.

4. The (branch) _____ was bent by the heavy snow.

5. I do not (judge) _____ this situation dangerous.

Unit 5: Mysterious Worlds

"**A Dream Within a Dream**" by Edgar Allan Poe (text page 390)
"**The Spring and the Fall**" by Edna St. Vincent Millay (text page 391)
"**Ankylosaurus**" by Jack Prelutsky (text page 392)

Build Spelling Skills: The Sound *ow* Spelled *ough*

Spelling Strategy The words *bough* and *drought* use *ough* to spell the sound *ow*. How-ever, the *ow* sound is usually spelled *ow*, as in *vow*, or *ou* as in *noun*.

Examples: b<u>ough</u>, dr<u>ough</u>t, pl<u>ough</u>/pl<u>ow</u>, gr<u>ou</u>nd, h<u>ou</u>se, f<u>ou</u>nd, ab<u>ou</u>t, <u>ou</u>t, h<u>ow</u>, n<u>ow</u>, v<u>ow</u>, all<u>ow</u>

Exceptions: Not all words spelled with *ough* make the *ow* sound. The words *cough*, *though*, and *through* are three examples.

A. Practice: Add the letters *ough*, *ou*, or *ow* to the incomplete word in each sentence.

1. I made a v_____ to always to tell the truth.

2. It finally rained, ending the month of dr_____.

3. He lives in the h_____ on the corner.

4. The farmer went out to pl_____ the field.

5. I will all_____ her one more chance.

6. The b_____ was covered with pink blossoms.

B. Practice: In the following paragraph, cross out the misspelled words, and write the word correctly above the line.

In "A Dream Within A Dream," the poet has fownd owt something important abought

life: time changes everything. Like sand, everything he cares about slips through his fingers,

no matter hough tightly he grasps it. Nou, as he comes to this realization, he feels boughed

doun with sadness.

Challenge: In most words, the *ow* sound is spelled *ou* or *ow*. However, some words that have the *ow* sound are spelled with *au*. These are German words that have made their way into the English language and are used both in German-speaking and English-speaking countries.

hausfrau, a housewife
sauerkraut, shredded, salted cabbage
landau, an enclosed, four-wheeled carriage

DIRECTIONS: Use the information above to complete the sentences, filling in the blanks with one of the above words borrowed from German.

1. I like _____ on my hotdog,

2. Queen Elizabeth rode in a _____.

3. A _____ works hard managing a home.

"A Dream Within a Dream" by Edgar Allan Poe (text page 390)

"The Spring and the Fall" by Edna St. Vincent Millay (text page 391)

"Ankylosaurus" by Jack Prelutsky (text page 392)

Build Grammar Skills: Complete Sentences

A **complete sentence** expresses a complete thought and has at least one subject and one predicate, or verb. If a sentence is missing a subject or verb, you can tell that the sentence is incomplete.

> **Complete sentence**: The poet writes about the seasons.
>
> The subject is *poet*. The verb is *writes*. The sentence expresses a complete thought.
>
> **Incomplete sentence**: Uses beautiful words.
>
> No subject. The verb is *uses*. No complete thought.
>
> **Incomplete sentence**: But she, only she
>
> The subject is *she*. No verb. No complete thought.
>
> **Incomplete sentence**: Although the words rhyme.
>
> The subject is *words*, the verb is *rhyme*, but there is no complete thought. More words are needed: *Although the words rhyme, I don't like their sound.* .

While it is usually considered incorrect to use incomplete sentences, they are often used in dialogue, and in poetry to produce a special effect. For example, in "A Dream Within a Dream," Edgar Allan Poe uses the incomplete sentence "While I weep—while I weep!"

A. Practice: In the blanks, write C if the sentence is complete, or I if it is incomplete.

____ 1. I weep.   ____ 4. He hurt her in little ways.

____ 2. Because she was lonely.   ____ 5. Stomped around the forest making noise.

____ 3. This enormous dinosaur.   ____ 6. Sand crashes in the wave

B. Writing Application: Write complete sentences using the subjects and verbs given.

1. flower / give _____

2 bough / broke _____

3. ankylosaurus / waddled _____

4. she/ grasped _____

5. friend / laughed _____

Unit 5: Mysterious Worlds

"A Dream Within a Dream" by Edgar Allan Poe (text page 390)
"The Spring and the Fall" by Edna St. Vincent Millay (text page 391)
"Ankylosaurus" by Jack Prelutsky (text page 392)

Reading Strategy: Make Inferences

Rather than plainly and directly stating exactly what they mean, poets often use language that is indirect and words that can have several meanings. The reader is expected to **make inferences**, or draw conclusions, about the meaning, based on details in the poem. When you do so, you arrive at a deeper understanding of a poem and find greater pleasure in reading it.

DIRECTIONS: As you read the poems, use the chart below to note details and make inferences based on those details. Three details are given, and the first inference has been made for you.

"A Dream Within a Dream"

Detail	Inference
The speaker gives someone a parting kiss.	The poet is sad to say good-bye to someone he once cared for.

"The Spring and the Fall"

Detail	Inference
"He laughed at all I dared to praise."	

"Ankylosaurus"

Detail	Inference
"Ankylosaurus was built like a tank."	

"A Dream Within a Dream" by Edgar Allan Poe (text page 390)
"The Spring and the Fall" by Edna St. Vincent Millay (text page 391)
"Ankylosaurus" by Jack Prelutsky (text page 392)

Literary Focus: Rhyme

Words that **rhyme** end with the same sound. For example the word *bough* rhymes with *allow* because both end with the sound *ow*, even though the sound is spelled differently in each word.

- Rhyming words may be spelled alike: *cake, make, sake, mistake*
- Or they may be spelled differently: *go, know, toe, although*
- Some words have similar spellings, but do not rhyme: *earth, hearth; wear, near*

A. DIRECTIONS: For each line, circle the letter of the line that rhymes with it.

1. The ankylosaurus grew in weight

   a. More quickly than it grew in height   b. The more it ate and ate and ate

2. He made a vow

   a. That I'll allow   b. When he felt low

3. It stomped through forests long ago

   a. It had so many things to do   b. The sky above, the earth below

4. In the fall of the year

   a. It was hard to bear   b. She shed a tear

5. He broke a bough

   a. She remembers it now   b. And she'd had enough

B. DIRECTIONS: In the paragraph below, circle all the words that rhyme with the word *show*.

The violinist's career had been slow to grow, but he had made a vow that he would allow

himself five years to achieve success. Now the time had come for him to wow his audience.

Every row in the concert hall was filled. With a slight bow of his head, he raised his bow,

and the sounds began to flow. By the end of the evening, he would know if he'd made it.

Name _____ Date _____

Build Vocabulary: Compound Adjectives

When two or more words work together as one to modify a noun or pronoun, the word is called a **compound adjective**. The word *airtight*, for example, combines two words, *air* and *tight*. This word describes something so tight no air can get in.

Compound adjectives are useful in writing, because they can replace a whole phrase or group of words. For example, it's shorter and clearer to say "The compartment was airtight," than "The compartment was so tight that no air could get into it." Here is another example.

It was breezy, so I packed up my jacket *that was light in weight* and red.
It was breezy, so I packed up my *lightweight* red jacket.

A. DIRECTIONS: Replace the italicized words with a compound adjective from the list below.

watertight   carefree   windblown

1. The passengers had a conversation *that was free of care*. _____

2. The ship's compartments were *made tight so that no water could get in.* _____

3. I need a comb because my hair is *blown by the wind.* _____

Using the Word Bank

majestically	drawing	collision	novelty	rapidly	watertight

B. DIRECTIONS: Use a word from the Word Bank above to answer the following riddles, filling in the blank space.

1. How is a high, snow-capped mountain like a king wearing velvet robes? They are both _____ dressed.

2. Two skaters with bad vision might have a _____.

3. How is an artist using a pencil like a horse pulling a cart? They both are _____ something.

4. To someone who studies all the time, having no homework is a _____

5. A fish is very happy inside a _____ container.

6. How would you remove your finger from a hot stove? _____

Recognizing Antonyms

C. DIRECTIONS: Circle the letter of the word that is most *opposite* in meaning to the word in CAPITAL LETTERS.

1. RAPIDLY: a. quickly   b. slowly   c. nervously   d. calmly

2. WATERTIGHT: a. dry   b. damp   c. leaky   d. desert

3. MAJESTICALLY: a. modestly   b. grandly   c. magically   b. sadly

4. COLLISION: a. crash   b. separation   c. plot   d. collection

from *Exploring the* Titanic by Robert Ballard (text page 398)

Build Spelling Skills: The Sound *zhun* Spelled *-sion*

Spelling Strategy The Word Bank word *collision*, meaning "a crash," spells the *zhun* sound with *-sion*. Other words that have this sound and spelling include *illusion*, *vision*, and *confusion*.

• **Exception:** If the *-sion* is preceded by an *s*, it is pronounced *-shun*: admi<u>ssion</u>, discu<u>ssion</u>.

A. Practice: Add *-sion* to the word parts in parentheses; then use each word in a sentence.

1. (deci) _____

2. (confu) _____

3. (explo) _____

4. (inva) _____

5. (illu) _____

B. Practice: In the paragraph below, fill in the blanks with a word that uses the spelling *-sion* from the following list:

vision   conclusion   collision   illusion

Most people on the Titanic were under the _____ that the Titanic was

"unsinkable". A passenger remembers that the night was brilliant and starry. Apparently

there was a clear line of _____ from the crow's nest, but the lookout only

saw the iceberg seconds before the _____ occurred. The

_____ of the voyage was a disaster rather than a celebration.

Challenge: In *Exploring the* Titanic, the ship's radio is called a "wireless set." In Great Britain today, a radio is still called a "wireless." Though Americans and the British share a common language, you may find when reading English literature that some words are used differently in Great Britain. Here are some examples of British words and their American equivalents.

lorry (truck)   **torch** (flashlight)   **boot and bonnet** (car trunk and hood)
lift (elevator)   **chips** (French fries)   **crisps** (potato chips)

DIRECTIONS: Write a sentence using each of the above words in its British meaning.

1. _____

2. _____

3. _____

4. _____

5. _____

6. _____

Unit 5: Mysterious Worlds

from *Exploring the* Titanic by Robert Ballard (text page 398)

Build Grammar Skills: Kinds of Sentences

A **sentence** is a group of words that expresses a complete thought. There are four kinds of sentences: declarative, imperative, interrogative, and exclamatory.

- A **declarative** sentence makes a statement:

  Bride watched the crewmen steer the ship towards New York.

- An **imperative** sentence commands:

  Go back to your cabins.

- An **interrogative** sentence asks a question and ends with a question mark:

  Why were the iceberg warnings ignored?

- An **exclamatory** sentence expresses abruptness or excitement and ends in with exclamation mark:

  Move out quickly! Water is pouring into the forward holds!

A. Practice: Circle the letter of the sentence that correctly answers the question about its type.

1. Which sentence below is interrogative?

   a. When did the temperature start to drop?   b. When he got the message he passed it on.

2. Which sentence below is imperative?

   a. Reverse the engines.   b. Reverse the engines?

3. Which sentence below is declarative?

   a. The crew braced for the collision.   b. Turn the ship's wheel hard.

4. Which sentence below is exclamatory?

   a. There weren't enough lifeboats for everyone.   b. What a tragedy!

B. Writing Application: On the lines provided, rewrite the following sentences, changing each to the type of sentence indicated in parentheses. The first one is done for you.

1. Jack Thayer put on his coat. (imperative)

   Put on your coat, Jack Thayer. _____

2. Harold Bride was only twenty-two years old. (interrogative)

   _____

3. Captain Smith was on duty on the bridge. (exclamatory)

   _____

4. Were the stars shining brightly? (declarative)

   _____

5. Will you send the call for assistance? (imperative)

   _____

from *Exploring the* Titanic by Robert Ballard (text page 398)

Reading Strategy: Fact vs. Opinion

Nonfiction writing, such as *from Exploring the* Titanic, is based on **facts**, information that is true and can be proven. For example, the following sentence expresses a fact:

The *Titanic* sank.

In addition to facts, nonfiction writers express **opinions**, or statements about what someone thinks or believes. Opinions cannot be proven, but can be supported, or backed up, by reasons and arguments. For example, the sentence below expresses an opinion:

The captain of the *Titanic* acted foolishly.

This statement can't be proven, but it can supported, or backed up, by saying, "He should have paid more attention to the warnings." You might disagree with this opinion by arguing, "But he believed the ship was unsinkable."

A piece of nonfiction writing that includes opinions is more interesting than one that includes facts only. Opinions give the reader more to think about. It's important to know the difference between facts and opinions so that you can think about whether you agree with the writer's opinions rather than simply accept them as proven facts. *Exploring the* Titanic contains both facts and opinions.

A. DIRECTIONS: Identify the following passages from the selection as fact or opinion by writing *F* or *O* on the lines provided.

_____ 1. It was a sunny but cold Sunday morning . . .

_____ 2. It was the kind of night that made one glad to be alive.

_____ 3. At 7:30 P.M. the radio room received three more warnings . . .

_____ 4. . . . such a close call at the beginning of a maiden voyage was a very bad omen.

_____ 5. As it was Sunday, church services had been held in the morning . . .

B. DIRECTIONS: Robert Ballard fills *Exploring the* Titanic with many kinds of interesting facts. Read through the selection, and find at least two facts to fill in at each category in the chart below.

1. Facts about the collision:
2. Facts about the officers and crew:
3. Facts about the passengers:

Unit 5: Mysterious Worlds

Name _____ Date _____

from *Exploring the* **Titanic** by Robert Ballard (text page 398)

Literary Focus: Suspense

Suspense is the sense of nervous expectation you feel when you are waiting to find out what will happen next in a story. When writing is suspenseful, you are excited and drawn into the action, and you want to find out what happens next. Often when reading nonfiction, you know what will happen in the end, but suspense-filled details make you want to find out how and when it will happen. For example, you know that the *Titanic* sank. But when you read that it was in danger of colliding with another ship first, you want to know if the collision actually occurred.

DIRECTIONS: As you read *from Exploring the* Titanic, use the chart below to help you note elements that add suspense to the writing. The left-hand column, **What I Know**, lists details you learn as you read. In the right-hand column, list what each detail makes you **want to know**. The first example has been done for you.

What I Know	What I Want to Know
The pull created by the *Titanic* broke the docking ropes of another ship.	Did the two ships collide?
Bride gives an iceberg warning to the captain.	
The lookouts were ordered to watch for ice.	
The watertight compartments were closed.	
The stokers were hit by a jet of icy water.	

"Orpheus" by Alice Low (text page 409)

Build Vocabulary

The words below are used in "Orpheus." Read the words and their definitions. Knowing the meanings of these words will help you understand and enjoy the selection.

presided: directed, commanded

inspiration: motivation, something that encourages creativity or action

entranced: enchanted, charmed

underworld: in Greek mythology, the place of the dead

mortal: human, fated to die (as opposed to the gods, who were considered *immortal*—who could not die)

quench: satisfy, relieve

A. DIRECTIONS: For each of the following definitions, write the correct word from the list above in the spaces provided. Then, on the line below, copy the letters you wrote in the *circled* spaces, and you will find the name of one of those who were charmed by the music of Orpheus in the Underworld.

1. charmed, enchanted __ __ ⃝ __ ⃝ __ __ __ __

2. satisfy, ease __ __ __ ⃝ __ __

3. motivation __ __ __ __ __ __ __ __ ⃝ __ __

4. human __ __ __ __ ⃝⃝ __

5. place of the dead ⃝ __ __ __ __ __ __ __ __ __

6. commanded, led __ __ __ ⃝ __ __ __ __

One of those who was charmed by Orpheus's music was __ __ __ __ __ __ __ __.

B. DIRECTIONS: Complete each of the following sentences by filling in the blank with one of the words from the list above. Use each word once.

1. She took a long drink of water to _____ her thirst after being out in the hot sun.

2. The life of Jackie Robinson has been an _____ to many young athletes.

3. The vice-president of the United States has always _____ over sessions of the Senate.

4. In Greek mythology, the dead were taken by Charon across the River Styx to reach the _____.

5. Unlike the gods, who would never die, human beings were _____.

6. We were _____ by the beauty of the scenery.

Unit 5: Mysterious Worlds

"**Orpheus**" by Alice Low (text page 409)

Connecting a Myth to Social Studies

In "Orpheus," you read that the nine Muses were the daughters of the god Zeus. Another god mentioned in the selection is Hades, god of the underworld. The most important Greek gods are the twelve who were believed to live on Mount Olympus, a high mountain in Greece. Each of the twelve Olympian gods was believed to be responsible for specific aspects of nature or human activities. They are named and identified in the following list:

Zeus (ZOOS) the king of the gods; controlled weather, especially thunder and lightning

Aphrodite (aff-roh-DIE-tee) the goddess of love

Apollo (ah-POLL-oh) the god of light, medicine, and poetry

Ares (EH-reez) the god of war

Artemis (AHR-tuh-miss) the goddess of hunting and of childbirth

Athena (ah-THEE-nah) the goddess of wisdom and crafts; also the goddess of war

Demeter (Dih-MEE-ter) the goddess of agriculture and the harvest

Hephaestus (heh-FESS-tus) the blacksmith of the gods; also the god of crafts

Hera (HEH-rah) the queen of the gods and the protector of women and marriage

Hermes (HUHR-meez) the messenger for the gods and protector of travelers; also the god of commerce and science

Hestia (HESS-tee-ah) the goddess of the hearth and of fire

Poseidon (poh-SIGH-duhn) the god of the sea, of earthquakes, and of horses

Directions: Use the information above to fill in the blanks in the following sentences.

1. Before going into battle, a Greek general might have prayed to _____ and _____.

2. A Greek woman about to have a baby would have made an offering to _____.

3. The most powerful of the Olympian goddesses was _____.

4. A Greek leaving on a journey would hope that _____ would watch over him or her.

5. If lightning struck a Greek's house, the owner would wonder how he had offended _____.

6. When lighting a fire to cook over, a Greek might offer a prayer to _____.

7. A Greek farmer would have prayed to _____ to bring him a good harvest.

8. While they were at sea, Greek sailors hoped that _____ would not get angry with them.

9. If a Greek got sick, he or she would pray to _____ for good health.

10. A Greek man might have prayed to _____ to help him win the love of a certain woman.

"**Breaker's Bridge**" by Laurence Yep (text page 420)

Build Vocabulary

Using Related Words: Forms of *execute*

The Word Bank word *executioner* is a noun that means "one who carries out a death penalty." It is a form of the word *execute*, which means "put to death.." The word *execute* has other meanings as well. It can be used to mean "carry out," or simply "do."

The death penalty in a state allows it to *execute* convicted criminals. (*execute* = put to death)

We worked hard to *execute* our plan. (*execute* = carry out, do)

Several other English words are based on the word *execute*. Here are some of them:

The convicted man's *execution* will take place at midnight. (*execution* = putting to death)

The *executive* worked hard to make his company successful. (*executive* = person who manages)

Fred was the *executor* of our project. (*executor* = person who performs a job or assignment)

A. DIRECTIONS:

Use one of the words above to complete each of the sentences below.

1. The highest _____ in state government is the governor.

2. The school principal will _____ the order for a school uniform.

3. The _____ felt pity for the condemned man, but carried out the sentence.

4. The prisoner was allowed to choose the means of his _____.

Using the Word Bank

obstacle	writhing	piers	executioner	immortals

B. DIRECTIONS: Use one word from the Word Bank to replace the word or words in parentheses in the following sentences.

1. The town closed the bridge when several of its (supports) _____ cracked.

2. The dead hero is now one of the (beings who live forever) _____.

3. The biggest (barrier) _____ to our baseball team reaching the championship was a rival team.

4. The kite was (twisting and turning) _____ in the strong winds.

5. The identity of the (person who carries out the death sentence) _____ is often kept a secret.

Sentence Completions

C. DIRECTIONS: Circle the letter of the word that best completes each sentence.

1. If a car breaks down on a busy road, it could become a dangerous ____ .
   a. writhing   b. piers   c. immortals   d. obstacle

2. I was ____ with pain as the doctor examined by injured shoulder.
   a. writhing   b. piers   c. immortals   d. obstacle

"Breaker's Bridge" by Laurence Yep (text page 420)

Build Spelling Skills: *i* Before *e* Rule and Exceptions

Spelling Strategy A famous rhyme says, "Put *i* before *e* except after *c*, Or when sounded like *a* as in *neighbor* and *weigh*."

Examples: *i* **before *e*—** piers, piece, believe, field
except after *c*— receive, conceited, deceive
or when sounded like *a*— rein, sleigh, neighbor, weigh

Here are some exceptions to the rhyme:

either   financier   foreign   forfeit   height   heir   leisure
sheik   sovereign   their   weird   neither   protein   seize

A. Practice: Complete the words by adding *i* and *e* in the correct order.

1. It is better to give than to rec____ve.

2. My little brother has a w____rd way of tying his shoelaces.

3. I grabbed the r____ns of the horse and held tight.

4. The arrow p____rced the bull's eye on the target.

5. The American people bel____ve in the principles of democracy.

B. Practice: Proofread the following paragraph carefully, looking for misspelled words containing the *ie* combination. Cross out the misspelled words, and write them correctly above the line.

Engineers have concieve and build impressive suspension bridges. Some, such as the

Golden Gate Bridge in San Francisco and the Verrazano Narrows Bridge in New York City,

span waterways at a great height. The cheif users of these bridges are commuters on thier

way to and from work. Some beleived the wide lanes would help them receive some releif

from rush-hour congestion. However, to their greif, traffic still creeps along, morning and

evening.

Challenge: In the Word Bank word *writhing*, and in other words beginning with *wr*, the *w* is silent. On the lines below, write five sentences using the following *wr* words.

wrong   write   wrath   wreath   wrap

1. _____

2. _____

3. _____

4. _____

5. _____

"**Breaker's Bridge**" by Laurence Yep (text page 420)

Building Grammar Skills: Direct and Indirect Objects

You know that a verb is the action word in a sentence. A **direct object** is a noun or pronoun that *receives* the action of the verb. In other words, the verb tells what happens. The thing or person the action *happens to* is the direct object. It answers the question *what?* or *whom?*

The old man *held* the <u>crutch</u>.

What was held? A crutch. The crutch *receives* the action of the verb *held*.

Indirect objects are nouns or pronouns that name the person or thing *to whom* or *for whom* an action is done. Indirect objects may come before or after the direct object. Now look at these sentences:

The old man gave <u>the emperor</u> advice.   The old man gave advice <u>to the emperor</u>.

In the sentence, *gave* is the verb. *Advice* is the direct object. *To whom* did the old man give the advice? The answer is *the emperor*. *Emperor* is the indirect object of both sentences.

A. Practice: In each of the following sentences, underline the direct object once. Underline the indirect object twice. On the lines following each sentence, write the question each object answers. Choose from the questions *What? To whom?* and *For whom?* The first example has been done for you.

1. The old man gave <u>Breaker</u> the <u>pellets</u>.

Question answered by direct object <u>what?</u>   Question answered by indirect object <u>to whom?</u>

2. Breaker built the emperor a bridge.

Question answered by direct object_____   Question answered by indirect object_____

3. Breaker offered the crutch to the old man.

Question answered by direct object_____   Question answered by indirect object_____

4. The emperor wrote him a letter.

Question answered by direct object_____   Question answered by indirect object_____

B. Writing Application: Combine each of the following sentence pairs into one sentence with both a direct object and an indirect object. The first sentence has been done for you.

1. My sister threw the ball. She threw it to the puppy.
   <u>My sister threw the puppy the ball.</u>

2. My father built a desk. He built it for me.

_____

3. I gave a wonderful present. I gave it to my best friend.

_____

4. The babysitter told a bedtime story. She told it to the children.

_____

"Breaker's Bridge" by Laurence Yep (text page 420)

Reading Strategy: Cause and Effect

It's time for school and you're running late. You'd be on time if you'd remembered to turn on your alarm clock. The alarm clock failing to go off is a cause. The effect was that you were late for school. A **cause** is a reason that something happens. An **effect** is the thing that happens.

Recognizing cause and effect relationships when you read helps you to connect one event to another in a story. For example, in "Breaker's Bridge," the dam on the river breaks. The effect is that the water rushes down and destroys the two piers Breaker has built for his bridge.

DIRECTIONS: Read each passage below. On the lines following each passage, write the cause and the effect. The first one has been modeled for you.

1. "But Breaker was as clever as he was clumsy. When he grew up, he managed to outlive his nickname. He could design a bridge to cross any obstacle. No canyon was too wide. No river was too deep. Somehow the clever man always found a way to bridge them all.
   Eventually the emperor heard about this clever builder and send for him."

Cause: ___Breaker proves himself a clever bridge builder._____

Effect: ___The emperor sends for Breaker._____

2. "The river was too wide to span with a simple bridge. Breaker would have to construct two piers in the middle of the river. The piers would support the bridge like miniature stone islands."

Cause: _____

Effect: _____

3. "The old man looked at the branches that grew from the sides of his new crutch. `A little splintery.'
   Breaker angrily took his cut finger from his mouth. `Don't insult someone who's doing you a favor.'"

Cause: _____

Effect: _____

"Breaker's Bridge" by Laurence Yep (text page 420)

Literary Focus: Character Traits

Character traits are the qualities that make up an individual's personality. Fictional characters demonstrate their character traits through how they act and speak. Read the following passage from "Breaker's Bridge" about Breaker.

> Although it was hard to see, Breaker found a tall-straight sapling and tried to trim the branches from its sides; but being Breaker, he dropped his knife several times and lost it twice among the old leaves on the forest floor. He also cut each of his fingers. By the time he was ready to cut down the sapling, he couldn't see it. Of course, he cuts his fingers even more.

In the passage, Breaker drops his knife and loses it and cuts his fingers twice. Based on this behavior, you could say that clumsiness is one of Breaker's character traits.

A. DIRECTIONS: On the lines below each excerpt, write the actions of the character as described. Then write a word or words describing the character trait that these actions illustrate.

1. But before Breaker could straighten, the old man's left hand shot out and caught hold of Breaker's wrist. The old man's grip was as strong as iron. "Even the least word from me will remind that river of the law."

Breaker tried to pull away, but as strong as he was, he could not break the old man's hold. "Let me go."

But the crooked old man lowered his right hand so that Breaker could see that he had rubbed some of the dirt and sweat from his skin. "We are all bound together," the old man murmured, "and by the same laws."

The Old Man's Actions

1. _____

2. _____

3. _____

Character Trait: _____

2. "There is river in the hills," the emperor said to him. "Everyone tells me it is too swift and deep to span. So I have to go a long way around it to get to my hunting palace. But you're famous for doing the impossible."

The kneeling man bowed his head to the floor. "So far I have been lucky. But there is always a first time when you can't do something."

The emperor frowned. "I didn't think you were lazy like my other bridge builders. You can have all the workers and all the materials you need. Built the bridge and you'll have your weight in gold. Fail and I'll have your head."

The Emperor's Actions and Words

1. _____

2. _____

3. _____

Character Trait: _____

"The Fairies' Lullaby" by William Shakespeare (text page 431)
"Someone" by Walter de la Mare (text page 432)
"Who Has Seen the Wind?" by Christina Rossetti (text page 433)

Build Vocabulary

Using Old-Fashioned Words

When you read "The Fairies' Lullaby" and "Someone," you will come across the old-fashioned words *nigh*, *hence*, and *nought*. *Nigh* means "near," *hence* means "away," and *nought* means "nothing." These and other old-fashioned words are often found in poems that were written long ago and poems that have a special old-fashioned or storytelling style.

A. DIRECTIONS: Show the meanings of the old-fashioned words by matching the sentences in the left column to the sentences in the right column.

_____ 1. The fairies cry "*Hence*, spiders, *hence!*"

_____ 2. They listen for dangers coming *nigh*.

_____ 3. *Nought* is stirring in the dark night.

a. Nothing is moving out there.

b. They are on the alert for whatever comes near.

c. They tell the creatures to go away.

Using the Word Bank

offense	nigh	hence	nought

B. DIRECTIONS: Imagine that you are writing a play that is set in the distant past. The cast of characters includes a king, a queen, a knight, and several mythical creatures. Use each of the Word Bank words to write a sentence that might appear in the dialogue, according to instructions given.

1. Use *offense* in a sentence in which the king states that one of the mythical creatures has done something harmful or wrong.

   _____

2. Use *nought* in a sentence in which the queen disagrees with the king.

   _____

3. Use *nigh* in a sentence in which the knight provides says something about the creature.

   _____

4. Use *hence* in a sentence in which the knight continues to speak about the creature.

   _____

"The Fairies' Lullaby" by William Shakespeare (text page 431)
"Someone" by Walter de la Mare (text page 432)
"Who Has Seen the Wind?" by Christina Rossetti (text page 433)

Build Spelling Skills: Spelling the *awt* Sound With *ought*

Spelling Strategy The *awt* sound is sometimes spelled *ought*, as in the Word Bank word *nought*. For example, the *awt* sound is also spelled in this way in the words *thought* and *bought*. Notice that both these words are the past tense form of irregular verbs. *Thought* is the past tense of *think*. Of what verb is *bought* the past tense form?

A. Practice: Write a word in which the *awt* sound is spelled *ought*, according to the each clue given below. Write your answers on the lines.

1. This word is the past tense form of *bring*. _____

2. This word is the past tense form of *fight*. _____

3. This word is the past tense form of *seek*. _____

4. This word may be used instead of *should*, and is usually followed by the word *to*.

   _____

B. Practice: Complete each sentence by correctly spelling the word that contains the awt sound.

1. As you (awt) _____ to know, this play was written by William Shakespeare.

2. Millions of copies of his plays have been (bawt) _____ in stores and (brawt) _____ home from schools and libraries to be read and enjoyed.

3. Shakespeare is generally (thawt) _____ to be the greatest playwright in English literature; many people think that he is the greatest poet as well.

Challenge: In "The Fairies' Lullaby," the fairies command the small creatures of the woods to "do no offense," or harmful act, to their queen. In the word *offense* and several other words, such as *defense* and *suspense*, the *ens* sound is spelled *ense*. In many words, such as *difference* and *conference*, however, the *ens* sound is spelled *ence*.

Correctly spell each of these words that contain the *ens* sound. Use a dictionary to look up any words you are not sure of and to check your work.

1. int + (ens) _____

2. differ + (ens) _____

3. confid + (ens) _____

4. mm + (ens) _____

5. persist + (ens) _____

6. ess + (ens) _____

7. audi +(ens) _____

8. infer + (ens) _____

"The Fairies' Lullaby" by William Shakespeare (text page 431)
"Someone" by Walter de la Mare (text page 432)
"Who Has Seen the Wind?" by Christina Rossetti (text page 433)

Build Grammar Skills: Direct Objects

A **direct object** is a noun or pronoun that appears with an action verb and receives the action of the verb. It answers the question *what?* or *whom?*

Examples:

The fairies sing a <u>lullaby</u>. (answers the question *Sing what?*)

They lull the <u>queen</u> to sleep with their song. (answers the question *Lull whom?*)

They protect <u>her</u> as she sleeps in the forest. (answers the question *Protect whom?*)

A. Practice: Look at the underlined action verb in each sentence. Then draw an arrow to the direct object. The first one is done for you.

1. In the morning, the fairies gently <u>awaken</u> the queen.

2. They <u>greet</u> her with another song.

3. In the forest, spiders <u>spin</u> delicate, lacy webs.

4. The queen's protectors <u>warn</u> the hedgehogs not to approach.

5. The creatures of the forest <u>obey</u> the fairies.

6. They do not <u>offend</u> their queen.

7. Did Shakespeare <u>write</u> any other lullabies?

8. You can <u>find</u> all of his plays at the library.

B. Directions: Write a sentence about each topic suggested below. After you have written your sentences, underline the action verbs you used that have direct objects. Draw an arrow to noun or pronoun that receives the action of the verb.

1. Write a sentence to answer the question "What do you read in your spare time?"

_____

2. Write a sentence that explains when and where you met one of your friends.

_____

3. Write a sentence in which you use the noun *riddle* as a direct object.

_____

4. Write a sentence that names three things you do when you get ready for school each morning.

_____

"The Fairies' Lullaby" by William Shakespeare (text page 431)
"Someone" by Walter de la Mare (text page 432)
"Who Has Seen the Wind?" by Christina Rossetti (text page 433)

Reading Strategy: Paraphrase

One way in which you can make sure you know what's going on in a poem is to **paraphrase** —restate the lines of the poem into your own words. Suppose, for example, that you wanted to paraphrase the following lines from "The Fairies' Lullaby." What ideas and meanings would you find in them? How might you express these in your own words?

Philomel, with melody
Sing in our sweet lullaby;
Lulla, lulla, lullaby, lulla, lulla, lullaby.
Never harm, nor spell, nor charm,
Come our lovely lady nigh.
So, good night, with lullaby.

Here is one way to paraphrase the lines:

Nightingale, please join our lullaby with your own beautiful song; Lullaby…lullaby.
May our song keep all dangers and harmful magic spells from coming near our queen. We sing her good night with our lullaby.

Notice that when you paraphrase lines like these you can replace difficult and old-fashioned words such as *nigh* and *philomel* with more everyday words. You can also change the order of words and ideas to make them simpler and clearer.

DIRECTIONS: Use the chart below to paraphrase difficult lines from "The Fairies' Lullaby," "Someone," or "Who Has Seen the Wind?" One set of notes, based on the first two lines of "The Fairies' Lullaby," has been modeled for you.

Lines From the Poem	Paraphrase
The Fairies' Lullaby" You spotted snakes with double tongue, Thorny hedgehogs, be not seen.	Go away, you spotted snakes with your forked tongues and you prickly hedgehogs.
"Someone"	
"Who Has Seen the Wind?"	

"The Fairies' Lullaby" by William Shakespeare (text page 431)
"Someone" by Walter de la Mare (text page 432)
"Who Has Seen the Wind?" by Christina Rossetti (text page 433)

Literary Focus: Repetition

Poets often use **repetition** to make their poems more memorable and effective. The repeating of certain words, phrases, and lines creates a musical quality and helps to emphasize ideas within the poem. Notice Christina Rossetti's use of repetition in "Who Has Seen the Wind?" Think about the effects that the repetition creates.

Who has seen the wind?
   Neither I nor you:
But when the leaves hang trembling,
   The wind is passing through.

Who has seen the wind?
   Neither you nor I:
But when the trees bow down their heads,
   The wind is passing by.

By repeating the question and answer within the poem, the poet emphasizes their importance while creating a pleasant, musical effect. Also, by slipping slight variations in wording into these repeated structures, she creates a lively and playful effect that is appropriate to her subject.

A. DIRECTIONS: Read the following passages from "The Fairies' Lullaby" and "Someone." One the lines provided, briefly describe the repetition that you see. Then write a sentence or two describing the effect of the repetition.

1. Philomel, with melody
Sing in our sweet lullaby
   Lulla, lulla, lullaby, lulla, lulla, lullaby.

_____

_____

2. Someone came knocking
   At my wee, small door;
Someone came knocking,
   I'm sure—sure—sure;

_____

_____

B. DIRECTIONS: Read the full text of either "Who Has Seen the Wind?" or "The Fairies' Lullaby." One the lines below, briefly describe how the structure of the poem is like the structure of many songs.

_____

_____

_____

"The Loch Ness Monster" by George Laycock (text page 438)
"Why the Tortoise's Shell Is Not Smooth" by Chinua Achebe (text page 442)

Build Vocabulary

Using Forms of *orate*

The words *orate* and *oration* are related to the Word Bank word *orator*. Look at the meaning of each word. Which one is a verb? Which one is an adjective? Which two are nouns?

orate: to deliver a speech
orator: speaker
oratorical: having to do with formal speaking
oration: formal speech

A. DIRECTIONS: Use one of the forms of *orate* to complete each sentence. Write your answers on the lines provided.

1. Pericles, a leader in ancient Greece, was a famous _____.

2. He was known to _____ on many subjects; sometimes he spoke in tribute of people he knew, and sometimes he tried to persuade others to agree with his views on government.

3. His most famous _____ honored a fellow Greek at the time of his funeral.

4. Everyone who heard Pericles speak was impressed by his _____ gifts.

Using the Word Bank

elusive	abundant	famine	orator	eloquent

B. DIRECTIONS: Match each word in the left column with its definition in the right column.

____ 1. abundant   a. always escaping

____ 2. eloquent   b. shortage of food

____ 3. elusive   c. speaker

____ 4. orator   d. able to speak effectively

____ 5. famine   e. plentiful

Sentence Completions

C. DIRECTIONS: Circle the letter of the word that best completes each sentence.

1. I think that Felicia should join debating team because she is such a(n) ____ speaker.
    a. abundant   b. elusive   c. orator   d. eloquent

2. The villagers held a feast to celebrate the unusually ____ harvest that they enjoyed.
    a. eloquent   b. abundant   c. famine   d. elusive

3. The rains ended the drought that had caused years of ____.
    a. oratory   b. famine   d. eloquence   d. abundance

"The Loch Ness Monster" by George Laycock (text page 438)
"Why the Tortoise's Shell Is Not Smooth" by Chinua Achebe (text page 442)

Build Spelling Skills: Words Ending in *ent* and *ant*

Spelling Strategy The letters *ent* and *ant* usually have the same sound at the end of words—*eloquent* and *abundant*, for example. There is no easy way to know when to use *ent* or *ant*; therefore, it is important to try to learn the correct spelling of these words when you come across them. If you're not sure whether a word is spelled with *ent* or *ant*, look in a dictionary.

A. Practice: Use the clues in the sentences below to help you correctly complete the spelling of the following words. Write the complete word on the lines provided. You can use a dictionary to check your work..

intellig __ __ __   independ __ __ __   descend __ __ __

assist __ __ __   oppon __ __ __   excell __ __ __

1. This word means "free from the control of others" and is spelled with three e's in a row.
   _____

2. This word means "outstandingly good" and is also spelled with three e's in a row.
   _____

3. This word is similar in meaning to the word *aunt*, because both have to do with family relationships; its ending is spelled with an *a*, as in *aunt*. _____

4. This word means "smart" and is spelled with two *i*'s and two *e*'s. _____

5. This word means "one who opposes" and, like *opposes*, is spelled with an e in its ending.
   _____

6. This word means "helper"; like *abundant*, it has an *a* at its beginning and in its ending.
   _____

B. Practice: Revise the following sentences to correct the errors in the spelling of words that have the *nt* sound. Write any misspelled words correctly on the lines. If there are no misspelled words in a sentence, write *no error*. Use a dictionary to check any spellings that you are not sure of.

1. The tortoise in "Why the Tortoise's Shell Is Not Smooth" is an eloquant speaker.
   _____

2. One day, he thinks of a brilliant plan. _____

3. He convinces the birds to invite him to their feast by insisting he is a changed man.
   _____

4. He also tricks the birds into helping him make an efficiant pair of wings.
   _____

5. The clever and confidant tortoise manages to eat most of the food. _____

6. It becomes apparant to the birds that the tortoise had not changed after all.
   _____

"The Loch Ness Monster" by George Laycock (text page 438)
"Why the Tortoise's Shell Is Not Smooth" by Chinua Achebe (text page 442)

Build Grammar Skills: Subject Complements

A **linking verb** is a word such as *be*, *feel*, *appear*, or *seem* that tells what the subject of a sentence is or is like. A **subject complement** is a word that comes after a linking verb and identifies or describes the subject. In the following sentences, the subject complement is underlined.

Loch Ness is a <u>lake</u> in Scotland. (*identifies* the subject, Loch Ness)

Loch Ness is very <u>deep</u>. (*describes* Loch Ness)

There are two kinds of subject complements: predicate nouns and predicate adjectives. A **predicate noun** follows a linking verb and identifies or renames the subject. A **predicate adjective** follows a linking verb and describes the subject.

A. Practice: Look at the underlined subject complement in each sentence. Draw an arrow to the word or phrase that it renames or describes. Then write whether the subject complement is a *predicate noun* or a *predicate adjective*. The first one is modeled for you.

1. George Laycock is a professional <u>writer</u>. _____ predicate noun _____

2. He is also an avid <u>photographer</u>. _____

3. He became <u>curious</u> about the Loch Ness monster. _____

4. The creature is <u>famous</u> throughout Scotland and throughout the world. _____

5. Nessie is the <u>nickname</u> that most people use when referring to it. _____

6. Nessie appears <u>huge</u> in several famous photos. _____

7. According to one theory, Nessie is a giant <u>reptile</u> that surfaces to breathe. _____

8. The tales of the Loch Ness Monster are <u>fascinating</u>. _____

9. In fact, Nessie has become the most valuable <u>animal</u> in all of Scotland. _____

10. No one has proved its existence, and so Nessie remains a <u>mystery</u>. _____

B. Writing Application: Complete the following sentences with phrases of your choice. After you have completed each sentence, underline the subject complement that you used. Then, after the sentence, write *PN* if it is a predicate noun, or *PA* if it is a predicate adjective.

_____ 1. To me, the Loch Ness monster is _____.

_____ 2. The scientists who study Nessie are _____.

_____ 3. To those who have seen the Loch Ness monster, Nessie looks
_____.

_____ 4. The waters of Loch Ness must feel _____.

_____ 5. It seems _____ that the Loch Ness monster really
exists.

"The Loch Ness Monster" by George Laycock (text page 438)
"Why the Tortoise's Shell Is Not Smooth" by Chinua Achebe (text page 442)

Reading Strategy: Author's Purpose

Every author writes for a reason, or **purpose**, which may to be inform, teach, persuade, entertain, or even to make readers laugh or cry. The details that the author includes, the direct statements he or she makes, and his or her attitude can help you recognize this purpose.

Consider the following detail from "The Loch Ness Monster," which George Laycock includes just after describing several sightings of Nessie by people who were traveling in and near Loch Ness. What do you think the detail reveals about Laycock's purpose for writing the article?

But the lecturer who was to tell us about the Loch Ness monster that night in Oxford, Ohio, had brought scientific methods to the search for Nessie, and people were eager to hear his message. All the seats were filled and students stood around the walls and sat in the aisles to listen to the story Robert H. Rines had to tell.

This important detail introduces the scientific side of the search for the Loch Ness monster. It reveals that Laycock's purpose is to inform readers—specifically to inform them about how science has approached the question of whether Nessie really exists.

DIRECTIONS: Use the chart below help you recognize the author's purpose as you read "The Loch Ness Monster" or "Why the Tortoise's Shell Is Not Smooth." In first column, jot down details that helped to reveal the purpose. In the second column, describe the purpose. One set of notes, based on another detail from the beginning of "The Loch Ness Monster," has been modeled for you.

Details	Purpose
"The Loch Ness Monster" Laycock describes how the team of scientists used sonar equipment to learn about the lake, and he explains what sonar equipment is	to <u>inform</u> readers about the scientists' work and to explain their methods
"Why the Tortoise's Shell Is Not Smooth"	

© Prentice-Hall, Inc.

"The Loch Ness Monster" by George Laycock (text page 438)
"Why the Tortoise's Shell Is Not Smooth" by Chinua Achebe (text page 442)

Literary Focus: Oral Tradition

The Nigerian tale "Why the Tortoise's Shell Is Not Smooth" is part of the oral tradition. Stories, songs, and poems that belong to this tradition are passed from generation to generation by word of mouth and may be hundreds or even thousands of years old. Today, writers such as Chinua Achebe collect and write down these traditional works so that today's readers and future generations will continue to know and enjoy them.

DIRECTIONS: Answer the following questions about how the oral tradition is reflected in "Why the Tortoise's Shell Is Not Smooth" and "The Loch Ness Monster." Write your responses on the lines provided.

1. Explain in your own words what is happening in the opening passage from "Why the Tortoise's Shell Is Not Smooth," which is reprinted below. In what way does the action illustrate what happens in the oral tradition?

> Low voices, broken now and again by singing, reached Okonkwo from his wives' huts as each woman and her children told folk stories. Ekwefi and her daughter, Ezinma, sat on a mat on the floor. It was Ekwefi's turn to tell a story.
> "Once upon a time," she began, "all the birds were invited to a feast in the sky...

_____
_____
_____
_____
_____
_____
_____

2. Chinua Achebe has written, "Our ancestors created their myths and legends and told their stories for a purpose. . . . Any good story, any good novel, should have a message." In a sentence or two, summarize what you think the message of "Why the Tortoise's Shell Is Not Smooth" is.

_____
_____
_____

3. Which of the following do you think is part of the oral tradition—George Laycock's article about the Loch Ness monster or the stories of sailors and other people in Scotland that described sightings of the creature? Explain your answer.

_____
_____
_____

"**Dragon, Dragon**" by John Gardner (text page 461)

Build Vocabulary

Using Forms of *tyrant*

The Word Bank word *tyrant* means "a cruel, unjust ruler." Look at the meanings of the following words related to *tyrant*. What idea or ideas do all of them have in common?

tyranny: a cruel, unjust reign or rule   **tyrannize:** to rule unjustly and cruelly
tyrannical: having the qualities of one who rules unjustly and cruelly
tyrannically: in the manner of one who rules unjustly and cruelly

A. DIRECTIONS: Use one of the forms of *tyrant* to complete each sentence.

1. The king in "Dragon, Dragon" declared that he was not a _____.

2. He did not believe in behaving _____; therefore, he did not feel he could force his knights to slay the dragon.

3. The king did believe that if the dragon were to gain complete control of the kingdom, he would surely _____ everyone who lived in it.

4. Fortunately, the young man who won half of the kingdom was wise and fair; he was not at all _____.

Using the Word Bank

plagued	ravaged	tyrant	reflecting	craned

B. DIRECTIONS: Choose the word from the Word Bank that answers each question below. Write your answers on the lines.

1. Which word names the way someone might have moved his or her neck? _____

2. Which word could describe an unfair and unpopular ruler? _____

3. Which word might you use if you were talking about someone who is thinking seriously about his or her future? _____

4. Which word might you use if you were looking for another way to say that a kingdom was "tormented by a dragon"? _____

5. Which word could name the way that a powerful hurricane affected an area? _____

Analogies

C. DIRECTIONS: Circle the letter of the pair of words that expresses a relationship most similar to that expressed by the pair in CAPITAL LETTERS.

1. CRANED : NECK
   a. snapped : fingers   b. washed : soap   c. removed : gone   d. whistled : ears

2. RAVAGED : DESTROYED
   a. built : rebuilt   b. led : followed   c. poured : dripped   d. helped : assisted

Name _____ Date _____

"Dragon, Dragon" by John Gardner (text page 461)

Build Spelling Skills: Spelling the Long *i* Sound with a y

Spelling Strategy The long *i* sound is sometimes spelled with a *y*, as it is in the word *tyrant*. Pronounce each of the following words to yourself. Notice that in each one the long *i* sound is spelled with a *y*.

dynamic   why   bicycle   typhoon   rhyme   deny   style   type

A. Practice: Use the clues to fill out the puzzle below. *Hint:* You can find all of the words in the above list.

Across

4. energetic, forceful
5. for what reason?
6. fashion

Down

1. The words *bad, sad, glad,* and *dad* do this
2. a vehicle with two wheels and pedals
3. another word for *hurricane*
7. kind

B. Practice: Revise the following sentences to correct the errors in the spelling of words that have the long *i* sound. Cross out each misspelled word and write it correctly above the line. Write C next to the sentence if it contains no errors.

_____ 1. The king in "Dragon, Dragon" does not wish to be thought of as a tierant.

_____ 2. Forcing his knights to slay the dragon is not his stile, so he looks for someone else.

_____ 3. The cobbler's three dinamic sons step forward to apply for the job.

_____ 4. Only one of them, however, was the tipe of person the king wanted.

_____ 5. You can't deny that this story took place in bygone days.

"**Dragon, Dragon**" by John Gardner (text page 461)

Build Grammar Skills: Clauses

A **clause** is a group of words that contains a subject and verb. An **independent clause** can stand on its own as a complete sentence. A **subordinate clause** cannot stand on its own; it needs an independent clause to complete its meaning. Subordinate clauses begin with **subordinating conjunctions**. Here are some common subordinating conjunctions: *who, whose, where, which, that, after, as, because, if, unless, whenever,* and *when.*

In the following example, the subject of each clause is underlined once and the verb twice; the subordinating conjunction is in italics.

┌──── subordinate clause ────┐┌──── independent clause ────┐
When <u>everything</u> <u>was</u> ready, the <u>son</u> <u>went</u> for a last talk with his father.

A. Practice: Circle the independent clause in each sentence. Then underline the subordinate clause.

1. The dragon caused trouble wherever it went.

2. The king's wizard was unable to help because he had misplaced his book of spells.

3. The king called everyone in the kingdom together so that he could ask for help.

4. There lived in the village a cobbler who had three sons.

5. Although he thought of himself as an unimportant person, the cobbler came to the king's meeting.

6. The king began to speak when all the people were assembled.

7. The frustrated ruler had put up with the dragon as long as he could.

8. Surely there must be a hero in the kingdom who could slay the terrible monster.

9. In order to encourage a volunteer to step forward, the king offered a huge reward.

10. If anyone could get rid of the dragon, he would win half of the kingdom and the princess's hand in marriage.

B. Writing Application: Build your own sentences by adding a subordinate or independent clause to each clause given below. After you have completed each sentence, circle the independent clause and underline the subordinate clause.

1. The king stared at the queen _____.

2. _____ the cobbler's eldest son volunteered to go out and slay the dragon.

3. The cobbler's middle son decided that it was his turn to try

_____.

4. Although he was nervous and timid, _____.

5. The youngest son was glad that he had listened to his father

_____.

Reading for Success: Strategies for Reading Fiction

Fiction, which includes short stories and novels, is filled with made-up characters and events. Reading a work of fiction is like exploring a new world. As you read, your imagination creates a map of this world. The following strategies will help you find your way in a work of fiction.

- **Identify** with the characters or the situation. Put yourself in the characters' place or imagine yourself in their situation.

- **Predict.** As the events in the story unfold, ask yourself what will happen next. Be on the lookout for clues that are hints of events to come.

- **Make inferences.** Writers seldom tell you everything directly. Often, you need to draw conclusions based on the details the author provides.

- **Envision** the action and setting. Use details that the author provides to help you picture in your own mind the places, people, and events in a piece of writing. Try to experience sounds, tastes, smells, and physical sensations as well.

DIRECTIONS: Read the following passage from "The Wish" by Roald Dahl, and use the reading strategies to increase your comprehension. In the margin, note where you identify with the characters or the situation, predict, make inferences, and envision the action and setting. Finally, write your response to the selection on the lines provided.

from "The Wish" by Roald Dahl

You see, he told himself, I know how it is. The red parts of the carpet are red-hot lumps of coal. What I must do is this: I must walk all the way along it to the front door without touching them. If I touch the red I will be burnt. As a matter of fact, I will be burnt up completely. And the black parts of the carpet . . . yes, the black parts are snakes, poisonous snakes, adders mostly, and cobras, thick like tree trunks round the middle, and if I touch one of *them*, I'll be bitten and I'll die before tea time. And if I get across safely, without being burnt and without being bitten, I will be given a puppy for my birthday tomorrow.

He got to his feet and climbed higher up the stairs to obtain a better view of this vast tapestry of color and death. Was it possible? Was there enough yellow? Yellow was the only color he was allowed to walk on. Could it be done? This was not a journey to be undertaken lightly; the risks were too great for that. The child's face—a fringe of white-gold hair, two large blue eyes, a small pointed chin—peered down anxiously over the banisters. The yellow was a bit thin in places and there were one or two widish gaps, but it did seem to go all the way along to the other end. For someone who had only yesterday triumphantly traveled the whole length of the brick path from the stables to the summer-house without touching the cracks, this carpet thing should not be too difficult. Except for the snakes. The mere thought of snakes sent a fine electricity of fear running like pins down the backs of his legs and under the soles of his feet.

He came slowly down the stairs and advanced to the edge of the carpet. He extended one small sandaled foot and placed it cautiously upon a patch of yellow. Then he brought the other foot up, and there was just enough room for him to stand with the two feet together. There! He had started! His bright oval face was curiously intent, a shade whiter perhaps than before, and he was holding his arms out sideways to assist his balance. He took another step, lifting his foot high over a patch of black, aiming carefully with his toe for a narrow channel of yellow on the other side. When he had completed the second step he paused to rest, standing very stiff and still. The narrow channel of yellow ran forward unbroken for at least five yards and he advanced gingerly along it, bit by bit, as though walking a tightrope. Where it finally curled off sideways, he had to take another long stride, this time over a vicious looking mixture of black and red. Halfway across he began to wobble. He waved his arms around wildly, windmill fashion, to keep his balance, and he got across safely and rested again on the other side. He was quite breathless now, and so tense he stood high on his toes all the time, arms out sideways, fists clenched. He was on a big safe island of yellow. There was lots of room on it—he couldn't possibly fall off—and he stood there resting, hesitating, waiting, wishing he could stay forever on this big safe yellow island. But the fear of not getting the puppy compelled him to go on.

Step by step, he edged further ahead, and between each one he paused to decide exactly where next he should put his foot. Once, he had a choice of ways, either to the left or right, and he chose the left because although it seemed more difficult, there was not so much black in that direction. The black was what made him nervous. He glanced quickly over his shoulder to see how far he had come. Nearly halfway. There could be no turning back now. He was in the middle and he couldn't turn back and he couldn't jump off sideways either because it was too far, and when he looked at all the red and all the black that lay ahead of him, he felt that old sudden sickening surge of panic in his chest—like last Easter time, that afternoon when he got lost all alone in the darkest part of Piper's Wood.

He took another step, placing his foot carefully upon the only little piece of yellow within reach, and this time the point of the foot came within a centimeter of some black. It wasn't touching the black, he could see it wasn't touching, he could see the small line of yellow separating the toe of his sandal from the black; but the snake stirred as though sensing the nearness, and raised its head and gazed at the foot with bright beady eyes, watching to see if it was going to touch.

"I'm not touching you! You mustn't bite me! You know I'm not touching you!"

Another snake slid up noiselessly beside the first, raised its head, two heads now, two pairs of eyes staring at the foot, gazing at a little naked place just below the sandal strap where the skin showed through. The child went high up on his toes and stayed there, frozen stiff with terror. It was minutes before he dared to move again.

_____

_____

_____

_____

_____

_____

_____

_____

_____

_____

_____

_____

_____

_____

_____

_____

Name _____ Date _____

"Dragon, Dragon" by John Gardner (text page 461)

Literary Focus: Plot

When you read a story like "Dragon, Dragon," you follow a series of events in which a problem is introduced and characters try to solve it. This sequence of events is known as the story's **plot**. As the characters attempt to solve their problem, the events lead to a climax, or turning point; this is the moment of highest tension in the story. The events are then wrapped up in a part of the story known as the resolution or conclusion.

DIRECTIONS: Use the organizer below to identify the problem, significant events, the turning point and the conclusion as you read "Dragon, Dragon." Note that two of the events have been filled in for you as examples.

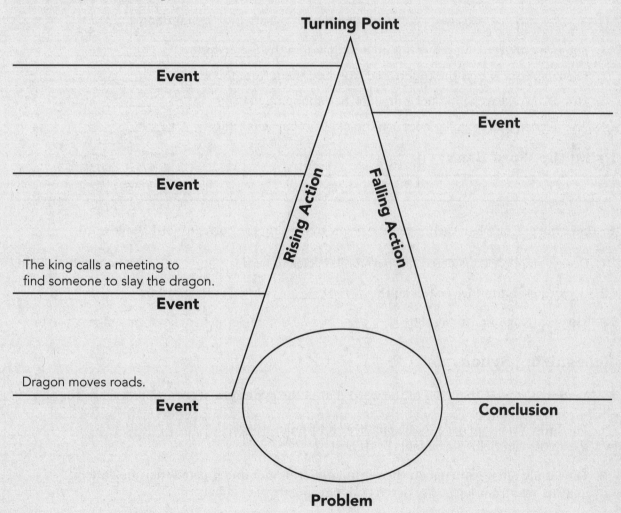

Turning Point

_____ Event

Event _____

_____ Event

Rising Action   Falling Action

The king calls a meeting to
find someone to slay the dragon.
_____ Event

Dragon moves roads.
_____ Event

Conclusion _____

Problem

"Becky and the Wheels-and-Brake Boys" by James Berry (text page 473)

Build Vocabulary

Using Regional Synonyms

Speakers of the same language may use different words to name or describe something. Depending upon the area where you live, you might call the same tasty breakfast food a *pancake*, a *flapjack*, or a *griddle cake*; you might call the same big sandwich a *hero*, a *hoagie*, a *grinder*, or a *sub*. These words are called **regional synonyms** because the word you use depends on the region, or area, where you live. The Word Bank word *veranda* and the word *porch* are examples of regional synonyms.

A. DIRECTIONS: Replace each underlined word with one of the following regional synonyms:

> seesaw   frying pan   sofa   handbag

1. The two children enjoyed going up and down on the <u>teeter-totter</u>. _____

2. Their parents sat on the <u>couch</u> and watched them from the window. _____

3. Mrs. Brown searched in her <u>purse</u> for her shopping list. _____

4. She needed a new <u>skillet</u> because the old iron one was rusty. _____

Using the Word Bank

veranda	menace	reckless

B. DIRECTIONS: Complete each sentence below by writing the correct Word Bank word.

1. Becky's mother considered the boys on bicycles to be a _____ to the neighborhood.

2. Becky's grandmother rested on the _____ while Becky played.

3. They watched a particularly _____ boy do dangerous tricks on his bike.

Recognizing Synonyms

C. DIRECTIONS: Circle the letter of the word that is the **synonym** of the underlined word.

1. The bully was a <u>menace</u> to the smaller children in the class.
   a. threat   b. help   c. teacher   d. pest

2. The family often gathered on the <u>veranda</u> after dinner and greeted their neighbors.
   a. attic   b. front lawn   c. porch   d. pavement

3. The parents in the neighborhood did not like the <u>reckless</u> way some of the children rode their bicycles and scooters.
   a. careful   b. sloppy   c. ridiculous   d. careless

"Becky and the Wheels-and-Brake Boys" by James Berry (text page 473)

Build Spelling Skills: *ace* and the *is* Sound

Spelling Strategy The letters *ace* are sometimes used to spell the *is* sound when it comes at the end of a word. The Word Bank word *menace*, for example, spells the *is* sound with the letters *ace*. The words *surface* and *necklace* are other examples. Some words, however, spell the *is* sound at the end of a word with the letters *iss*, as in *miss*; some use the letters *is*, as in *Paris*.

Remembering that the *is* sound is sometimes spelled with *ace* may help you to avoid some spelling mistakes. If you are not sure how to spell the *is* sound at the end of a word, look up the word in a dictionary until you find the correct spelling.

A. Practice: Fill in the following words on the chart below. Sort the words into columns according to the way they spell the *is* sound:

menace   palace   kiss   tennis   dismiss   terrace   grimace   synopsis   Swiss

ace	iss	is

B. Practice: Proofread the following paragraph about Becky. Correct any misspelled words.

Becky did not want an expensive neckliss or a new dress to wear. She did not care to live in a mansion or a palis. She only wanted a bicycle of her own. Becky did not plan to be a menace to the neighborhood. She would never ride on the sidewalk, but only on the paved surfiss of the road. She knew she would always be careful.

Challenge: Unscramble each of the following words in Column A. Write the word on the line next to the correct definition in Column B. Clue: Every word on the list can be found in the story "Becky and the Wheels-and-Brake Boys."

Column A	**Column B**
namece	careless of danger _____
ndavera	opposite of "outdoors" _____
sebuol	another word for firefighter _____
leksrcses	a girl's shirt _____
doinros	threat or danger _____
nmaefri	porch of a house _____

"Becky and the Wheels-and-Brake Boys" by James Berry (text page 473)

Build Grammar Skills: Independent Clauses

An **independent clause** must have both a subject and a verb, and make sense by itself as a complete sentence. In the following sentences from "Becky and the Wheels-and Brake Boys," the independent clause is underlined.

> I only want a bike because I want it, and I want it, and I want it.
> When she can borrow a bike, Shirnette comes too.

The groups of words that are not underlined in the sentences above are called **dependent clauses**. Even though a dependent clause has a subject and a verb, it doesn't make sense when you read it by itself. It needs to be joined with an independent clause. "When she can borrow a bike," doesn't stand alone as a sentence, but "Shirnette comes too" does. Notice that the independent clause does not always come first and is not necessarily the longest clause in a sentence.

A. Practice: Underline the independent clause in each of the following sentences. Then write its subject and the verb on the lines provided.

1. Becky wanted a bicycle badly, no matter what her mother and grandmother said.
   Subject_____   Verb_____

2. The Wheels-and-Brake Boys had so much fun when they rode together.
   Subject_____   Verb_____

3. After she watched the boys ride, Becky asked her mother for a bicycle.
   Subject_____   Verb_____

4. Although she felt sorry for Becky, her mother said no at first.
   Subject_____   Verb_____

5. Because Granny-Liz could not understand Becky's wish, she considered it foolish.
   Subject_____   Verb_____

6. Becky knew she had to get a bike somehow, as soon as possible.
   Subject_____   Verb_____

7. When she asked them to teach her to ride, the boys ignored Becky.
   Subject_____   Verb_____

8. Things certainly changed for Becky after she got her own bicycle.
   Subject_____   Verb_____

B. Writing Application: The following sentences are about "Becky and the Wheels-and-Brake Boys." Complete each sentence with an independent clause.

1. _____ whenever Becky came to watch them.

2. If Becky could only have a bike of her own, _____.

3. When Becky asked her mother for a bike, _____.

4. _____ when she tried to do her homework.

5. When Becky and Shirnette asked the boys to teach them to ride,

   _____.

Name _____ Date _____

"Becky and the Wheels-and-Brake Boys" by James Berry (text page 473)

Reading Strategy: Predict

As you read a story, you probably find yourself predicting what characters will do or what events will occur next. The predictions you make are logical guesses based on information and details in the story, or on your own experience. For example, at the beginning of "Becky and the Wheels-and-Brake Boys," you might wonder if Becky will get the bike she wants. Based on clues in the story, such as the words of Becky's mother, "Becky, d'you think you're a boy?" you might predict that she won't get the bike. But based on your own experience with asking for things you want very much, you might predict that Becky will get her bike in the end.

DIRECTIONS: As you read "Becky and the Wheels-and-Brake Boys," use the chart below to help you to predict the events in the story. Fill in the chart with details the author includes, predictions you can logically make based upon these details, and your reasons for making these predictions. The first row in the chart has been filled in as an example.

Detail	Prediction	Reason for Prediction
Becky wants a bike very much.	Becky will find some way to get her bike.	Becky is a strong-minded and persistent character.

"Becky and the Wheels-and-Brake Boys" by James Berry (text page 473)

Literary Focus: Conflict

In most short stories there is a **conflict**, a struggle between two forces, that will be resolved in the end. In "Becky and the Wheels-and-Brake Boys," the two opposing forces are Becky's fierce desire for a bicycle and her mother's belief that the family's small income should not be wasted on what she considers a boy's possession. This conflict determines the **action**, or series of events in the story. Some events contribute to the conflict; others occur as a result of the conflict. For example, in "Becky and the Wheels-and-Brake Boys," Becky's grandmother's opinion about girls riding bikes contributes to the conflict. Becky and her mother make friends with Mr. Dean as a result of the conflict.

DIRECTIONS: Look through "Becky and the Wheels-and-Brake Boys." Note the forces that are either for or against Becky's side of the conflict. List the forces you note on the organizer below. An example of each has been filled in for you.

Forces for Becky's Side of Conflict	Forces Against Becky's Side of Conflict
Becky's determined personality	Mother's and grandmother's feeling that bikes are only for boys

"Overdoing It" by Anton Chekhov (text page 483)
"Eleven" by Sandra Cisneros (text page 488)

Build Vocabulary

Using the Prefix *fore-*

A **prefix** is a word part added to the beginning of a word. A prefix has a meaning of its own and changes the meaning of a base word when added to it. The prefix *fore-* adds the meaning, "coming before" or "happening at an earlier time." For example, *foretell* means to tell about an event or action that will happen *before* it actually happens. Here are more examples.

see: "to understand, recognize, or know"
foresee: "to understand, recognize, or know beforehand"
　We *foresee* a difficult time if the tornado hits our city.
shadow: "a faint image," "a hint"
foreshadow: "give a hint of an idea beforehand".
　The sunrise and the rainbow in the story *foreshadow* its happy ending.

A. DIRECTIONS: Complete each sentence below by writing one of the appropriate words from the following list.

　　forewarned　　　　　　forecast　　　　　　foreshadow　　　　　　foretell

1. Knowing the weather _____ helps us know what clothing to wear.

2. No one can _____ the future, although many people wish they could.

3. I was _____ about the icy sidewalk, so I walked carefully.

4. At the beginning of the movie, the stranger's words _____ the strange events that take place later on.

Using the Word Bank

prolonged	emaciated	obstructed	wry	emerged	meditated	foresee

B. DIRECTIONS: Use a word from the Word Bank to replace the italicized word or words in each sentence below.

1. The horse looked so *thin and sickly* _____ that I couldn't believe it would be able to pull the wagon.

2. She sat at her desk and *thought seriously and carefully* _____ for hours about how she could help her friend.

3. We *know beforehand* _____ that we are going to have a great school year.

4. After the talks were *extended for days* _____, the two nations reached an agreement.

5. The man's body was so large that he *blocked* _____ our view of the road ahead.

6. The lady made a *twisted and distorted* _____ face by wrinkling her brow and turning down her mouth in disgust.

7. The animal *came out of and into view* _____ slowly from the forest.

　　　　　　　　　　　　　　　　　　　Selection Support **187**

Name _____ Date _____

Build Spelling Skills: Homophones with *r* and *wr*

Spelling Strategy The **sound *r*** at the beginning of words can be spelled *r* as in *right* or *wr* as in *write*. The words *right* and *write* are **homophones**—words have the same sound, but different spellings and meanings. The meaning of a sentence lets you know which homophone is the correct one to use.

Here are some examples of other homophones with the sound *r*.

rap to tap; a kind of music	**wrap** to enclose in a covering
ring bell sound; jewelry for the finger	**wring** to twist
rest to relax	**wrest** to take forcefully
write to form letters	**right** correct, opposite of left
rye a type of grain	**wry** bent, twisted

A. Practice: In each sentence below, replace the italicized word or words with one of the homophones in parentheses. Write the correct homophone on the line next to each sentence.

1. Please *place a covering around* this birthday gift. (rap/wrap) _____

2. I hear *a quick, sharp tap* on the door. (rap/wrap) _____

3. We heard the telephone *make a sound like a bell.* (ring/wring) _____

4. You need to *twist* the clothes before hanging them out to dry. (ring/wring)
   _____

5. He wants *to form letters or words on a surface, as with a pen or pencil* a story about his experience. (right/write) _____

6. This is not the *correct* answer. (right/write) _____

7. The baker wants to use *a special kind of grain* to make a tasty party bread. (rye/wry)
   _____

8. The actor's face showed a *twisted and distorted* smile to show disapproval. (rye/wry)
   _____

9. The police officer tried *forcefully to take away* the money from the thief. (rest/wrest) _____

10. After such a long trip, we need to *relax* for a while. (rest/wrest) _____

B. Practice: Complete the following short passage with the correct homophones from the list above. Remember to use sentence meaning to help you know which homophone to write.

To _____ a story as good as those of Anton Chekhov is not easy. You have to find just the _____ blend of narration and dialogue, and you need to create believable characters. Chekhov doesn't _____ his characters in any kind of wordy descriptions; he portrays them directly through their words and actions. In "Overdoing It," for example, the _____ face that Klim makes after listening to the land surveyor lets readers know he is not happy with his passenger, while the passenger's words show that he is afraid that Klim wants to _____ his possessions from him. I think that the way Chekhov had both characters react to being scared was brilliant.

"**Overdoing It**" by Anton Chekhov (text page 483)
"**Eleven**" by Sandra Cisneros (text page 488)

Build Grammar Skills: Subordinate Clauses

A **subordinate clause**, or dependent clause, is a group of words that has its own subject and verb but cannot stand as a complete sentence by itself. It is dependent on the rest of the sentence to complete its meaning. A subordinate clause usually begins with a **subordinating conjunction**. Here are some of the most common subordinating conjunctions: *who, whose, which, while, that, before, after, during, if, because, wherever, when, whenever,* and *until.*

In the following examples, the subordinate clauses are underlined, and the subordinating conjunction is in italics. Notice that when a subordinate clause appears first in a sentence, the clause is usually followed by a comma.

> The land surveyor could not tell what was ahead *because* his field of vision was completely obstructed.

> Rachel cried *until* there weren't any more tears left in her eyes.

> *When* Rachel's papa comes home from work, they will eat the cake.

A. Practice: Underline the subordinate clause in each sentence.

1. Because there was no one in sight, the surveyor felt nervous.

2. After he heard the surveyor's words, Klim ran away.

3. The surveyor was surprised that Klim ran off.

4. The surveyor couldn't find his way unless he got Klim to come out of the forest.

5. It sometimes takes months to say eleven when they ask you.

6. You don't feel smart until you're almost twelve.

7. Rachel has to wear the sweater if Mrs. Price insists.

8. When Rachel tried to speak, nothing came out of her mouth.

B. Writing Application: Join the independent clause with the subordinate clause to form a sentence. Write each complete sentence on the line, and be sure to use the correct punctuation.

1. he bragged about his guns   because he wanted to hide his fear

   _____

2. Klim emerged from the forest   after a period of time

   _____

3. everyone knows   that the red sweater is ugly

   _____

4. the worst part of the day was lunchtime   when Phyllis Lopez claimed the sweater

   _____

"Overdoing It" by Anton Chekhov (text page 483)
"Eleven" by Sandra Cisneros (text page 488)

Reading Strategy: Identify With Characters

Often, you can **identify with a character** by putting yourself in the character's place and sharing the character's thoughts and feelings. You think to yourself, "I know just how that character feels because I've felt that way, too."

Think about the land surveyor, Gleb Smirnov, in "Overdoing It." He was alone with a stranger in an isolated place, and he was afraid. But to hide his fear, he pretended he had guns and bragged how brave he was. Have you ever tried to hide the fact that you were afraid of something? When you put yourself in his place, you can sympathize with him.

Now think about Rachel in "Eleven." Her birthday was supposed to be a happy day, but it turned out to be a very painful one instead. Have you ever felt so embarrassed that you feel like crying? When you put yourself in Rachel's place, you can sympathize with her and understand how she wished that she was far away from her eleventh birthday and that unhappy experience.

DIRECTIONS: Match each experience with the name of the character from one of the stories with which that person could identify. On each line, write K for Klim, G for Gleb Smirnov, or R for Rachel.

_____ being treated unfairly

_____ trying to scare someone you're really scared of yourself

_____ being embarrassed in front of your friends

_____ looking forward to something and being disappointed

_____ finding out you've been fooled by someone

"Overdoing It" by Anton Chekhov (text page 483)

"Eleven" by Sandra Cisneros (text page 488)

Literary Focus: Characterization

The ways in which an author reveals what a character is like is called **characterization**. An author might use **direct characterization** by making direct statements about a character's personality and appearance. For example, an author might say, "The man was frightened." More often, however, an author uses **indirect characterization** by revealing a character's traits through the character's own words and actions, through what other characters say and think about her or him, and through the other characters' reactions to what she or he does and says. For example, in "Overdoing It," Anton Chekov uses Smirnov's own words and actions to let you know Smirnov is lying to hide his fear. In "Eleven," Sandra Cisneros indirectly characterizes Mrs. Price as an unsympathetic character by her words, "You put that sweater on right now and no more nonsense."

DIRECTIONS: In each part of the pyramid below, jot down words, thoughts, actions, and direct statements to either tell about Gleb Smirnov or Rachel.

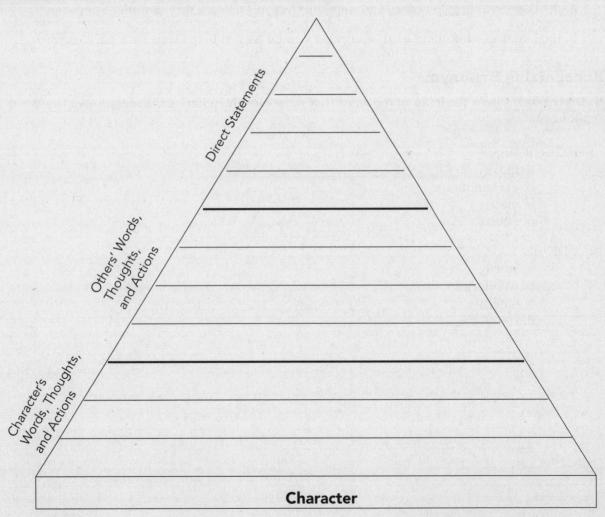

"Dentistry" by Mark Twain (text page 495)

Build Vocabulary

Using the Word Bank

odious	exertions

A. DIRECTIONS: Answer each of the following questions to demonstrate your understanding of the Word Bank words. Circle the letter of your choice.

1. Which of the following describes something that Tom Sawyer would find *odious*?

   a. the taste of a bitter medicine that a doctor gave him to treat a stomachache

   b. the smell of a freshly baked pie

2. Which of the following could be described as *exertions*?

   a. the day-dreaming, relaxing, and napping that you do on a lazy summer afternoon

   b. the bending, stretching, and lifting that you do as you help clean up a park or yard

Recognizing Synonyms

B. DIRECTIONS: Circle the letter of the word that most closely matches the meaning of the Word Bank word.

1. EXERTIONS:
   - a. ideas
   - b. exclamations
   - c. motions
   - d. efforts

2. ODIOUS:
   - a. smelly
   - b. wonderful
   - c. hateful
   - d. round

"Dentistry" by Mark Twain (text page 495)

Connecting Fiction to Social Studies

In this selection, Tom will go to almost any lengths to avoid going to school. Understanding more about United States education in the 1870's might explain why going to school seemed more unpleasant to Tom than it does to most students in modern times. There are three characteristics of public education at that time that might help explain Tom's dislike of school: less variety in courses of study, more emphasis on discipline, and more emphasis on memorization. It was not until the early 1900's that courses in elementary school were broadened to include subjects such as geography, history, and science; before that, children concentrated mainly on the "3 R's": reading, (w)riting, and (a)rithmetic. Children were expected to sit still most of the day, be quiet, and do little except listen to the teacher. Furthermore, children were expected to memorize everything they learned, often without having the opportunity to ask questions and understand what they were being taught.

A. DIRECTIONS: Using the information above, give a possible explanation for why Tom did not want to go to school.

_____

_____

_____

B. DIRECTIONS: On the lines below, or on a separate sheet of paper, write an essay or an outline for an essay in which you compare and contrast schools in the 1870's and modern schools of today. Base your essay or outline on the information above. You may do further research, if you wish, to find out more about education in the United States before 1900.

_____

_____

_____

_____

_____

_____

_____

_____

_____

_____

_____

_____

_____

_____

"**The Lawyer and the Ghost**" by Charles Dickens (text page 504)
"**The Wounded Wolf**" by Jean Craighead George (text page 511)

Build Vocabulary

Using the Prefix *in-*

If you did not know the meaning of the Word Bank word *inconsistent*, you could probably figure it out by looking at its two parts. The prefix *in-* means "no," "not," "without," "the lack of," or "the opposite of." The word *consistent* means "staying the same" or "making sense." Therefore, *inconsistent* means "not always the same" or "not making sense."

A. DIRECTIONS: Complete each sentence by combining the word in parenthesis with the prefix *in-*. Write the new word in the blank.

1. It was very _____ of Jim to watch television while we talked to our guests. (considerate)

2. Laura felt _____ and nervous on the high diving board. (secure)

3. The story was so strange, it was _____ . (credible)

Using the Word Bank

sufficient	expend	inconsistent	massive
stoic	barren	gnashes	

B. DIRECTIONS: Use one word from the Word Bank to complete each of the following sentences.

1. We entered the _____ building through the huge, heavy doors.

2. The dog _____ and grinds his teeth as he chews up a bone.

3. I will _____ every ounce of energy I have to win the race.

4. Margarite was _____ and did not cry when the doctor gave her an injection.

5. The dinner was _____ and satisfied my appetite.

6. Joseph is _____ in his schoolwork, doing well in some subjects but not in others.

7. The explorers marched across the flat, frozen, and _____ landscape.

Recognizing Antonyms

C. DIRECTIONS: Circle the letter of the word that is most nearly *opposite* to the word in CAPITAL LETTERS.

1. INADEQUATE

   a. sufficient

   b. expend

   c. inconsistent

   d. massive

2. FRUITFUL

   a. inconsistent

   b. massive

   c. stoic

   d. barren

"The Lawyer and the Ghost" by Charles Dickens (text page 504)
"The Wounded Wolf" by Jean Craighead George (text page 511)

Build Spelling Skills: The Sound *shent* Spelled *cient*

Spelling Strategy Many words that end in the sound *shent* are spelled *cient*, such as the Word Bank word *sufficient*. Other examples are *efficient*, *proficient*, and *deficient*.

A. Practice: Write the word from the list that best completes each sentence below.

proficient: skilled, accomplished

sufficient: enough

inefficient: wasteful, not productive

deficient: lacking

efficient: productive, orderly

prescient: foresighted, able to make predictions

1. The assembly line is _____ and needs to be redesigned to work better.

2. Viewers believe that the accurate weather forecaster must be _____ .

3. José is _____ in both Spanish and English.

4. To stay healthy, you should get _____ exercise daily.

5. The car has a very _____ engine and goes far on one tank of gas.

6. The man took vitamins because his diet was _____ in many ways.

B. Practice: Complete the following advertisement. Using the context clues, choose four words from the list above to fill in the blanks.

Have you always wanted to be _____ in another language? Have you visited a foreign land and felt _____ because you couldn't communicate with the people? Your worries are over! Our new Learn-a-Language program will have you talking confidently in the language of your choice in just seven days or your money back. In just one short week, you will have _____ vocabulary to speak like a native! Other language programs are _____ and take far too long for results. Learn-A-Language is the most effective language program on the market today. Won't you give it a try?

Challenge: The Word Bank word *gnashes* begins with the two letters *gn*. When this combination begins a word, the *g* is almost always silent. Other similar words are: *gnarled*, *gnat*, *gnaws*, and *gnome*.

On the lines below, write a short paragraph using all five of these words beginning with *gn*. If you are unfamiliar with the meaning of a word, look it up in a dictionary.

_____

_____

_____

_____

"The Lawyer and the Ghost" by Charles Dickens (text page 504)
"The Wounded Wolf" by Jean Craighead George (text page 511)

Build Grammar Skills: Simple Sentences

A **simple sentence** is a sentence containing just one independent clause, and no dependent clauses. Some simple sentences have a **compound** subject, or more than one subject. Some simple sentences have a **compound verb**, or more than one verb. In the following three examples, the subjects are underlined once and the verbs twice.

Weakness overcomes him. (one subject, one verb)

The ravens and the fox move in on Roko. (compound subjects: *ravens* and *fox*)

The raven flies and circles back. (compound verbs: *flies* and *circles*)

The following sentences are not simple sentences because they contain more than one clause. In each, one clause is in italics and the other is underlined.

Roko stops and his breath comes hard.

It penetrates the rocky cracks where the Toklat ravens nest.

A. Practice: Write SS for each simple sentence. Underline all compound subjects once. Underline all compound verbs twice. Put an X next to each sentence that is not a simple sentence. The first sentence has been done for you.

1. They plunge and turn. ___SS___

2. The ravens and the owl stare at Roko. _____

3. Young Roko glances down the valley. _____

4. He gnashes, gorges, and shatters bits upon the snow. _____

5. The ravens fly overhead, and the white fox waits in the snow. _____

6. Roko growls. _____

B. Writing Application: Rewrite each pair of sentences as one simple sentence. Follow the directions in parentheses. The first pair of sentences has been rewritten for you.

1. The ghost appeared. The ghost spoke to the lawyer. (Simple sentence with one subject and a compound verb) The ghost appeared and spoke to the lawyer.

2. The ghost had a conversation. The lawyer had a conversation. (Simple sentence with a compound subject and one verb) _____

3. The ghost left. He left the lawyer alone. (Simple sentence with one subject and one verb)

_____

4. The ravens alight upon the snow. They follow the wolf. (Simple sentence with one subject and a compound verb) _____

5. The wolf answers. He answers the call of the pack. (Simple sentence with one subject and one verb) _____

6. Roko ran down the Ridge. Kiglo ran down the Ridge. (Simple sentence with a compound subject and one verb) _____

"The Lawyer and the Ghost" by Charles Dickens (text page 504)
"The Wounded Wolf" by Jean Craighead George (text page 511)

Reading Strategy: Envision Action and Setting

When you read, you see more than words on a page. The words create images, or pictures that you "see" in your head like a movie. Good writers use clear, colorful words to make you **envision** what is happening. They use words that appeal to your senses of sight, hearing, smell, touch, and taste.

Here is an example from "The Lawyer and the Ghost":

> He had hardly spoken the words, when a sound resembling a faint groan, appeared to issue from the interior of the case.

The passage above appeals to your sense of sound. As you read it, you can almost hear the sound the ghost makes from inside the case.

Look for passages in your reading that make the action and setting real to you by appealing to your senses of sight, sound, touch, taste, and smell.

DIRECTIONS: Read each passage below. The first is from "The Wounded Wolf," and the second is from "The Lawyer and the Ghost." In the first column of the organizer, fill in the details that appeal to your senses. Then write how you envision the action or the setting in the second column.

1. "Young Roko glances down the valley. He droops his head and stiffens his tail to signal to his pack that he is badly hurt. Winds wail. A frigid blast picks up long shawls of snow and drapes them between young Roko and his pack. And so his message is not read."

2. "At that moment, the sound was repeated: and one of the glass doors slowly opening, disclosed a pale and emaciated figure in soiled and worn apparel, standing erect in the press. The figure was tall and thin, and the countenance expressive of care and anxiety; but there was something in the hue of the skin, and gaunt and unearthly appearance of the whole form, which no being of this world was ever seen to wear."

Passage 1—Details	Passage 2—Details
Hearing:	**Sight:**
Sight:	
How I Envisioned the Action:	**How I Envisioned the Action:**
How I Envisioned the Setting:	**How I Envisioned the Setting:**

"The Lawyer and the Ghost" by Charles Dickens (text page 504)
"The Wounded Wolf" by Jean Craighead George (text page 511)

Literary Focus: Setting

Every story has a **setting**—the place and time in which it takes place. The place can be a kind of environment, such as Toklat Ridge in "The Wounded Wolf" or the tattered room where the story "The Lawyer and the Ghost" takes place. The time of the setting can be a historical era, like 19th-century England, or a time of year or season.

Sometimes the author will state the setting directly. Other times you will have to be a literary detective and look for clues that tell you what the place and time are. As you read, look for these clues provided by the author.

Read the following passage from "The Wounded Wolf."

A wounded wolf climbs Toklat Ridge, a massive spine of rock and ice. As he limps, dawn strikes the ridge and lights it up with sparks and stars. Roko, the wounded wolf, blinks in the ice fire, then stops to rest and watch his pack run the thawing Arctic valley.

Details about place include:

1. Toklat Ridge is made of rock and ice
2. It is an Arctic valley

Details about time include:

1. dawn strikes the ridge
2. the thawing Arctic valley

From these details, you can determine that the setting is Toklat Ridge in the frozen Arctic regions. You can also determine that it is dawn and that the valley is starting to thaw, indicating that spring is coming.

A. DIRECTIONS: On the lines below each excerpt, write the details that are clues to the setting of place and time. Then write what the setting is.

1. The hours pass. The wind slams snow on Toklat Ridge. Massive clouds blot out the sun. In their gloom Roko sees the death watch move in closer.

Details about place setting

1. _____

2. _____

Details about time setting

1. _____

2. _____

Conclusion: _____

_____

2. "I knew [a] man—let me see—it's forty years ago now—who took an old, damp, rotten set of chambers, in one of the most ancient Inns, that had been shut up and empty for years and years before. There were lots of old women's stories about the place, and it certainly was very far from being a cheerful one; but he was poor, and the rooms were cheap.

Details about place setting

1. _____

2. _____

Details about time setting

1. _____

2. _____

Conclusion: _____

_____

"The All-American Slurp" by Lensey Namioka (text page 518)
"The Stone" by Lloyd Alexander (text page 526)

Build Vocabulary

Using Related Words: Forms of *migrate*

The Word Bank word *migrate* is a verb that means "to travel." *Migrate* is related to the verbs *emigrate* and *immigrate*. When a person *emigrates*, he or she moves *away from* one place to settle somewhere else. The person *leaving* the place is an *emigrant*. When a person *immigrates*, he or she moves *to* another country in order to live there. That person arriving in the new country is known as an *immigrant*. Notice the way each of these words is used in the sentence below.

migrate: Each year in late autumn, many birds *migrate* to warmer climates.

emigrate: Though the Lins chose to *emigrate* from China, they still missed their old life there.

immigrate: When people *immigrate* to a new country, they must get used to new customs.

emigrant: Saying good-bye to loved ones at home is often a sad experience for an *emigrant*.

immigrant: For the *immigrant* entering a new country, a new language can be a challenge.

A. DIRECTIONS: Use the correct word to complete each sentence. Write your answers on the lines.

1. Some species of birds (migrate, immigrate) _____ for the winter.

2. The Lins (immigrated, emigrated) _____ from China.

3. At the airport, the Lins' relatives kissed the (immigrants, emigrants) _____ good-bye.

4. A U.S. customs inspector checked the passports of each (emigrant, immigrant) _____ .

Using the Word Bank

B. DIRECTIONS: Choose the word from the Word Bank that has the same meaning as the underlined word or words in the following sentences. Write the new sentence on the lines provided.

etiquette	emigrated	plight	consumption
jubilation	fallow	mortified	rue

1. When our great-grandparents left one country to settle in another, they did not forget their old habits and customs. _____

2. Sometimes, they had trouble with acceptable social manners . _____

3. Once or twice, my great-grandmother was extremely embarrassed, because she did not understand a custom of this country. _____

4. The eating and drinking of strange foods can be difficult at first. _____

5. At times, a person may regret an embarrassing action. _____

6. Mastering a new language can lead to a feeling of triumph . _____

7. When a person is in a difficult situation, it's best to ask for help. _____

8. The main character's fields are unproductive as a result of a foolish wish. _____

"The All-American Slurp" by Lensey Namioka (text page 518)
"The Stone" by Lloyd Alexander (text page 526)

Build Spelling Skills: The *k* Sound Spelled *qu*

Spelling Strategy In some words, such as the Word Bank word *etiquette*, the *k* sound is spelled *qu*. Other words that use *qu* to spell the *k* sound are *racquet*, *physique*, and *plaque*. Notice that the *u* in these words is silent. Some other ways the *k* sound can be spelled are *c* as in *cat*, *k* as in *fake*, and *ck* as in *back*.

Since there is no rule to let you know when to use *qu* to spell the *k* sound, look a word up in the dictionary if you are not sure how the *k* sound should be spelled.

A. Practice: Look at the following words. They all have the *k* sound. In the chart, sort the words according to the way the *k* sound is spelled.

| plaque | stack | steak | racquet | castle | antique | slick |
| etiquette | quake | tackle | crumb | physique | blank | |

k sound spelled *qu*	*k* sound spelled *k*	*k* sound spelled *c*	*k* sound spelled *ck*

B. Practice: Revise the following sentences to correct the errors in the spelling of words that have the *k* sound. Write any misspelled words correctly on the lines. If there are no misspelled words in a sentence, write OK.

1. The plack on the wall said the gymnasium had been built one year before. _____

2. The new Chinese gazed around in confusion._____

3. She had a strong, athletic physike and loved sports._____

4. Yet, she did not fully understand the etikette in her new school._____

5. She was good at rackit sports and hoped to make the tennis team. _____

Challenge: The Word Bank word *rue* dates back to Old English, or English as it was spoken before the year A.D. 1150, more than 800 years ago. In Old English, *rue* was spelled *hreow*. Rue, meaning "regret," can be a noun or a verb. Compare these two sentences:

Poor Maibon felt *rue* for his hasty wish. (used as noun)

The miserable man *rued* the moment he set eyes on the magic stone. (used as verb)

Rue is also related to *rueful*, which means *sorry* or *regretful*.

On the lines below, write a sentence for each of the following words: *rue*, *rued*, and *rueful*.

1. _____

2. _____

3. _____

"The All-American Slurp" by Lensey Namioka (text page 518)
"The Stone" by Lloyd Alexander (text page 526)

Build Grammar Skills: Compound Sentences

A compound sentence is two or more **independent clauses** joined by a coordinating conjunction or a semicolon (;). The **coordinating conjunctions** are *and*, *but*, *or*, *nor*, *yet*, and *for*. In the following sentences, each independent clause is underlined. The coordinating conjunctions are italicized. Notice that each independent clause could stand on its own as a complete sentence.

Mother didn't tell me how the rest of the dinner went, *and* I didn't want to know.

Those eggs should have hatched by now, *but* the hen is still brooding on her nest.

Notice that a comma is used before the coordinating conjunction in a compound sentence.

A. Practice: Write a C on the line for each compound sentence. If a sentence is compound, underline each independent clause once. Underline the coordinating conjunction twice. For sentences that are not compound, write NC on the line.

_____ 1. My mother also puts everything on the table and hopes for the best.

_____ 2. I got acquainted with a few other kids, but Meg was still my only real friend.

_____ 3. Mrs. Gleason announced that dinner was served and invited us to the table.

_____ 4. Then I picked up a stalk, and my brother did too.

_____ 5. The dwarf squeezed shut his bright red eyes and began holding his breath.

_____ 6. You'll stay as you are, but I'll turn old and gray.

_____ 7. The weeds aren't growing, but neither is the wheat.

_____ 8. Never again did Maibon meet any of the Fair Folk, and he was just as glad of it.

B. Writing Application: Rewrite each pair of sentences below as a compound sentence. Use the coordinating conjunction in parentheses to join the two independent clauses in each compound sentence that you write. Remember to use a comma before the coordinating conjunction.

1. Maibon could have chosen a practical wish. Instead, he chose a foolish one. (but)

_____

2. Maibon's wife wanted him to get rid of the stone. It caused nothing but trouble. (for)

_____

3. The eggs weren't hatching. The wheat wasn't growing. (and)

_____

4. Maibon had to get rid of the stone. Nothing would grow. (or)

_____

5. Maibon tried to get rid of the stone. It kept coming back. (yet)

_____

"**The All-American Slurp**" by Lensey Namioka (text page 518)
"**The Stone**" by Lloyd Alexander (text page 526)

Reading Strategy: Making Inferences

Authors do not always come right out and state simply and directly what they mean. You often have to figure out the meaning of what you are reading by making **inferences**, or judgments, based on the details and information the author does give you.

Read this passage from "The All-American Slurp." What can you infer from the details the author provides?

> My brother didn't have any problems making friends. He spent all his time with some boys who were teaching him baseball, and in no time he could speak English much faster than I could—not better, but faster.

The author doesn't come right out and explain the personality differences between the narrator and her brother, but from this passage, you can make the inference that the brother is outgoing and athletic, while the sister is probably more shy and reserved. As you continue reading, you gather further details and information that support your understanding of the characters.

DIRECTIONS: As you read each of the stories, complete one of the flow charts below. Each chart should contain two details and one inference that can logically be drawn from these details.

"The All-American Slurp"

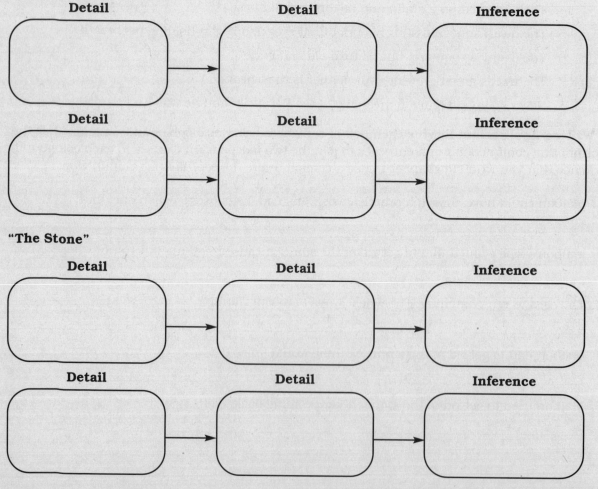

"The Stone"

"The All-American Slurp" by Lensey Namioka (text page 518)

"The Stone" by Lloyd Alexander (text page 526)

Literary Focus: Theme

A **theme** is the message or main insight about life that an author wishes to communicate to readers. In a story, the author usually does not state the theme directly, but implies or suggests it by showing how characters react to the events, people, and places in their lives.

For example, as you read "The All-American Slurp," by Lensey Namioka, you will notice events and details that suggest the story's main theme—the challenges of adjusting to a new country and culture.

DIRECTIONS: Read the following passages from "The All-American Slurp" and "The Stone." Make a list of three events or details that suggest each story's theme. On the last line provided, write a sentence stating the theme.

"The All-American Slurp"

All of us, our family and the Chinese guests, stopped eating to watch the activities of the Gleasons. I wanted to giggle. Then I caught my mother's eye on me. She frowned and shook her head slightly, and I understood the message: the Gleasons were not used to Chinese ways, and they were just coping the best they could. For some reason I thought of celery strings.

Detail: _____

Detail: _____

Detail: _____

Theme: _____

"The Stone"

Maibon gave a joyful cry, for at that same instant the fallow field was covered with green blades of wheat, the branches of the apple tree bent to the ground, so laden they were with fruit. He ran to the cottage, threw his arms around his wife and children, and told them the good news. The hen hatched her chicks, the cow bore her calf. And Maibon laughed with glee when he saw the first tooth in the baby's mouth.

Detail: _____

Detail: _____

Detail: _____

Theme: _____

"The Shutout" by Patricia C. McKissack and Frederick McKissack, Jr. (text page 547)

Build Vocabulary

Using the prefix *ir-*

The prefix *ir-*, like the prefixes *un-* and *in-*, means "not." It is attached only to words beginning with *r*.

Examples: *ir-* + *rational* = *irrational*; *ir-* + *relevant* = *irrelevant*
- Not all words beginning with *r* use *ir-* as a negative-forming prefix. Many use *un-*.

Exceptions: *un-* + *reasonable* = *unreasonable*; *un-* + *related* = *unrelated*
　　　　　　　　un- + *reliable* = *unreliable*; *un-* + *responsive* = *unresponsive*
- Whenever you're not sure of a spelling, look in a dictionary.

A. DIRECTIONS: Make a new word by adding the prefix *ir-* to each word in the chart below. Then write the meaning of the new word. The first row has been filled in for you.

Word	Meaning	New word with *ir-*	Meaning of new word
regular	normal	irregular	not normal
responsible	trustworthy		
replaceable	able to be replaced		
resolvable	able to be resolved		
retrievable	able to be gotten back		

Using the Word Bank

anecdotes	evolved	irrational	diverse	composed

B. DIRECTIONS: Complete each sentence with a word from the Word Bank.

1. A winning baseball team is often _____ of the best players.

2. Many people prefer _____ to long, serious stories.

3. If you were sad after hitting a home run, your reaction would be _____.

4. American baseball _____ over a period of time.

5. I'm tired of pizza and would like to see a more _____ menu.

Recognizing Synonyms

C. DIRECTIONS: Circle the letter of the word that is closest in meaning to the word in CAPITAL LETTERS.

1. IRRATIONAL: a. soggy b. insane c. reasonable d. nervous

2. EVOLVED: a. rotated b. concerned c. judged d. changed

3. DIVERSE: a. different b. alike c. careful d. rhyming

"The Shutout" by Patricia C. McKissack and Frederick McKissack, Jr. (text page 547)

Build Spelling Skills:
Using the prefix *ir-* with words that begin with *r*

Unit 7: Nonfiction

Spelling Strategy The prefix *ir-*, meaning "not," is used only with words that begin with the letter *r*. When you add *ir-* to a word, remember to keep both *r*'s. In the examples below, notice how both *r*'s are kept when the prefix *ir-* is added.

Examples: *ir* + *replaceable* = *irreplaceable* (not able to be replaced)

ir + *revocable* = *irrevocable* (not able to be revoked or taken back)

ir + *responsible* = *irresponsible* (not responsible, not trustworthy)

A. DIRECTIONS: On the line following each sentence, rewrite the italicized word as a negative by adding *ir-* or *un*.

1. The *responsible* player was often late for practice. _____

2. The game was one of the most *exciting* ones I've seen. _____

3. The excellent coach was *replaceable*. _____

4. The fans found the long wait *interesting*. _____

5. The disagreement between them was *reconcilable*. _____

B. DIRECTIONS: Proofread the following paragraph. Cross out each misspelled word that begins with *ir-*. Then write the correctly spelled word above it.

The people who began organizing professional baseball leagues irationally excluded non-

white athletes. However, at the time, the decision to segregate teams was irevokable. For

talented African American players, life without baseball was an ireconcilable notion. They

decided to organize a league of their own.

Challenge: In the essay, the word *shutout* describes the way African American athletes were excluded from professional baseball. In sports, the word is more commonly used to describe a game in which one side doesn't score at all. Baseball is filled with words that are used uniquely in the game. The word *strike* for instance, ordinarily means "to hit." In baseball, however, a strike is a perfectly batter swings at and misses. The word *fly*, usually a verb, becomes a noun in baseball and refers to a ball that is hit high in the air. Similarly, the word *run*, usually used as a verb, is a noun referring to a point scored when a player crosses home plate.

On the lines below, write three sentences using the following words as they are used in baseball: *strike*, *fly*, *run*. Use a different word in each sentence.

_____

_____

_____

"The Shutout" by Patricia C. McKissack and Frederick McKissack, Jr. (text page 547)

Build Grammar Skills: Subject Pronouns

A **subject pronoun** is always used as a *subject* in a sentence or as a *subject complement* following a *linking verb*, often a form of the verb *to be*. The subject pronouns are *I, you, he, she, it, we, you* (plural), and *they*. In the following sentences, subject pronouns are used as subjects and as subject complements.

Subject: <u>She</u> was a great pitcher. (The subject pronoun *she* is the subject.)

Subject complement: It was <u>she</u> who won the game for us. (The subject pronoun *she* is a subject complement. The linking verb is *was*.)

Subject complement: The only pitcher to strike out Jill was <u>she</u>. (The subject pronoun *she* is a subject complement. The linking verb is *was*.)

A. DIRECTIONS: Underline the subject pronoun in each sentence below. On the lines, write *S* if the subject pronoun is used as the subject; write *SC* if it is used as a subject complement. The first sentence has been done as an example.

_S_ 1. <u>It</u> was African American ball players who organized their own league.

____ 2. The most important players were he and his brother.

____ 3. Despite an injury, he played an excellent game.

____ 4. You had a rough first inning.

____ 5. The ones who deserved to win were they.

____ 6. We gained a much better understanding of the game.

B. Writing Application: Follow the directions below to write five sentences about watching or playing a sport.

1. Use the subject pronoun *I* as the subject of the sentence.

_____

2. Use the subject pronoun *they* as a subject complement.

_____

3. Use the subject pronoun *we* as the subject of the sentence.

_____

4. Use the subject pronoun *she* or *he* as a subject complement.

_____

5. Use the subject pronoun *he* or *she* as the subject of the sentence.

_____

Reading for Success: Strategies for Reading Nonfiction

You're bombarded with facts and ideas at all times and from every direction. When you scan a cereal box, read a textbook, or cruise the internet, you make decisions about what, who, and how much to believe. These strategies will help you read the nonfiction you encounter every day.

- **Set a purpose for reading**. Before you begin, set a goal for reading a work of non-fiction. Your goal may be to find facts, to analyze a writer's theory, to understand an opinion, or simply to be entertained. Keep your purpose in mind as you read.
- **Understand the author's purpose.** Authors of nonfiction have a reason, or a pur-pose, for writing. Their details and information support their purpose. They also adopt a tone, or attitude, toward their topic and their reader. Consider the details and tone to determine an author's purpose.
- **Identify the author's main points.** Ask yourself what the author wants you to learn or think as a result of reading his or her nonfiction work. These main points are the most important ideas in the piece.
- **Identify the evidence for the author's main points.** The author should present evidence—facts or arguments—supporting each main point.

DIRECTIONS: Read the following selection from "Misunderstood 'Monsters'" by Doug Perrine, and use the reading strategies to increase your comprehension. In the margin, note your purpose for reading, and where you understand the author's purpose, identify the author's main points, and identify the evidence for the author's main points. Finally, write your response to the selec-tion on the lines provided.

from "Misunderstood 'Monsters'" by Doug Perrine

The following passage describes some facts about sharks.

Sharks rarely offer any threat to human beings. We had to be very careful with the lemon sharks that we worked with because they are prone to bite in self-defense when being han-dled. However, if left alone to mind their own business, they avoided humans whenever they could. Their long sharp teeth may look scary, but are actually perfectly adapted for seizing the small fish and octopus that make up most of their diet.

When I first learned to scuba dive in the early 1970's, I believed, like most people at the time, that if a shark saw you in the water, you were as good as dead. On my second scuba dive in the ocean, I swam around a coral head and came face to face with a small blacktip reef shark. Terrified, I bolted in the opposite direction. Looking over my shoulder to see if the fearsome beast was gaining on me, I saw the shark fleeing in the opposite direction. Obviously the shark felt it had more to fear from people than the other way around. As it turned out, the shark was right.

When people find out that I spend a good portion of my time photographing sharks, the first question they nearly always ask is, "Have you ever been bitten?" I'm embarrassed to admit that the answer is yes. Embarrassed because it was my own fault. Any large animal, domestic or wild, is potentially dangerous. The accident happened on a dive trip after one of the crew told me that there was a shark behind the boat. I was foolish enough to grab my camera and jump into the water without asking more questions or observing the shark's behavior. I only learned after I came back out of the water that my shipmates had been teasing it with a stringer of freshly-speared fish, dropping the fish into the water and then pulling them back out just as the shark charged. By the time I found this out, I had spent the most terrifying few minutes of my life defending myself with my camera as the shark

(continued next page)

circled closer and closer, snapping at my exposed arms. The encounter ended when I slammed the camera into the shark's mouth and sustained a gash that required eight stitches to close as I pulled my hand back out of the open jaws.

The shark that bit me was a Caribbean reef shark, a species considered dangerous because it sometimes attacks spear-fishermen when competing for their catch. However, the shark which is responsible for most shark bites is the nurse shark. This species is usually considered harmless because it feeds on bottom-dwelling shellfish, mostly at night, and spends most of the day sleeping with its head under a ledge or coral head. Many divers can't resist the urge to pull the shark's tail when they see it sticking out of a cave, although the result seems quite predictable. Most injuries from sharks should be called 'shark defenses,' rather than 'shark attacks', because the shark is defending itself against a provocation by a human.

Other 'shark attacks' occur when sharks and other sea creatures begin to scavenge the body of a person who has drowned or died of other causes. In most cases, an autopsy[1] is not conducted. Because of the presence of shark bites on the body, the death is then listed in shark attack files which show that, worldwide, there are around 50–75 unprovoked shark attacks per year, 10–15 of which are fatal. Many other animals, including dogs, pigs, and deer, kill more people than this each year. Statistically, the most deadly creature in the world (apart from humans) is the common honey bee.

Many books and articles about sharks continually refer to 'the shark,' suggesting all sharks behave the same. A class[2] is a very large grouping of animals and sharks and rays comprise the class *Chondrichthyes*. Another example of a class is *Mammalia*[3]. To talk about 'the shark' is equivalent to making a statement about 'the mammal', implying that it is equally true of whales and rats. Apart from the nearly 500 species of skates and rays which are not biologically distinct from sharks, only differently shaped, there are about 375–475 species of sharks. This number is approximate because there are species which have not yet been cataloged, and certainly species which have not yet been discovered. Also, scientists do not agree entirely on which sharks should be classified as separate species, and which may be lumped together as a single species.

Between three and five new species of sharks are discovered each year. Among all these different types of sharks there is tremendous diversity. The whale shark is the largest fish in the ocean, while the pygmy shark grows to no more than 27cm (11 inches). Some sharks live at the surface of the ocean; others in its deepest depths. Some swim constantly; others lie on the bottom. Some sharks feed on plankton that they strain out of the water; others bite off large chunks of fish, turtles, and marine mammals.

_____

_____

_____

_____

_____

_____

_____

_____

_____

_____

[1] autopsy: investigation into the cause of death.
[2] class: group into which similar animals and plants are placed.
[3] Mammalia: class of animals which give birth to live young, including humans.

"The Shutout" by Patricia C. McKissack and Frederick McKissack, Jr. (text page 547)

Literary Focus: History Essay

A **history essay** is a short piece of nonfiction about events that happened in the past. The author of a history essay includes **facts**, such as the date when an event occurred, names of people who were involved, and the place where the event occurred. The author usually includes **evidence** to show that the facts are true. A history essay also includes **explanations**, such as the reason that something happened or how one event was the cause of another. In addition, the author usually includes personal **insights**—the meaning that he or she finds in the event. Following are examples of these kinds of information included in "The Shutout."

Facts:
Date: National Association of Base Ball Players formed 1857–1858
Name: Samuel Hopkins Adams, who stated that his grandfather was playing baseball in the 1820's
Place: New York, where the New York Knickerbocker Club was organized.

Evidence: Report of baseball being played in the 1820's is evidence that it was founded before 1839.

Explanation: Exclusion from major-league teams was the reason that African Americans organized their own teams.

Insight: Irrational, racist thinking was behind the December 1867 vote to exclude African Americans from major-league baseball.

DIRECTIONS: On the lines below, write additional examples of facts (dates, names or places), evidence for facts, explanations, and insights found in "The Shutout."

Facts

1. _____

2. _____

Evidence

3. _____

4. _____

Explanation

5. _____

Insight

6. _____

"Letter to Scottie" by F. Scott Fitzgerald (text page 556)
"Letter to Joan" by C. S. Lewis (text page 558)
"Olympic Diary" by Amanda Borden (text page 559)

Build Vocabulary

Using Forms of *document*

The word *document* is a noun that means "something that is printed or written," often something that can be used to prove a fact or identity—a library card, a birth certificate, or a passport, for example. Here are several other forms of the word *document*, along with their meanings and examples of their use:

- **document** (*verb*) A person can *document* (prove) the fact that he or she graduated from high school by showing a diploma.
- **documented** (*adjective*) When you write a report, make sure your facts are *documented* (backed up with proof).
- **documentation** (*noun*) I proved my identity by showing the proper *documentation* (written evidence).
- **documentary** (*noun*) I saw a *documentary* (film or TV show that shows a visual record of an event or time period) about dog shows.
- **undocumented** (*adjective*) Too many facts in the students' reports were *undocumented* (not backed up with proof or documentation).

A. DIRECTIONS: Complete each of the following sentences by filling in the blank with the correct form of *document* from the list above. *Hint: Document* may be used as a noun or a verb.

1. His birth certificate served as _____ that he was twelve years old.

2. The class watched a _____ about desert animals.

3. A driver's license is a _____ that all drivers should carry with them.

4. Many of the statements the reporter made were _____.

5. She showed her passport to _____ her citizenship.

6. My report card would serve as _____ that I had taken a science class.

Using the Word Bank

implement	documentation	compulsory	intrigued

Sentence Completions

B. DIRECTIONS: Complete each sentence with a word from the Word Bank.

1. Great Britain tried to _____ a harsh tax policy on the colonies.

2. In gymnastics competitions, some exercises are _____.

3. At airports, travelers must produce _____ to prove their identity.

4. We were _____ by the rhythms of the electronic keyboard.

Name _____ Date _____

"Letter to Scottie" by F. Scott Fitzgerald (text page 556)
"Letter to Joan" by C. S. Lewis (text page 558)
"Olympic Diary" by Amanda Borden (text page 559)

Build Spelling Skills: Spelling the *g* Sound as *gue*

Spelling Strategy In some words the hard *g* sound is spelled *gue*.

Examples: intrigue   league   vague   guess   guest

If you are not sure of how to spell the *g* sound in an unfamiliar word, check the spelling in a dictionary.

A. Practice: Rewrite each of the following words, filling in the missing *gue*.

1. lea____   _____league_____   5. pla____   _____

2. monolo____   _____   6. va____   _____

3. fati____   _____   7. ____ess   _____

4. ____st   _____   8. vo____   _____

B. Practice: Complete each of the following sentences. Add the letters that spell the *g* sound to the word parts in parentheses, and write the completed word in the space provided.

1. Amanda Borden worked hard and learned to fight (fati + *g* sound) _____fatigue_____.

2. While training, she was (pla+ *g* sound + ed) _____ with injuries.

3. Borden hints that (intri + *g* sound)_____ kept her off the 1992 U.S. Olympic team.

4. In letters, Fitzgerald and his daughter established a (dialo + *g* sound) _____.

5. C. S. Lewis advises Joan to avoid using (va + *g* sound) _____ words.

Challenge: The middle syllable of the word *implement* is spelled with the vowel *e*, but the syllable is pronounced *uh*. This vowel sound is called a **schwa** and is often represented by a the symbol ∂. For example, the phonetic spelling of *implement* looks like this: im′ pl∂′ ment. Sometimes, as in *implement*, you spell the schwa sound with the letter *e*. At other times, the schwa sound may be spelled with an *a* (**a**pply), an *o* (daff**o**dil), or a *u* (s**u**ppose). You use the schwa sound in pronouncing all the words below. In the space provided, write each word, replacing the symbol ∂ with the correct vowel. If you are not sure how to spell a word, look it up in the dictionary. The first one has been done as an example.

1. poss∂ble   _____possible_____   5. socc∂r   _____

2. ∂mazing   _____   6. t∂mato   _____

3. comparis∂n   _____   7. s∂pply   _____

4. ben∂fit   _____   8. syst∂m   _____

© Prentice-Hall, Inc.   Selection Support **211**

"Letter to Scottie" by F. Scott Fitzgerald (text page 556)
"Letter to Joan" by C. S. Lewis (text page 558)
"Olympic Diary" by Amanda Borden (text page 559)

Build Grammar Skills: Object Pronouns:
Direct and Indirect Objects

An **object pronoun** is used as a *direct object* (receiving the action of the verb) or an *indirect object* (the person, animal, place, or thing to or for whom an action is done). The object pronouns are *me, you, him, her, it, them,* and *us.* For example, the pronoun *me* is the direct object in the sentence, "Will you please help <u>me</u>?" It is an indirect object in this sentence: "Throw <u>me</u> the ball."

Direct objects: I watched <u>her</u> in the 1984 Olympics and thought she was amazing.

                         Am I trying to make my body a useful instrument, or am I neglecting <u>it</u>?

Indirect objects: When the doctor gave <u>me</u> the OK to start again, I pulled my hamstring.

                         Tell your story to <u>them</u>.

A. Practice: Complete each of the following sentences by filling in the blank with the object pronoun form of the pronoun in parentheses. The first one has been done as an example.

1. The teacher gave (I) _____ an extra assignment in science.

2. We told (she) _____ me _____ that she was invited to the party.

3. The museum tour guide gave (they) _____ a lecture about dinosaurs.

4. I wanted to thank (you) _____ for helping clean up my room.

5. The judges awarded (he) _____ first prize at the science fair.

6. A woman made a speech welcoming (we) _____ to the meeting.

7. The puppy jumped up and knocked (I) _____ down.

8. The librarian can teach (you) _____ how to use the computer to find books.

B. Writing Application: Fill in the blanks in the following sentences with the correct object pronouns.

1. In the letter to his daughter, Fitzgerald gives _____ some valuable advice.

2. Fitzgerald does not like it when Scottie calls _____ "Pappy."

3. If you follow C. S. Lewis's suggestions, they can help _____ be a better writer.

4. When gymnasts must deal with problems, it helps make _____ better people.

5. To compete in the Olympics would give _____ the biggest thrill of my life.

6. We had 22,000 fans cheering _____.

7. Borden is grateful to the people who helped _____ become a world-class athlete.

"**Letter to Scottie**" by F. Scott Fitzgerald (text page 556)
"**Letter to Joan**" by C. S. Lewis (text page 558)
"**Olympic Diary**" by Amanda Borden (text page 559)

Reading Strategy: Understand the Author's Purpose

C. S. Lewis devotes most of his "Letter to Joan" to an evaluation of her writing and to suggestions for improving her skills. Lewis's main **purpose** for writing the letter is to give Joan information that will help her become a better writer. Authors have different purposes in mind when they write. In addition to giving information, they may want to entertain readers or persuade readers to think or act in a certain way. Sometimes, an author may have more than one purpose; for example, Lewis tries to persuade Joan, early in the letter, to read a poem by Wordsworth. He also tries to encourage her to become a good writer and do her best.

DIRECTIONS: Two of Amanda Borden's purposes in writing her "Olympic Diary" were to make readers understand the challenges she faced as a gymnast, and to give readers an idea of the emotions she felt. Fill out the graphic organizer below by writing, under the appropriate heading, some details from the selection that serve to accomplish either of these purposes. One detail has been given under each heading as an example. Add three additional details under the one that is given.

"OLYMPIC DIARY"

Challenges	Feelings
Breaking elbow before U.S. Championship.	Unhappy at not making 1992 team.

"**Letter to Scottie**" by F. Scott Fitzgerald (text page 556)
"**Letter to Joan**" by C. S. Lewis (text page 558)
"**Olympic Diary**" by Amanda Borden (text page 559)

Literary Focus: Letters and Journals

Unlike stories, essays, and poems, **letters and journals** are "private" writing, usually meant to be read by no more than one person other than the writer. Several characteristics distinguish the writing in letters and journals from public writing: the expression of personal feelings, the inclusion of details that are meaningful only to the writer and the person addressed, and a more informal tone than would be used in "public" writing.

DIRECTIONS: In the left column of the chart below, write a detail from each piece in this selection that is more typical of a letter or journal than of "public writing." In the right column, explain why you chose these details. One has been done for each piece as an example.

Detail	Reason for Choosing
"Letter to Scottie"	
Author dislikes the name "Pappy."	Only the writer's daughter would know about this.
"Letter to Joan"	
Lewis thanks Joan for photos.	Other readers don't know about the photos.
"Olympic Diary"	
"Wow! Did my life change!"	Use of informal language is appropriate to private writing.

"My Papa, Mark Twain" by Susy Clemens (text page 567)
"The Drive-In Movies" by Gary Soto (text page 570)

Build Vocabulary

Using the Word Root -sequi-

The Word Bank word *consequently*, which comes from the Latin root *sequi*, means "to follow." *Consequently* is an adverb meaning "following as a result."

Example: Jen practiced more often; *consequently*, her guitar playing improved.

In the sentence above, Jen's improved guitar playing *followed as a result* of her increased practice. Other words formed from the word root *-sequi-* also show the order of events. *Sequence*, for example, is a noun that means "a series in which one thing follows another."

A. DIRECTIONS: Complete each sentence with one of the following words.

consequently   sequel   sequence

1. Did Gary Soto write a _____ to his book *Crazy Weekend*?

2. I slept too late this morning; _____ I missed the school bus.

3. I alphabetized my CDs so that they are all in correct _____.

Using the Word Bank

incessantly	consequently	consumed	prelude
crescent	pulsating	vigorously	

B. DIRECTIONS: In the following paragraph, cross out each underlined word or phrase and write an appropriate Word Bank word above the line. Be sure to choose the word that makes the most sense.

When Eleanor babysat for her baby brother Jake, he cried <u>without ceasing</u>. As the <u>introduction</u>, he screamed when he saw his parents going out the door. He yelled even more <u>forcefully</u> when Eleanor tried to amuse him with toys. He hurled his <u>moon-shaped</u> teething ring across the room. <u>Following as a result</u>, Eleanor started to get a headache. After an hour, her head was <u>throbbing</u>. Jake finally fell asleep about five minutes before Eleanor's parents came home. By that time, every bit of her energy had been <u>used up</u>, and she needed a nap herself.

C. DIRECTIONS: Circle the letter of the word that is most opposite in meaning to the word in CAPITAL LETTERS.

1. VIGOROUSLY: a. harshly   b. weakly   c. energetically   d. quickly

2. CONSUMED: a. opened   b. completed   c. replaced   d. used up

3. INCESSANTLY: a. barely   b. often   c. occasionally   d. without stopping

4. PRELUDE: a. intermission   b. middle   c. opening   d. ending

Unit 7: Nonfiction

"My Papa, Mark Twain" by Susy Clemens (text page 567)
"The Drive-In Movies" by Gary Soto (text page 570)

Build Spelling Skills: Words with *cess*

Spelling Strategy Remember that the letter sequence *cess* is spelled with one *c* and two *s*'s. For example:

That squirrel outside my window chatters in<u>cess</u>antly.

Our class always goes to the park during re<u>cess</u>.

There is an ex<u>cess</u> of clothing in this suitcase.

A warm coat is a ne<u>cess</u>ity for a winter in the Northeast.

A. Practice: Read the definition of each word below, then fill in the missing letters.

1. something that is needed and essential: ne____ ____ ____ ____ity

2. the time when children leave their classroom to play outdoors: re____ ____ ____ ____.

3. without stopping: in____ ____ ____ ____antly

4. too much of something: ex____ ____ ____ ____.

B. Practice: Cross out each misspelled word in the following paragraph, and write it correctly above the line.

At a very early age, biographers often begin the writing prosess by making notes about

people. A child who becomes such a writer may be more interested in listening to people's

conversations than in playing kickball during recces. For a sucsessful writer, the ability to

observe is a nesesity. Some writers admit that they watch and listen to others inseccantly.

Perhaps an excces of curiosity is a gift to anyone who wants to write about a person's life.

Challenge: The word *vigorously*, meaning "forcefully" or "powerfully," contains the noun *vigor* and the adjective *vigorous*, which come from the Latin word for "liveliness" or "energy." The words *invigorate* and *invigorated* also come from the same Latin root. Use a dictionary to find the definitions of these two words; then write a sentence using each one.

1. _____

_____

2. _____

_____

"My Papa, Mark Twain" by Susy Clemens (text page 567)
"The Drive-In Movies" by Gary Soto (text page 570)

Build Grammar Skills:
Object Pronouns: Objects of Prepositions

Object pronouns are *me, you, him, her, it, us,* and *them.* When the object of a preposition is a pronoun, use an object pronoun. Look at the following sentences. Each prepositional phrase is underlined, and the object of the preposition is in italics.

Papa knows that I am writing this biography <u>of *him*</u>, and he said this <u>for *it*</u>.

With hands on her aproned hips, Mother came out and looked <u>at *us*</u>.

Notice that the words *of, for,* and *at* are prepositions. Some other prepositions are *with, from, on, about, by* and *in.*

A. Practice: In each sentence, draw a line under the prepositional phrase, and circle the object pronoun.

1. The teacher recommended "My Papa, Mark Twain" to us.

2. She found more information regarding Twain's life for me.

3. We all enjoy Twain's stories as well as this lively biography of him.

4. My sister read the stories first and told me about them.

5. I admire Twain's style and like any story written by him.

6. Reading about drive-in movies was a new experience for me.

7. My parents go to indoor theaters with us.

8. Would a drive-in movie seem strange to you?

9. Young Gary loved his mother and certainly worked hard for her.

10. He also loved the movies and went to them whenever he could.

B. Writing Application: Each sentence below contains one or more prepositional phrases with a common noun or proper noun as the object. Rewrite the sentences, replacing each object of a preposition with an object pronoun.

Example: Gary's brother polished the family car with Gary.

Rewritten sentence: Gary's brother polished the family car with him.

1. I enjoyed reading the selection about Mark Twain.

2. Do you know some other stories by Twain?

3. Gary Soto clearly recalls that day when he worked so hard for his mother.

4. My parents also gave a list of chores to my brother and me.

5. This book has a story by Gary Soto in the book.

"My Papa, Mark Twain" by Susy Clemens (text page 567)
"The Drive-In Movies" by Gary Soto (text page 570)

Reading Strategy: Author's Evidence

When authors tell stories of their own lives or the lives of other people, they often make statements about their subjects' appearance or personalities. For example, Susy Clemens says of Mark Twain that he is "a very striking character." She then goes on to give details about his hair, nose, eyes, mustache, head, and profile. Without the **evidence**, the story of her father's life would not be very believable or interesting. It would just be a string of statements with no interesting details to back them up.

DIRECTIONS: Read the following passage from "My Papa, Mark Twain." Then find the evidence the author uses to support the statement she makes about her father. Record your findings on the chart provided.

Papa is very fond of animals particularly of cats, we had a dear little gray kitten once that he named "Lazy". . . and he would carry him around on his shoulder, it was a mighty pretty sight! the gray cat sound asleep against papa's gray coat and hair. The names that he has give our different cats are really remarkably funny, they are named Stray Kit, Abner, Motley, Fraeulein, Lazy, Buffalo Bill, Soapy Sall, Cleveland, Sour Mash, and Pestilence and Famine.

STATEMENT:	Evidence:
	Evidence:
	Evidence:
STATEMENT:	Evidence:
	Evidence:
	Evidence:

"My Papa, Mark Twain" by Susy Clemens (text page 567)
"The Drive-In Movies" by Gary Soto (text page 570)

Literary Focus: Biography and Autobiography

Biography and **autobiography** are two kinds of literature that tell the story of a person's life. In a biography, readers see the subject and the events and people in the subject's life through the eyes of the author. In an autobiography, the subject is the author, so readers share the author's thoughts and feelings about his or her own life.

In "My Papa, Mark Twain," Twain's daughter Susy Clemens writes from the point of view of a thirteen-year-old who deeply loved and admired her father. We see the famous author, Mark Twain, through her eyes. In "The Drive-In Movies," author Gary Soto recalls a day from his childhood. We learn what he was thinking and feeling that day through his own memories, which other people would not know unless he had told them himself.

DIRECTIONS: Read the following passages from "The Drive-In Movies." After each one, write the letter AO (for *author only*) if the passage provides information that only the author would know about himself; write SE (for *someone else*) if the passage provides information that someone else could have written.

_____ 1. For our family, moviegoing was rare.

_____ 2. So on Saturday we tried to be good.

_____ 3. One Saturday I decided to be extra good.

_____ 4. . . . my brain was dull from making the trowel go up and down . . .

_____ 5. I made a face at them when they asked how come I was working.

_____ 6. I . . . was ready to cry when Mother showed her face at the window.

_____ 7. My arms ached from buffing, which though less boring than weeding, was harder.

_____ 8. After lunch, we returned outside with tasty sandwiches.

_____ 9. I promised myself I would remember that scene with the golf tees and promised myself not to work so hard the coming Saturday.

_____ 10. Twenty minutes into the movie, I fell asleep with one hand in the popcorn.

"**Space Shuttle *Challenger***" by William Harwood (text page 584)
"**Central Park**" by John Updike (text page 588)
"**Noah Webster's Dictionary**" by Charles Kuralt (text page 590)

Build Vocabulary

Using Homophones

Say the following words to yourself: *cite, sight, site.* What do you notice about the way the words sound? Now look at the spellings of the words. What do you notice?

The words *cite, sight,* and *site* are **homophones**—words that sound alike but have different meanings and, usually, different spellings. The Word Bank word *cite* means "to give as an example," the word *sight* means "the ability to see," and *site* means "a place."

A. DIRECTIONS: Choose the correct homophone to complete each sentence. You can use a dictionary to check any spellings that you are not sure of.

1. I just repaired the (brake, break) _____ on my bicycle.

2. Now that it's fixed, I hope it doesn't (brake, break) _____ again for awhile.

3. Washington, D.C., is the (capital, capitol) _____ city of the United States.

4. The (Capital, Capitol) _____ is the building where the U.S. Congress meets.

5. If an object is (stationary, stationery) _____, it is fixed in place.

6. She wrote her thank-you notes on flowered (stationary, stationery) _____.

Using the Word Bank

futile	monitoring	occasionally	moot
peripheral	catastrophic	cite	atrocious

B. DIRECTIONS: Demonstrate your understanding of the Word Bank words by writing T for each true statement and F for each false statement.

_____ 1. If you were *monitoring* birds' habits, you would be ignoring the birds.

_____ 2. It's wise to spend many hours discussing a *moot* point.

_____ 3. Good *peripheral* vision lets you see things at the edge of your field of view.

_____ 4. A scarf in an *atrocious* color would make a good gift.

_____ 5. If you *cite* soccer as a team sport, you are offering it as an example.

_____ 6. Reading about *catastrophic* events in the newspaper cheers people up.

_____ 7. You would be frustrated after making several *futile* attempts to phone your friend.

Name _____ Date _____

"Space Shuttle *Challenger*" by William Harwood (text page 584)
"Central Park" by John Updike (text page 588)
"Noah Webster's Dictionary" by Charles Kuralt (text page 590)

Build Spelling Skills: Consonant Patterns

Spelling Strategy Thinking about patterns can help you remember the spellings of long words that contain both doubled and single consonants. For example, in the Word Bank word *occasionally*, two single consonants come between two doubles. In the word *parallel*, the pattern is two single consonants, a double, then another single.

A. Practice: The following words contain the same pattern of consonants as the word *parallel*: two singles, a double, then another single. Write one of the words in each numbered space in the puzzle, following the clues given.

beginner   colossal   disappear   disappoint   metallic   necessary

Across

3. needed

5. vanish

6. gigantic

Down

1. to let someone down

2. someone who is new at something

4. made of or resembling metal

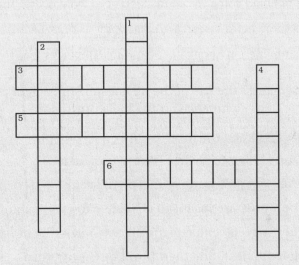

B. Practice: Use one of the words listed above to complete each sentence. Write your answers on the lines.

1. The metal rails in railroad tracks are always _____ to each other.

2. Silver or gold ink can be described as being _____ in appearance.

3. The new football stadium is _____; it can hold 50,000 people.

4. The new laundry detergent will make stains _____.

5. It is _____ to use a password to access your e-mail.

6. Are you a _____ or an intermediate tennis player?

7. I'm sorry to _____ you, but the movie is sold out.

Unit 7: Nonfiction

Name _____ Date _____

"Space Shuttle *Challenger*" by William Harwood (text page 584)
"Central Park" by John Updike (text page 588)
"Noah Webster's Dictionary" by Charles Kuralt (text page 590)

Build Grammar Skills: Apostrophes

An **apostrophe** is used with singular or plural nouns to show a relationship or possession. It also indicates missing letters in a contraction.

Relationship or possession:

The students in <u>Matthew's</u> class are compiling a dictionary.

Do you know anything about this <u>word's</u> origin?

Where should we put the <u>authors'</u> names?

Contraction:

<u>They're</u> defining computer terms. (replaces the *a* in *are*: They are)

<u>Let's</u> do some more research. (replaces the *u* in *us*: Let us)

<u>We'll</u> be meeting in Room 402 next week. (replaces the *wi* in *will*: We will)

A. Practice: Identify the use of the apostrophe in each of the underlined words. Write P for *possession* or C for *contraction* on the lines provided.

____ 1. Ms. <u>Feldman's</u> class is holding a spelling bee.

____ 2. <u>Who's</u> going to go first, Team A or Team B?

____ 3. Team <u>A's</u> first word is phosphorescent.

____ 4. The words are meant to challenge the <u>contestants'</u> skills.

____ 5. <u>They'll</u> keep competing until only one student is left.

____ 6. Moira is next, and then it will be <u>Steve's</u> turn.

____ 7. Field day is coming up soon; in fact, <u>it's</u> scheduled for May 2.

____ 8. Next <u>week's</u> games will give the teams some practice.

B. Writing Application: Write a sentence about each topic suggested below, using words that contain apostrophes as indicated.

1. Use at least one contraction in a sentence about a weekend activity. _____

_____

2. Use a possessive in a sentence that tells about something belonging to a friend of yours.

_____

3. Use a contraction in a sentence that tells about today's weather. _____

_____

4. Use a possessive in a sentence about an animal or a plant. _____

_____

Name _____ Date _____

"**Space Shuttle *Challenger***" by William Harwood (text page 584)
"**Central Park**" by John Updike (text page 588)
"**Noah Webster's Dictionary**" by Charles Kuralt (text page 590)

Reading Strategy: Set a Purpose

When you **set a purpose for reading**, you decide why you are reading. Your purpose for reading "Central Park" and the other media accounts in this group, for example, might be to broaden your experience. While reading each of these works, you can focus on details, impressions, and reactions that help you achieve this purpose.

Directions: Use the chart below to help you achieve the purpose of broadening your experience as you read the selections in this grouping. A few entries are modeled for you.

Title: "Noah Webster's Dictionary"
Detail: spelling bee held in West Hartford
Writer's Reaction: impressed by kids from all over the country
My Impression: sounds interesting and exciting
My Reaction: I'd enjoy participating.
Title:
Detail:
Writer's Reaction:
My Impression:
My Reaction:
Title:
Detail:
Writer's Reaction:
My Impression:
My Reaction:

"**Space Shuttle *Challenger***" by William Harwood (text page 584)
"**Central Park**" by John Updike (text page 588)
"**Noah Webster's Dictionary**" by Charles Kuralt (text page 590)

Literary Focus: Media Accounts

Media accounts are reports, explanations, opinions, or descriptions written for television, radio, newspapers, and magazines. Some media accounts report only facts, while others include the author's thoughts, feelings, and reflections. Through these accounts, which range from reports of major events such as the *Challenger* tragedy to descriptions of the sights and sounds in a city park on the first day of spring, you can experience people, places, and events around the world.

A. DIRECTIONS: Read the following passages from "Space Shuttle *Challenger*." Then, on the lines below, list two facts and two thoughts or feelings that the author conveys in his accounts.

As night gave way to day, the launch team was struggling to keep the countdown on track. Problems had delayed fueling and launch—originally scheduled for 9:38 a.m.—for two hours to make sure no dangerous accumulation of ice had built up on Challenger's huge external tank. Finally, all systems were "go" and the countdown resumed at the T-minus nine-minute mark for a liftoff at 11:38 a.m. Battling my usual pre-launch jitters, I called UPI national desk editor Bill Trott in Washington about three minutes before launch.

And then, in the blink of an eye, the exhaust plume seemed to balloon outward, to somehow thicken. I recall a fleeting peripheral impression of fragments, of debris flying about, sparkling in the morning sunlight. And then, in that pregnant instant before the knowledge that something terrible has happened settled in, a single booster emerged from the cloud, corkscrewing madly through the sky.

I sat stunned. I couldn't understand what I was seeing.

Facts:

_____

_____

Thoughts or feelings:

_____

_____

B. DIRECTIONS Read the following passage from "Noah Webster's Dictionary." Then write a sentence in which you identify a new fact or idea that you found.

In the Italy of Noah Webster's day, there were so many dialects that many Italians couldn't talk to one another. The same thing, to a lesser degree, was true in Great Britain. America's common language, with more or less agreed-upon rules for spelling and punctuation, was the work of Noah Webster. He wanted us to be one nation, a new nation, and he showed us how.

_____

_____

"Restoring the Circle" by Joseph Bruchac (text page 597)
from "In Wildness is the Preservation of the World"
by Henry David Thoreau and Eliot Porter (text page 600)
"Turkeys" by Bailey White (text page 603)
"How the Internet Works" by Kerry Cochrane (text page 606)

Build Vocabulary

Using Forms of *tolerate*

The word *tolerate* means "to put up with" or "endure."

Example: I can usually tolerate (put up with) barking dogs , but not at night.

Forms of *tolerate* include the past-tense verb *tolerated*, the noun *tolerance*, the adjectives *tolerant*, *intolerant*, *tolerable* and *intolerable*, and the adverb *tolerably*.

A. DIRECTIONS: Write the correct word to complete each sentence.

1. The turkey could not (tolerate, tolerant) _____ the ornithologists around her nest.

2. She found them (intolerant, intolerable) _____ and wished they'd go.

3. I hate waiting and have little (tolerate, tolerance) _____ for crowds.

4. Thoreau (tolerate, tolerated) _____ inconveniences to live a simple life.

5. He survived in the wilderness (tolerably, tolerant) _____ well.

Using the Word Bank

tolerance	detrimental	imparted	destination
dilution	demise	vigilance	

B. DIRECTIONS: Fill in each blank with an appropriate word from the Word Bank..

1. I had to use _____ to keep the puppy from getting out of the yard.

2. Eating too much candy can be _____ to your teeth.

3. I wasn't sorry to see the mosquito meet its _____.

4. When you add water to lemonade, you cause _____.

5. When you are patient with a younger child, you show _____.

6. The opposite of the point you start from is your _____.

7. Thoreau felt that nature _____ life's most important lessons.

"Restoring the Circle" by Joseph Bruchac (text page 597)
from "In Wildness is the Preservation of the World"
by Henry David Thoreau and Eliot Porter (text page 600)
"Turkeys" by Bailey White (text page 603)
"How the Internet Works" by Kerry Cochrane (text page 606)

Build Spelling Skills: Changing -ent and -ant
to -ence and -ance

When words that end in -ent and -ant are changed to related words that end in -ence and -ance, they keep the same vowel.

Examples: vigil<u>a</u>nt, vigil<u>a</u>nce   correspond<u>e</u>nt, correspond<u>e</u>nce

A. Practice: In each of the following sentences, change the word in parentheses from a word ending in -ant or -ent to a word ending in -ance or -ence.

1. (correspondent) Mom uses e-mail for her business __correspondence__ .

2. (assistant) They asked their older brother for his _____.

3. (resident) Another word for the place where you live is your _____.

4. (tolerant) Her mother had _____ for noise, but not for rudeness.

5. (insistent) Our teacher's _____ that we do our homework on time keeps us on schedule.

B. Practice: In the following paragraph, change each word ending in -ant or -ent to the related word ending in -ance or -ence to correctly complete the sentences.

Pure wild turkeys have become rare; so it is unusual to find a wild-turkey nest filled with

eggs. In "Turkeys," however, this is just what a group of ornithologists find, in (defiant)

_____ of the odds. Unfortunately, the mother turkey soon abandons the

nest, which has been her (resident) _____. The ornithologists worry about

the eggs, which, having little (resistant) _____ to cold, must be kept at a

warm and even temperature. Due to the kindliness and (tolerant) _____

of the author's mother, the eggs are saved in the end. With the (assistant)

_____ of the author, the eggs hatch overnight safely tucked next to her

feverish body.

"Restoring the Circle" by Joseph Bruchac (text page 597)
from "In Wildness is the Preservation of the World"
by Henry David Thoreau and Eliot Porter (text page 600)
"Turkeys" by Bailey White (text page 603)
"How the Internet Works" by Kerry Cochrane (text page 606)

Build Grammar Skills: Quotation Marks

Quotation marks are used to enclose the exact words of a speaker. In "Turkeys," for example, the author uses quotation marks to record the ornithologists' conversation:

"Feels just right, I'd say."
"A hundred and two—can't miss if we tuck them up close and she lies still."

A comma, question mark, or exclamation point always separates the speaker's words from the words that tell who said them. The punctuation appears inside the closing quotation marks, as in these examples:

"Does your little girl still have measles?" he asked.
"The ornithologists," I whispered.

If the sentence includes introductory words before the opening quotation marks, those introductory words are followed by a comma:

The ornithologist said, "I'll be right over."

A. Practice: Rewrite each of the following sentences, using quotation marks to set off the exact words of the speaker. Remember that punctuation after introductory words belongs before the opening quotation marks; punctuation at the end of a quote belongs inside the closing quotation marks.

1. Wild turkeys are very rare, the ornithologist told my mother.

2. They asked, Would you allow us to put the eggs in your daughter's bed?

3. Will they hatch overnight? my mother asked.

4. The ornithologist answered, Yes, with any luck.

5. Let's give it a try, said my mother.

B. Writing Application: The following sentences could be from an interview with the author of "Turkeys." Rewrite each of sentence, adding any necessary punctuation and placing the quotation marks correctly.

1. The interviewer asked Isn't there a vaccine for measles, now?

_____

2. Yes, but there wasn't a vaccine at that time the author answered.

_____

3. How did you feel when you woke up asked the interviewer.

_____

4. The author answered Well, I was rather surprised, at first!

_____

Name _____ Date _____

"Restoring the Circle" by Joseph Bruchac (text page 597)
from "In Wildness is the Preservation of the World"
by Henry David Thoreau and Eliot Porter (text page 600)
"Turkeys" by Bailey White (text page 603)
"How the Internet Works" by Kerry Cochrane (text page 606)

Reading Strategy: Identify Author's Main Points

The author of an essay usually has a message, or one important idea, he or she wants to get across to readers. To communicate that message, the author makes several main points—ideas that support the central message. To understand the message of an essay, you should **identify the author's main points**. As you read, you will notice certain points that the author explains in great detail, or backs up with examples. These are usually the main points.

In "Restoring the Circle," the author's message is the importance of passing down cultural traditions from one generation to the next in Native American cultures. As you read the selection, look for the author's main point. Also, look for the examples the author provides to back up that main point.

Think of an essay as a tree. The message would be the trunk; the largest limbs growing out of the trunk would be the main points; the smaller branches growing out of those limbs would be the examples and explanations that back up the main points. Fill in the branches as you need.

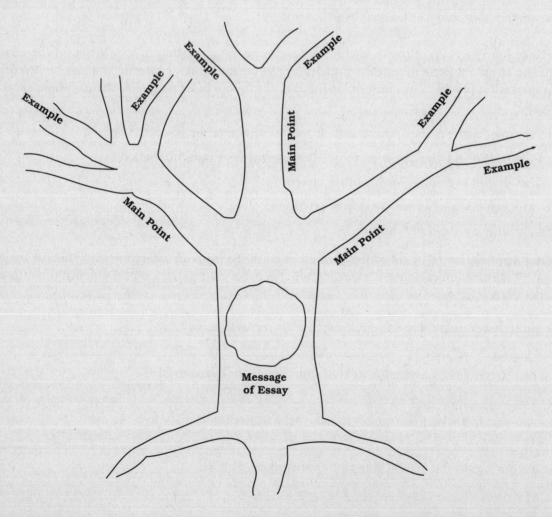

© Prentice-Hall, Inc.

"Restoring the Circle" by Joseph Bruchac (text page 597)
from "In Wildness is the Preservation of the World"
by Henry David Thoreau and Eliot Porter (text page 600)
"Turkeys" by Bailey White (text page 603)
"How the Internet Works" by Kerry Cochrane (text page 606)

Literary Focus: Types of Essays

Unit 7: Nonfiction

An essay is a short nonfiction work written about a particular subject. There are several different types of essays, each written for a different purpose.

Type of Essay	**Purpose**
Persuasive	To persuade, or convince, readers to act or think in a certain way
Visual	To make a point through photographs as well as words
Narrative	To tell a story about a true experience or event
Informational	To explain or inform

"Restoring the Circle" is an example of a **persuasive essay**; the author tries to convince readers to see the importance of cultural traditions. "In Wildness is the Preservation of the World" is a **visual essay**; the photographs back up the authors' points about the beauties and wonders of nature. "Turkeys" is a **narrative essay**; it is based on a memorable event in the author's life. "How the Internet Works" is an **informational essay**; it informs readers about a subject they might not understand.

DIRECTIONS: For each question below, circle the letter of the choice that best identifies the type of essay named.

1. Which of the following details from "Restoring the Circle" lets you know that the essay is persuasive?

   a. Native Americans envision life as a circle.
   b. The author explains damage caused by Native American stereotypes.
   c. More than 400 languages are spoken by Native Americans in North America.

2. Which of these statements indicates that "In Wildness is the Preservation of the World" is a visual essay?

   a. The author has a reverence for nature.
   b. The text is by Thoreau.
   c. The text is accompanied by photographs.

3. Choose the statement that indicates that "Turkeys" is a narrative essay.

   a. The author describes an event from her childhood.
   b. The author uses vivid language.
   c. The author includes dialogue in the essay.

4. Choose the statement that indicates "How the Internet Works" is an informational essay.

   a. The author uses the pronoun "I" in his writing.
   b. The author provides detailed facts and explanations about the Internet.
   c. The author has an Internet address of his own.

"Eulogy for Gandhi" by Jawaharlal Nehru (text page 613)

Build Vocabulary

The words defined below are from "Eulogy for Gandhi." Understanding their meanings will help you better understand the selection.

hamlet tiny village

immemorial ancient, before memory

ultimately finally

perilous dangerous

desolate abandoned, solitary

millennia thousands of years

A. DIRECTIONS: Write the correct vocabulary word from the list above in the appropriate "building" below. Fill in the letters of the words from top to bottom. The first one has been done as an example.

1. dangerous, risky

2. tiny village

3. thousands of years

4. solitary, abandoned

5. finally

6. ancient, before memory

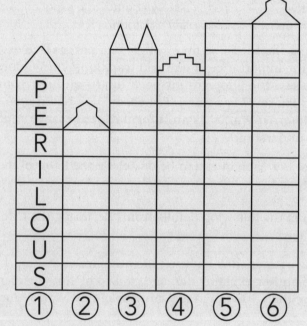

B. DIRECTIONS: Complete each sentence with the correct word from the vocabulary list.

1. Crossing the Atlantic Ocean by ship used to be considered _____, but modern inventions have made it much safer.

2. Since time _____, dogs and human beings have lived in communities together.

3. Los Angeles, California, is now a huge city, but it was once a tiny _____ with a population of only a few hundred.

4. The pyramids of Egypt were built about five _____ ago.

5. The Sahara desert is one of the most _____ places on earth.

6. If students neglect their studies, _____ it will have a bad effect on their grades.

"Eulogy for Gandhi" by Jawaharlal Nehru (text page 613)

Connecting a Eulogy to Social Studies

India began its fight for independence from England in the 1800's. However, two serious difficulties stood in India's way. First, the country was splintered into many independent districts that used hundreds of local languages, making communication difficult. In addition, the Hindus and Muslims, who made up the majority of the population, were bitter enemies. It seemed that these groups could never cooperate, until Gandhi entered Indian politics in 1915. Within five years he was the leader of the Indian independence movement. Gandhi was a Hindu, but preached that people of all religions could and should live together in peace. He also believed in and practiced nonviolent resistance. He and his followers would disobey laws they thought unjust, but would not commit any violent acts. Inspired by his teaching and example, hundreds of millions of people set aside their differences and worked together for the common cause of freedom. The Indian people's reverence for him led them to call him "Mahatma," meaning "great soul."

New violence broke out between Hindus and Muslims in the early 1940's, to Gandhi's sorrow. When England granted India independence in 1946, he was further saddened by Indian Muslims' insistence on a separate nation of their own, Pakistan. Gandhi was assassinated in 1948 by a member of a radical Hindu group who opposed Gandhi's idea of religious tolerance. His death, just as the two independent nations were being born, was a source of grief and shock for Indians and Pakistanis alike. The world joined them in mourning Gandhi's passing.

DIRECTIONS: Answer the following questions by writing details from Jawaharlal Nehru's "Eulogy for Gandhi" on the lines. (More than one detail might be correct.)

1. How does Nehru describe the Indian people's reaction to Gandhi's death?

   _____

   _____

2. How does Nehru describe the extent of Gandhi's influence in India?

   _____

   _____

3. Which passage might refer to the violence between Hindus and Muslims?

   _____

   _____

4. How does Nehru describe his concern for India's future at the time of Gandhi's death?

   _____

   _____

Unit 7: Nonfiction

The Phantom Tollbooth, Act I
based on the book by Norton Juster, by Susan Nanus (text page 630)

Build Vocabulary

Using the Prefix *pre-*

The prefix *pre-* means "before." When it is added to the beginning of a word, it adds the meaning of "before" or "in advance" to the word. In the Word Bank word *precautionary*, for example, cautionary means "with caution"; *precautionary* means "with caution beforehand," or "caution in advance."

Examples:

It's good to take *cautionary* measures in a dangerous situation, but it's even better to take *precautionary* measures beforehand.

You can *cook* a meal at the last minute, or you can *precook* some of the dishes and heat them up later.

We took *prefilled* bottles of milk along for the baby. When they were used up, we *filled* up some more.

Exception: Not all words that begin with the letters pre have the prefix *pre-*. For example, words such as *precious* and *pretty* do not have have meaning, *before*.

A. DIRECTIONS: Keeping in mind the meaning of the prefix *pre-*, write your definition for each underlined word in the sentences below.

1. Let's <u>prearrange</u> our plans for vacation. _____

2. We had a chance to <u>preview</u> the new hit movie. _____

3. Eleven- and twelve-year-olds are sometimes called <u>preteens</u>. _____

4. Don't <u>prejudge</u> a person before you get to know her. _____

5. I like to read about <u>prehistoric</u> times. _____

Using the Word Bank

ignorance	precautionary	misapprehension

B. DIRECTIONS: Complete each sentence with the Word Bank Word that makes the most sense.

1. A little _____ advice is always helpful when beginning a new experience.

2. Some say that experience is the best teacher, but reading can also put an end to

   _____ .

3. If you think you may have a _____ about something a friend said or did, it's best to clear it up right away.

The Phantom Tollbooth, **Act I**
based on the book by Norton Juster, by Susan Nanus (text page 630)

Build Spelling Skills: Spelling Words With *tion* and *sion*

Spelling Strategy The letters *tion* and *sion* can both be used to spell the sound *shun*.

- In the Word Bank word *precau**tion**ary* , the *shun* sound is spelled *tion*. Some other words that spell the *shun* sound *tion* are *predic**tion**s*, *expecta**tion**s*, *atten**tion***, and *ques**tion***.

- In the Word Bank word *misapprehen**sion***, the *shun* sound is spelled *sion*. Other words that spell the *shun* sound *sion* include *comprehen**sion***, *exten**sion***, *expan**sion***, and *suspen**sion***.

A. Practice: Read the following sentences, looking for errors in words spelled with the *shun* sound. Cross out the misspelled words, and write them correctly above the line. Write **C** next to any sentences that contain no errors. Use a dictionary if you are not sure whether to spell the shun sound *tion* or *sion*.

_____ 1. I am a globe has three. I have three dimenshuns.

_____ 2. If you have me, you have a misunderstanding. I am a misapprehention.

_____ 3. You can also make me about the end of a story you're reading. I am a predicshun.

_____ 4. word for me is *care*. I am causion.

_____ 5. If you're not sure of something, you ask me. I am a question.

_____ 6. I am something you should "pay" to your teacher. I am attension.

_____ 7. On a reading test, it's important to have me. I am comprehention.

_____ 8. I'm whatever you want to be when you grow up, I am your ambition.

B. Practice: In the following paragraph, you will find that some words are incomplete. Complete each word by adding the ending *-tion* or *-sion* to spell the *shun* sound. If you are not sure which spelling to use, check the words in the box below.

dimension misapprehension prediction caution question attention

Milo found it difficult to pay _____ to anything for more than a little while.

He had the _____ that there was nothing interesting to do with his time. One

day a talking clock and a mysterious package started him on a journey into another

_____, where he met all sorts of strange beings. Along the way, Milo had to use

_____ to avoid danger. When Milo met the Whether Man, he asked him a

_____ about the land of Expectations. The odd man made no

_____ about the adventures Milo would have in the future but said "Whether or

not you find your own way, you're bound to find some way."

The Phantom Tollbooth, Act I
based on the book by Norton Juster, by Susan Nanus (text page 630)

Build Grammar Skills: Subject and Verb Agreement

In a sentence, the verb and subject must **agree** in number. A **singular** subject refers to one person, place, or thing. A **plural** subject refers to more than one. If the subject of a verb in the present tense is *he, she, it,* or a singular noun or proper noun such a "the boy," or "Milo," the verb usually end in *s.* If the subject of a verb in the present tense is *they* or a plural noun or proper noun such as "people" or "the Smiths," or "Milo and Tock," the verb does not end in *s.*

Singular Subject	Singular Verb	
He	goe**s**	on a journey.
The boy	goe**s**	on a journey
Milo	goe**s**	on a journey

Plural Subject	Verb	
They	go	together.
The characters	go	together.
Milo and Tock	go	together.

A. Practice: In the blank following each sentence below, write **S** if the subject and verb are singular. Write **P** if the subject and verb are plural.

_____ 1. The boy begins the journey to strange lands. _____

_____ 2. The rule book and map prepare Milo for an unusual adventure. _____

_____ 3. The traveller soon arrives at his first destination. _____

_____ 4. The Whether Man speaks in a confusing manner. _____

_____ 5. The Lethargarians want to rest all day. _____

_____ 6. They wonder why anyone would want to be active. _____

_____ 7. Milo dislikes the sleepy land called the Doldrums. _____

_____ 8. The sleepy people annoy Milo with their incredible laziness. _____

B. Writing Application: Revise the following paragraph so that all subjects and verbs agree in number.

In *The Phantom Tollbooth,* a boy named Milo goes on a fantastic journey in which he learn some important lessons about life. His companion on his journey is a dog named Tock. Milo and Tock first goes to the land of Expectations, where they meets the Whether Man. He tells them that some people never goes beyond Expectations. Milo and Tock, however, do arrive at their first destination, Dictionopolis, where a king named Aziz rule over the land.

_____

_____

_____

_____

_____

_____

***The Phantom Tollbooth*, Act I**
based on the book by Norton Juster, by Susan Nanus (text page 630)

Reading Strategy: Summarize

When you **summarize**, you retell what has happened in your own words. A summary of a piece of literature should include details of important characters and review the important events in the order in which they occur in the original work. When you summarize, you should show how certain ideas and events are related, or belong together. For example, you should tell if one character is another's friend or enemy, or if one event is the cause of another.

DIRECTIONS: Use the roadmap below to note events and details that you find in Act I of *The Phantom Tollbooth.* Include the important information in the space provided on each signpost. You can choose any events and details that you find significant and interesting.

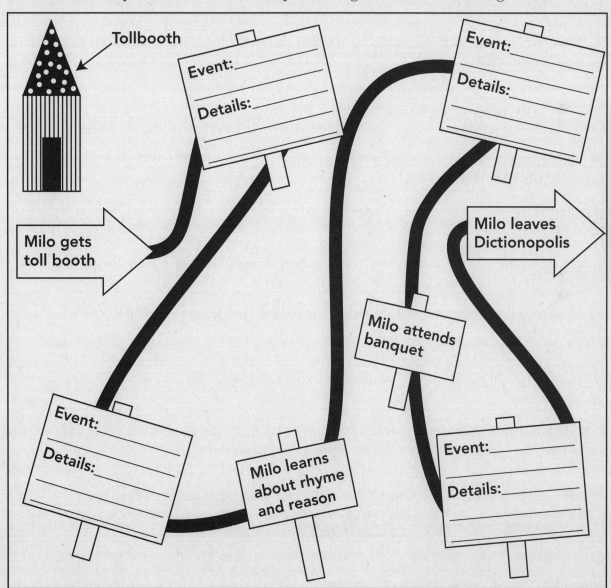

Name _____   Date _____

Literary Focus: Elements of Drama

Drama is a special literary form because unlike a story or poem, it is meant to be staged rather than read. An audience watches the **plot** unfold as actors "become" the **characters**, speaking lines of **dialogue** and expressing thoughts and emotions so that viewers can understand what is happening in the play. Like any story, a drama has a **setting**, or place where the action occurs. Unlike an ordinary story, much information about the characters, setting, and action is given in **stage directions**, and, in order to give a clear structure and sequence to a drama, the author may divide it into **acts** and **scenes**, rather than chapters.

A. DIRECTIONS: On the lines provided, answer the following questions about *The Phantom Tollbooth*, Act I.

1. Read the opening stage directions for **Scene i** and write the first sound the audience hears as the play begins.

   _____

2. What is the name of the main character in the play?

   _____

3. What is Milo's first line of dialogue in **Scene ii**?

   _____

4. What is the setting for the end of **Act I**?

   _____

5. What plot event prevents King Azaz and the Mathemagician from solving their arguments?

   _____

6. Read the stage directions that describe King Azaz of Dictionopolis, and describe what he looks like.

   _____

   _____

7. Read the stage directions that describe the Mathemagician, and describe what he looks like.

   _____

B. DIRECTIONS: Read the following passage from *The Phantom Tollbooth*, Act I. On the lines, write words from the passage that refer to plot, setting, and characters.

> The two princesses. They used to settle all the arguments between their two brothers who rule over the Land of Wisdom. You see, Azaz is the king of Dictionopolis and the Mathemagician is the king of Digitopolis and they almost never see eye to eye on anything. . . . But then one day, the kings had an argument to end all arguments . . .

Plot _____

Setting _____

Characters _____

Name _____ Date _____

Build Vocabulary

Using the Word Root *-son-*

The word root *-son-* comes from the Latin verb *sonare*, which means "to sound." Words formed from the word root *-son-* include the idea of sound in their meanings. For example, the word *dissonance* means "unpleasant sound." Other words built from the word root *-son-* are *resonate* ("make an echoing sound"), *super**son**ic* (faster than the speed of sound), ***son**orous* (rich and full in sound), and ***son**ata* (musical composition for one instrument). Here are other examples:

sonar: "an instrument that uses sound waves to detect underwater objects and to determine their location." (Short for *sound navigation ranging*) The scientists used *sonar* to follow the whale.

sonic boom: "a loud, explosive noise caused by an aircraft traveling at or above the speed of sound." When the jet hit the speed of sound, you could hear the *sonic boom*.

A. DIRECTIONS: Complete each sentence below by writing one of the following words. Use the meaning of the root *-son-* and sentence context to help you select the correct word.

sonar   resonate   consonant   dissonant   sonnet   sonata

1. I could no longer listen to the awful _____ sounds coming from the band room.

2. The letter *t* is a _____, while the letter *a* is a vowel.

3. When stretched tightly and then plucked, a rubber band will _____.

4. The poet wrote a beautiful _____.

5. The scientists are testing new _____ equipment for a deep-diving submarine.

6. The pianist played a very difficult _____ by Beethoven.

Using the Word Bank

dissonance	admonishing	iridescent	malicious

B. DIRECTIONS: Use one word from the Word Bank to replace the italicized word or words in each sentence below. Rewrite your new sentences on the lines provided.

1. The doctor in *The Phantom Tollbooth*, Act II, specialized in creating *a harsh or disagreeable combination of sounds.*

   _____

2. The stars in the sky were so bright they looked *shimmering.*

   _____

3. We couldn't believe that our friend could say anything so nasty and *spiteful.*

   _____

4. The teacher gave the noisy class a look, *warning* them to quiet down.

   _____

Unit 8: Drama

The Phantom Tollbooth, Act II
based on the book by Norton Juster, by Susan Nanus (text page 630)

Build Spelling Skills: The Sound *shəs* Spelled *cious*

Spelling Strategy The sound *shəs** at the end of a word can be spelled *cious* as in *malicious*, *precious*, and *gracious*. The *cious* spelling is always preceded by a vowel. This ending is used often used to form adjectives from nouns. Sometimes the *cious* ending is added to a word part such as *deli* to form an adjective, as in *delicious*. In the examples below, notice the spelling changes when *cious* is added.

noun or word part	adjective with *cious*	meaning
mali-	malicious	showing evil intentions
grace	gracious	well-mannered
space	spacious	roomy
suspicion	suspicious	believing someone is guilty
deli-	delicious	good tasting

A. Practice: In each sentence below, fill in the blank with an adjective formed by adding *cious* to the word in parentheses.

1. The stew tasted _____ (deli-)

2. That dog has a _____ streak, so don't get too near it. (mali-)

3. Our new apartment has _____ rooms. (space)

4. His face had a guilty expression that made me _____. (suspicion)

5. Our hosts were _____ and friendly to every guest in the room. (grace)

B. Practice: Complete the following short passage with the correct adjectives. Choose the adjectives from the ones that you wrote on the lines above. Use sentence context to help you know which adjective to write.

Milo has some interesting adventures in *The Phantom Tollbooth*, Act II. He visits the huge and _____ numbers mine. He wonders why the _____ stew he eats makes him more and more hungry. Before he leaves to rescue the princesses, he is _____ when the Mathemagician tells him he will have to overcome obstacles. Later, he finds out that the obstacles are _____ demons who chase him. When he finally succeeds in rescuing the princesses Rhyme and Reason, they are kind and _____ to him.

*The character ə is called *schwa* and represents the sound <u>uh</u>.

The Phantom Tollbooth, Act II
based on the book by Norton Juster, by Susan Nanus (text page 630)

Build Grammar Skills: Verb Agreement With Special Subjects

You know that the verb in a sentence must always **agree** with its subject in number (singular or plural). You also know that pronouns can take the place of nouns in sentences, and that a verb must always agree with the pronoun in number (singular or plural).

Milo hears a loud noise. *He looks* at the wagon. (singular subject, singular verb)
Milo, Humbug, and *Tock* look around for a creature. *They* open the door. (plural subject, plural verb)

It's important to remember that some pronouns are always singular even though the meaning may seem to be plural. These special pronouns are *everybody, everyone, everything, each, anybody, nobody,* and *somebody.* When these pronouns are used, they always take a singular verb.

Everyone looks for the creature.
Everything appears in shadow in the wagon.
Nobody can see a thing.
Anybody might make the noise, but who is it?

A. Practice: Write the correct form of the verb on the line following each sentence.

1. Everybody (think, thinks) that Kakafonous A. Dischord is weird. _____

2. Everything here in Digitopolis (is, are) quite precise. _____

3. Anybody who (is, are) in a hurry to travel should leave immediately! _____

4. Everyone (find, finds) Dodecaheron to be a very confusing character. _____

5. Nobody (understand, understands) the number problems. _____

6. Each (try, tries) to solve the problem. _____

7. Somebody (need, needs) to talk to Mathemagician. _____

8. (Is, Are) everything so confusing in Digitopolis? _____

B. Writing Application: Use each subject to create a sentence of your own about Digitopolis and its characters. Remember that the verb you use must agree with the subject. Write each sentence on the line.

1. Subject: Everything

_____

2. Subject: Anybody

_____

3. Subject: Everyone

_____

4. Subject: Each

_____

Unit 8: Drama

***The Phantom Tollbooth*, Act II**
based on the book by Norton Juster, by Susan Nanus (text page 630)

Reading Strategy: Envision

When you read a story, descriptive language in the narration and the characters' dialogue help you to **envision**, or picture in your mind, the sights, sounds, and actions in a scene. When you read a play, or drama, the descriptions in the stage directions and the characters' dialogue help you to envision a scene. The details include sights, sounds, colors, and shapes of things. The details tell about the sets and props. When you envision, you can gain better understanding and more pleasure from your reading experience.

For example, think about the details used in the stage directions to describe Dodecahedron:

(a 12-sided figure with a different face on each side, and with all the edges labeled with a small letter and all the angles labeled with a large letter. He wears a beret and peers at the others with a serious face.)

If you didn't know what Dodecaheron looked like, you would find his conversation with Milo quite confusing, and you wouldn't appreciate the humor in it.

DIRECTIONS: Fill in the chart below by writing details about three sets and props (sights, sounds, colors, shapes) that help you envision the characters and the action. You might start with the first scene with Milo, Tock, and Humbug approaching Digitopolis. Read the stage directions to find the props that are needed for Kakafonus A. Dischord. Then choose two other sets within Scene i, and two sets in Scene ii.

Scene	Change of Set	Use of Prop
Act II, Scene i		
Scene ii		

The Phantom Tollbooth, **Act II**
based on the book by Norton Juster, by Susan Nanus (text page 630)

Literary Focus: Staging

The term **staging** refers to the art of putting a play on the stage and making it come to life for an audience. Staging includes: the use of **sets** and **scenery** (tables, chairs, bookshelves, windows, trees, and background painted scenes); **costumes** (clothing appropriate for the characters, the place, and the time period); **props** (objects that are used as part of the play either for an action or simply to add to the effect of the set, such as a telephone); **lighting**; **sound effects**, and **special effects**.

Think about the character of Dodecaheron, who is a 12-sided figure with a different face on each side. The figure with its edges and angles labeled might be made out of a large piece of cardboard which an actor would wear. The scene with this character, Milo, Tock, and Humbug is on the road, at first by a sign post. So the scenery must show the outdoors, and the signpost is needed as a prop. To help Milo and his friends decide which way to go, Dodecaheron uses a blackboard that is wheeled out on stage, so another prop that is needed is a blackboard with wheels.

The examples above are just a few details of the staging. A director must consider all of the details the author gives and then decide how to bring those details to life.

DIRECTIONS: On the lines below, write the answers to each question about staging *The Phantom Tollbooth*, Act II. You will need to refer to details the author gives in the stage directions and the dialogue to answer the questions.

1. What prop does Mathemagician need to carry as he enters the numbers mine to talk to Milo and his friends?

   _____

2. How might the iridescent and glittery numbers be shown sparkling everywhere in the numbers mine?

   _____

   _____

3. What is needed for the scenery and props in the measuring room?

   _____

   _____

   _____

4. What should the stage look like for the opening of Scene ii and who is on stage?

   _____

   _____

   _____

5. Why is lighting important during the scene when the Terrible Trivium has Milo and his friends doing the tasks?

   _____

6. Why do you think the author made use of the whole theater for the chase scene when Milo and the others are escaping from the demons?

   _____

Unit 8: Drama

Anne of Green Gables
by L. M. Montgomery (text page 665)

Build Vocabulary

A. DIRECTIONS: For each of the definitions below, write the correct word from the following box. Write one letter of the word in each space. The circled letters will spell what Matthew had when he discovered that Anne was a girl.

excruciatingly   destiny   compel   founders   perish   strife   feuds   perpetually

1. fate, fortune ___ ___ (___) ___ ___ ___ ___

2. forefathers, originators ___ ___ (___) ___ ___ ___ ___ ___

3. conflict, disagreement ___ ___ (___) ___ ___ ___

4. force ___ ___ ___ (___) ___ ___

5. die, pass away ___ ___ (___) ___ ___ ___

6. very painfully ___ ___ ___ ___ ___ ___ ___ (___) ___ ___ ___ ___

7. fights, arguments ___ ___ ___ ___ (___) ___

8. always, forever ___ ___ ___ ___ (___) ___ ___ ___ ___ ___ ___

When Matthew found out that Anne was a girl, he had a

___ ___ ___ ___ ___ ___ ___ ___ .

B. DIRECTIONS: Complete each sentence by writing one word from the box above in the blank space.

1. Matthew could not _____ Anne to stop talking on the journey to the farm.

2. She seemed to talk on and on _____.

3. Anne showed her love for big words when she said that her suit case was _____ old.

4. She hoped it was her _____ to be either beautiful, clever, or good.

5. Anne sang a song about the first _____ of Prince Edward Island.

6. Many _____ between different groups of people lead to more serious conflicts

7. The _____ between the groups can even lead to war.

8. Some of the first settlers of the island had to _____ in battle.

Anne of Green Gables
by L. M. Montgomery (text page 665)

Connecting a Drama to Social Studies

Prince Edward Island, where Anne of Green Gables takes place, is the smallest but most heavily populated province of Canada. Its people usually call their province "The Island" or simply use its initials, "P.E.I." Farming is the chief source of income on the island, and its greatest natural resource is its fertile red soil. This *loam*, a mixture of clay, decayed matter, and sand, lies on beds of soft red or brown sandstone, which gives the soil its reddish color. Crops, grasses, and beautiful wild flowers thrive in the rich, red soil. Prince Edward Island has long stretches of red or white sandy beaches along its coasts with warm ocean currents offshore, which makes it a popular vacation spot for tourists. Many come to Prince Edward Island National Park where they visit Green Gables Farm, believed to be the scene of the story *Anne of Green Gables*.

DIRECTIONS: Answer the questions below. Base your answers on the information above. Write your answers on the lines.

1. In *Anne of Green Gables*, Anne asks why the roads are red. Matthew doesn't know the answer. Why are the roads red?

   _____

   _____

2. Where would you go on Prince Edward Island to visit the house where Anne will live with Matthew and his sister, Marilla?

   _____

   _____

3. If you lived on Prince Edward Island, what would your family probably do for a living?

   _____

   _____

4. If you lived on Prince Edward Island, what two nicknames might you use to refer to the place you lived?

   _____

   _____

Grandpa and the Statue by Arthur Miller (text page 677)

Build Vocabulary

Using the Word Root -scrib-

You can see the word root -scrib- in the Word Bank word *subscribe*. The word root, which may also be spelled -scrip-, as in *subscription*, comes from the Latin word *scribere*, meaning "to write." In the play, a neighbor asks Grandpa to *subscribe* to the fund to pay for a base for the Statue of Liberty. In other words, he wants Grandpa to sign or *write* his name on a list of people who promise to contribute money to the fund. Other useful words are also based on this root. Read the definitions and examples with the root in mind.

scribe: in ancient times, a person paid to copy books or documents

Before the invention of the printing press, books were copied by *scribes*.

scripture: writings important to a religion

Carrie went to the library to do research on ancient *scriptures*.

subscription: a signed agreement to pay for something in advance

We paid a year in advance for our newspaper *subscription*.

A. DIRECTIONS: Use the correct word to complete each sentence. Write your answer on the line.

scribe   scripture   subscription

1. Because they have a _____ to that magazine, my cousins get it every week.

2. In ancient times, a _____ wrote letters for people who did not know how to write.

3. The scholar had spent many years studying _____ of ancient religions.

Using the Word Bank

stingiest	subscribed	peeved	uncomprehending	tempest

B. DIRECTIONS: In the space following each of these sentences, write the Word Bank word that could replace the underlined word or words in each sentence.

1. Monaghan was <u>annoyed</u> with Sheean. _____

2. Monaghan expected that, in a <u>strong wind storm</u>, the Statue of Liberty would fall.
_____

3. August was <u>not understanding</u> about why Young Monaghan liked to spend hours looking at the Statue of Liberty. _____

4. Young Monaghan knew that his grandfather was called the <u>most miserly</u> man in Brooklyn.
_____

5. At the end of the radio play, Monaghan wishes that he had <u>signed up to give money</u> to the fund for the base of the Statue of Liberty. _____

Grandpa and the Statue by Arthur Miller (text page 677)

Build Spelling Skills: Adding *-er* or *-est*

Spelling Strategy When you add the ending *-er* or *-est* to an adjective that ends in *y*, change the *y* to *i* before adding the ending.

   Example: Although the comedian's jokes were **funny**, I've heard **funnier** jokes, and the jokes in this book are the **funniest** I've ever heard.

When the adjective ends in *y*, change the *y* to *i* before adding the ending.

   Exception: When you add *-er* or *-est* to a word ending in *y* preceded by a vowel, do not change the *y* to *i*.

   Example: The sky looked **gray** yesterday, but it looked even **grayer** today.

A. Practice: Add *-er* and *-est* to each adjective.

1. grouchy _____, _____

2. gray _____, _____

3. sturdy _____, _____

4. pretty _____, _____

5. grand _____, _____

6. likely _____, _____

7. manly _____, _____

8. young _____, _____

9. crummy _____, _____

B. Practice: In each sentence below, add the ending in parentheses to the underlined adjective. Write the adjective with its ending on the line.

1. Grandpa was <u>testy</u> when Sheean asked him for a donation, but he was even _____ when Sheean asked again. (*-er*)

2. The weather had been <u>windy</u> all week, but the day they went to see the Statue up close was the _____ day in a long time. (*-est*)

3. Buying peanuts made the boy <u>happy</u>, but he was even _____ to see his grandfather leave a coin on the base of the statue. (*-er*)

4. It's getting <u>sunny</u>, and later it will be even _____. (*-er*)

5. That is so <u>silly</u>, it's the _____ thing I've ever heard. (*-est*)

6. Before the storm, the <u>gray</u> sky turned even _____. (*-er*)

7. The teacher was <u>happier</u> with us this morning, and she was the _____ we've ever seen her this afternoon. (*-est*)

Grandpa and the Statue by Arthur Miller (text page 677)

Build Grammar Skills: Pronoun and Antecedent Agreement

A pronoun doesn't make sense by itself. It needs an **antecedent**, which is the noun or proper noun to which the pronoun refers. For a pronoun to make sense, it must **agree** with its antecedent in gender (masculine or feminine) and number (singular or plural). For example, in the following sentences from *Grandpa and the Statue*, each pronoun is underlined twice, and its antecedent is underlined once.

I didn't think there was a statue but there is. She's all broke, it's true . . .

The pronoun *she* refers to the noun *statue*. Because the noun *statue* is singular (there is only one) and feminine (this statue represents a woman), the pronoun is also singular and feminine (she).

"I don't really think your grampa knows what he's talkin' about.

The pronoun *he* refers to the noun *grampa*. Because the noun *grampa* is singular (he is just one person), and masculine (*grampa* means "grand**father**"), the pronouns is also singular and masculine (he). If the above sentence were written, "I don't really think your grampa knows what they're talkin' about," it would lose its intended meaning.

A. Practice: On the line following each sentence, write *A* if the pronoun and antecedent agree in gender and number. Write *X* if the pronoun does not agree with the antecedent. For each *X*, write the correct pronoun.

1. Young Monaghan tells a story about his grandfather. _____

2. All the people gave money because they wanted to be proud of Butler Street.

   _____

3. The statue needed a base, and the money would go to pay for them. _____

4. Each boy enjoyed their visit to the statue. _____

5. Finally, the grandfather admits that it was wrong about the statue. _____

B. Writing Application: Rewrite each sentence, filling in the blank with a pronoun that agrees in gender and number with the underlined antecedent.

1. When people listen to the play, _____ imagine being in Brooklyn long ago.

2. Sheean paid Grandpa's streetcar fare to the warehouse, but _____ wouldn't pay the return fare.

4. Everyone in my family except my youngest sister has been to the Statue of Liberty, but _____ hopes to go soon.

5. When my friend and I saw a film about the Statue of Liberty, _____ learned a lot.

6. By carefully reading what the characters said, I figured out the meaning of _____ words.

7. Each boy is eager to see the statue, and each hopes for _____ turn to go.

Grandpa and the Statue by Arthur Miller (text page 677)

Reading Strategy: Predict

When you read, you often make logical guesses, or **predictions**, about what will happen. Your predictions are based on clues, or details that the author provides to help you predict events in the story. The more an author can keep you guessing, the more you enjoy a story or play. And one reason to finish reading a story or play is to find out whether your predictions turn out to be correct. Even if you're wrong and the author surprises you, that's all part of the fun.

In _Grandpa and the Statue_, the big question is, "Will Grandpa give in and contribute money to the statue's base?" If you predicted that he would give in, you were wrong, because he does not give Sheean any money for the fund. But you'd be right, in a way, because finally, Grandpa puts a half dollar on the base of the statue—after it's already been built.

DIRECTIONS: For each of the following passages from _Grandpa and the Statue_, identify two details that give you clues as to what might happen later in the play. Then write the prediction you made based on those two details.

1. MONAGHAN. There's the Statue of Liberty out there. Don't you see it?

   AUGUST. Oh, that's it. Yeh, that's nice to look at.

   MONAGHAN. I like it. Reminds me of a lot of laughs

   AUGUST. Laughs? The Statue of Liberty?

   MONAGHAN. Yeh, my grandfather. He got all twisted up with the Statue of Liberty.

Detail 1: _____

Detail 2: _____

Prediction: _____

2. MONAGHAN. What I can't understand is what all these people see in that statue that they'll keep a boat like this full makin' the trip, year in year out. To hear the newspapers talk, if the statue was gone we'd be at war with the nation that stole her the followin' mornin' early. All it is is a big high pile of French copper.

   CHILD MONAGHAN. The teacher says it shows us that we got liberty.

   MONAGHAN. Bah! If you've got liberty you don't need a statue to tell you you got it; and if you haven't got liberty no statue's going to do you any good tellin' you you got it. It was a criminal waste of the people's money.

Detail 1: _____

Detail 2: _____

Prediction: _____

Selection Support   **247**

Grandpa and the Statue by Arthur Miller (text page 677)

Literary Focus: Dialogue

In a story, the author has many ways of giving you important information about the setting and action and the characters' thoughts and feelings. For example, an author might write, "Jerry was terrified, but he tried to look brave." In a play, the author has only one way of letting you know a character's feelings, and that is through **dialogue**, the conversation that takes place among characters in a play. By reading or listening to the dialogue, you find out where the characters are, how they feel about one another, what they are thinking and feeling, and other important information.

For example, in "Grandpa and the Statue," you know where the boy and his grandpa are when the boy says,

"Gee, it's nice ridin' on a boat, ain't it, Grandpa?"

Grandpa's answer lets you know that he is worried that the neighbors will find out about his trip to see the Statue of Liberty.

"Never said there was anything wrong with the boat. Boat's all right. You're sure now that Georgie's father is takin' the kids in the afternoon."

DIRECTIONS: Using the chart below, select a short piece of dialogue for each of the three characters on the chart. Write the dialogue you have selected in the first column. Write the information the dialogue provides in the second column.

Character's Dialogue	Information
Sheean:	
Grandpa Monaghan:	
Child Monaghan:	

"The Naming of Cats" by T. S. Eliot (text page 705)

Build Vocabulary

Using Forms of *scrutiny*

The word *scrutiny*, means "close observation." Various forms of *scrutiny* relate to the idea of observing or knowing. The word *scrutable*, for example, means "capable of being understood through study and observation". The word *inscrutable* means the opposite, "not able to be understood or known". Here are some other words related to scrutiny.

> **scrutinize:** to examine or observe with care
> I watched the cat *scrutinize* its dinner with distaste.
> **scrutinizer:** one who examines with care, or inspects critically
> It's good to be a *scrutinizer*, and double check all the facts.
> **inscrutability:** the quality of being mysterious or difficult to understand
> The *inscrutability* of the jumbled message was maddening.

A. DIRECTIONS: Choose the correct word to complete each of the sentences below, and write the word in the space provided.

> scrutiny   scrutinize   scrutable   inscrutable   scrutinizer   inscrutability

1. The translation was difficult, but after hours of study it was finally (scrutable, inscrutability) _____.

2. The silent cat watched the goldfish with (scrutinize, scrutiny) _____.

3. The (inscrutable, inscrutability) _____ of the word puzzle made me try harder.

4. I had to (scrutiny, scrutinize) _____ every detail before I was satisfied.

5. I was a real (inscrutability, scrutinizer) _____ and I checked the spelling twice.

6. I found the ancient Egyptian alphabet totally (scrutinize, inscrutable) _____.

Using the Word Bank

perpendicular	meditation	rapt	contemplation	inscrutable

B. DIRECTIONS: Circle the letter of the word that is most opposite in meaning to the word in CAPITAL LETTERS.

1. RAPT: a. absorbed   b. distracted   c. tapped   d. soothed

2. PERPENDICULAR: a. odd   b. hanging   c. horizontal   d. limited

3. INSCRUTABLE: a. understandable   b. unclear   c. thin   d. funny

4. CONTEMPLATION: a. thought   b. inattention   c. idea   d. lie

"The Naming of Cats" by T. S. Eliot (text page 705)

Build Spelling Skills: Spelling the *shun* Sound With *-tion*

Spelling Strategy When the sound *shun* comes at the end of a word, it is often spelled *-tion*, as in *meditation* and *contemplation*. Less frequently, the *shun* sound is spelled differently at the end of words such as *mission*, *magician* and *ocean*.

The following words spell the *shun* sound with *-tion*.

addition	contemplation	description	emotion	explanation
meditation	motion	obligation	position	recreation

A. Practice: In each sentence choose the ending in parentheses to correctly spell the italicized word. If you are not sure of the spelling, look at the words in the list above.

1. My cat sometimes will sleep in a strange *posi(-tion, -shun)* _____.

2. The new kitten was a wonderful *addi(-cian, -tion)* _____ to our family.

3. Many religions teach forms of *medita(-sion, -tion)* _____.

4. The poem was filled with *emo(-tion, -cian)* _____.

5. We played basketball in the *recrea(-shun, -tion)* _____ room.

B. Practice: Proofread the following paragraph. Cross out each misspelled word and write the correctly spelled word above it. If you are not sure how to spell a word, look at the words in the list above.

"The Naming of Cats" gives a funny explanasion of cats' behavior. The description of a

cat in meditashun is familiar to any cat lover: cats often sit for long periods of time without

making a single mosion. Is the cat, however, really sitting in comtemplacian of its name; or

does it just feel an obligasion to remain inscrutable?

Challenge: A number of English words incorporate the word cat to reflect various aspects of this fascinating animal's behavior. The word *catnap*, for example, means "a short nap," something real cats take often. The word *catty* means "cruel or spiteful." A *catwalk* means "a narrow platform or walkway," a reference to cats' excellent ability to balance. The word *caterwaul* means "to howl or screech."

In the space provided, write a sentence using each of the following words: *catty, catwalk, caterwaul,* and *catnap.*

_____

_____

_____

_____

_____

_____

"The Naming of Cats" by T. S. Eliot (text page 705)

Build Grammar Skills: Comparison of Adjectives and Adverbs

Most adjectives and adverbs have different forms when they are used to compare two items and when they are used to compare three or more items. The **comparative** form of an adjective or adverb is used to compare two items. The **superlative** form is used to compare three or more items. Short adjectives usually form the comparative by adding *-er* to the positive form of the adjective or adverb. For example, the comparative form of the adjective *strong* is *stronge*. Short adjectives usually form the superlative by adding *-est* to the positive. The superlative form of the adjective *strong* is *strongest*. Most adverbs add the word *more* to form the comparative, as in *more quickly*. Most adverbs add the word *most* to form the superlative, as in *most quickly*.

Comparative: Loulou is *livelier* than Spot. (adjective comparing two animals)
Loulou runs *more gracefully* than Spot. (adverb comparing two animals)

Superlative: Whiskers is the *liveliest* of all the cats. (adjective comparing more than two cats)
Loulou runs *most gracefully* of all the cats. (adverb comparing more than two cats)

Exceptions: There are a few adjectives that cannot take the comparative and superlative forms. The adjective *unique* means "one of its kind, or "without equal." Something that is *unique* cannot be compared to anything else. The sentence, "Out of all the jewels, the diamond was the most *unique*" is incorrect. The sentence should read "Out of all the jewels, the diamond was unique." Other adjectives that cannot be used in the comparative or superlative forms include *original, complete,* and *perfect*.

A. Practice: In each of the following sentences, underline the superlative or comparative form of the adjective or adverb. Write **C** after the sentence if it contains a comparative and **S** after the sentence if it contains a superlative. The first sentence has been done for you.

_C_   1. The name Quaxo is <u>funnier</u> than the name Peter.

____   2. Fareed thought cats were the haughtiest of all pets. _____

____   3. He has a deeper understanding of cats than I did. _____

____   4. Those were the cleverest names of any I had heard. _____

____   5. It uses wittier words than the other poem. _____

____   6. I thought it was the wittiest of all of them. _____

B. Writing Application: Choose either the comparative or superlative form of the adjective or adverb and write it in the space provided to correctly complete each of the following sentence.

1. Coricopat is (quieter, quietest) _____ than Jellylorum.

2. The sofa made a (warmer, warmest) _____ bed than the floor.

3. Augustus has the (stronger, strongest) _____ personality of all my cats.

4. Victor was (gentler, gentlest) _____ than Jonathan.

5. Those are the (sillier, silliest) _____ names of any I'd ever heard.

6. Aunt Hester thought cats were the (nobler, noblest) _____ of all animals.

Unit 9: Poetry

Reading for Success: Strategies for Reading Poetry

Poetry is different from other types of writing. Even plain, everyday words seem different in poems. These words stand out and seem to mean more than they usually do. These tips will help you figure out what's happening to the words in poetry:

- **Read lines according to punctuation.** Don't automatically stop at the end of every line. Pause like you always would, briefly for commas and semi-colons, and longer for end marks like periods and question marks.

- **Identify the speaker.** The voice that "says" the poem is the speaker, but the speaker isn't necessarily the poet. The speaker can be a character in an imaginary situation. Use clues to figure out who the speaker is.

- **Use your senses.** You must use your senses to experience the world that the poem introduces you to. Let your imagination create the sight, sounds and smells that the poem offers you.

- **Paraphrase the lines.** Restate a line or passage in your own words to be sure you understand it.

DIRECTIONS: Read the following poem by John Updike, and use the reading strategies to increase your comprehension. In the margin, note where you read lines according to punctuation, identify the speaker, use your senses, and paraphrase the lines.

"September" by John Updike

The breezes taste
    Of apple peel.
The air is full
    of smells to feel—

Ripe fruit, old footballs,
    Burning brush,
New books, erasers,
    Chalk, and such.
The bee, his hive
    Well-honeyed, hums,
And Mother cuts
    Chrysanthemums.

Like plates washed clean
    With suds, the days
Are polished with
    A morning haze.

"The Naming of Cats" by T. S. Eliot (text page 705)

Literary Focus: Rhythm in Poetry

Poetry uses many different kinds of **rhythm**, or patterns of stressed and unstressed syllables. When a poem has a regular rhythmic pattern, your ear recognizes it and begins to anticipate, or look forward to, the repeated pattern. Listen to the rhythm pattern in the following line from "The Naming of Cats." (The syllables in capital letters are stressed.)

> There are FANcier NAMES if you THINK they sound SWEETer,

The pattern of stressed and unstressed syllables is *da da DUM da da DUM da da DUM da da DUM da.* Except for the last two words of the line, the rhythm pattern is made up of two unstressed syllables followed by one stressed syllable. With slight variations, the poet uses this rhythm pattern throughout the entire poem. As you read the poem, notice how the slight variations in rhythm come like surprises, and add to the poem's humor.

A. DIRECTIONS: In the following passage from the poem, circle each stressed syllable and underline each unstressed syllable. The first line was been completed for you

> The Naming of Cats is a difficult matter
>
> It isn't just one of your holiday games:
>
> You may think at first I'm as mad as a hatter
>
> When I tell you, a cat must have THREE DIFFERENT NAMES.

B. DIRECTIONS: Circle the letter that identifies the correct rhythm pattern of the following lines. *Hint:* It may help you to tap out the rhythm with your finger as you read each line to yourself.

1. Else how can he keep up his tail perpendicular,

   a. DUM DUM da DUM DUM da DUM DUM da DUM DUM da da

   b. DUM DUM da DUM da da DUM DUM da da DUM da da

   c. da DUM da da DUM da da DUM da da DUM da da

2. Or spread out his whiskers or cherish his pride?

   a. da DUM da da DUM da da DUM da da DUM

   b. da da DUM da DUM DUM da DUM DUM da DUM

   c. DUM DUM da DUM DUM da DUM DUM da da DUM

3. Of names of this kind I can give you a quorum,

   a. da da DUM DUM DUM da da DUM DUM DUM da da

   b. da DUM da da DUM da da DUM da da DUM da

   c. DUM DUM da da da DUM DUM DUM da da DUM da

4. Such as Munkustrap, Quaxo, or Coricopat

   a. da da DUM da da DUM da da DUM da da da

   b. DUM da DUM da DUM da DUM da DUM da DUM

   c. da da DUM DUM da da DUM DUM da da DUM DUM

Selection Support **253**

"The Walrus and the Carpenter" by Lewis Carroll (text page 713)
"February Twilight" by Sara Teasdale (text page 716)
"Jimmy Jet and His TV Set" by Shel Silverstein (text page 717)
"The Geese" by Richard Peck (text page 718)

Build Vocabulary

Multiple Meanings

The Word Bank word antennae from "Jimmy Jet and His TV Set" can mean "metal rods that receive TV or radio signals" or "sense organs on the heads of insects." From the context of the poem, you can tell that the meaning being used is the first one.

Here are some other words from the selections with multiple meanings along with two definitions of each word.

odd: strange / not even, not evenly divisible by two
cold: chilly, at a low temperature / a virus producing coughing and sneezing
watch: to look at / a timepiece worn on the wrist
lure: a powerful attraction / artificial fishing bait

A. DIRECTIONS: Write the correct meaning of the italicized word from the definitions above in each sentence.

1. Will you *watch* the movie with me? _____

2. The magician asked a member of the audience to pick an *odd* number.

   _____

3. Mr. Sanchez tied the *lure* to the end of his fishing rod. _____

4. Hank stayed home from school with a bad *cold.* _____

Using the Word Bank

beseech	lean	antennae

B. DIRECTIONS: Use a Word Bank word to replace the italicized word or words in the following sentences. Write your words on the lines provided.

1. Don't overfeed your pet if you want to keep it *thin.* _____

2. "I *beg* of you to spare my life," the prisoner said to the king. _____

3. When dad raised the *metal rod*, the stations came in clearer on our car radio. _____

Analogies

C. DIRECTIONS: Circle the letter that best completes each analogy.

1. Tall is to short as fat is to _____.

   a. beseech   b. lean   c. antennae   d. odd

2. Sounds are to ears as signals are to _____.

   a. beseech   b. lean   c. antennae   d. watch

"The Walrus and the Carpenter" by Lewis Carroll (text page 713)
"February Twilight" by Sara Teasdale (text page 716)
"Jimmy Jet and His TV Set" by Shel Silverstein (text page 717)
"The Geese" by Richard Peck (text page 718)

Building Spelling Skills: long e sound (ee, ea)

Spelling Strategy The long e sound can be spelled in several ways. One way is ee, as in the Word Bank word be**see**ch, and the words k**ee**n and betw**ee**n. Another way is ea as in the Word Bank word l**ea**n and the words m**ea**n and cl**ea**n.

A. Practice: Complete the sentences below, using the following words.

mean   keen   between   clean   beseech   lean

1. The cottage stood on a hill _____ the lake and the woods.

2. I _____ you not to go out tonight.

3. Most dogs have a _____ sense of smell.

4. The runners in the race were all _____ and fit.

5. It was _____ of you not to invite Sally to the party.

6. Once a week I completely _____ my room.

B. Practice: Complete the following dialogue. Using the clues in parentheses for help, choose five words from your chart to fill in the blanks.

Walrus: My dear fellow, just (ee word) _____ you and me, I miss the poor oysters.

Carpenter: Yes, it was (ea word) _____ of us to eat them.

Walrus: I (ee word) _____ you, let us find some new little friends to walk with.

Carpenter: Let me ask the lobsters to join us.

Walrus: We can (ea word) _____ up our kitchen and have them to lunch.

Carpenter: Oh, dear. We won't stay very (ea word) _____ that way!

Challenge: The plural form of the Word Bank word *antenna* is *antennae* (pronounced an TEN ee). Words that end in *a* and form the plural by adding *e* come from the ancient language Latin. Other Latin words ending in *a* form the plural in the same way. For example, the plural of *formula* is *formulae* (pronounced FOR mew lee), and the plural of *alumna*, which means female graduate, is *alumnae* (pronounced uh LUM nee). On the lines below, write three sentences using the plural form of *antenna*, *formula*, and *alumna*.

_____

_____

_____

Name _____ Date _____

"The Walrus and the Carpenter" by Lewis Carroll (text page 713)
"February Twilight" by Sara Teasdale (text page 716)
"Jimmy Jet and His TV Set" by Shel Silverstein (text page 717)
"The Geese" by Richard Peck (text page 718)

Building Grammar Skills: Irregular Comparisons

Most adjectives and adverbs can be expressed in three forms: positive, comparative, and superlative. Usually, the comparative is formed by adding the ending *-er* or the word *more*; and superlative by adding the ending *-est* or the word *most*. Some adjectives, however, change completely in the comparative and superlative forms. These are called **irregular comparisons**. Here is an example:

Positive: The clams tasted <u>good</u>.
Comparative: The oysters tasted <u>better</u> than the clams.
Superlative: The lobsters tasted the <u>best</u> of all the food they ate. (superlative)

Because each irregular comparison is different, you should learn each one. Here are some others:

Positive	Comparative	Superlative
good / well	better	best
bad	worse	worst
many / much	more	most
little	less	least
far	farther	farthest

A. Practice: Replace the positive form of the modifier with the comparative or superlative form.

1. The walrus walked (far) _____ along the beach than the carpenter. (comparative)

2. The poor carpenter had the (bad) _____ stomach ache he had ever had. (superlative)

3. Jimmy Jet would be (well) _____ off, if he watched less television. (comparative)

4. We were left with the (little) _____ time to read "The Geese." (superlative)

5. "Jimmy Jet and His TV Set" is the (good) _____ of the four poems, in my opinion. (superlative)

B. Writing Application: Rewrite each sentence below changing the underlined word as indicated in parentheses. The first sentence has been done for you.

1. I think Lewis Carroll is a <u>better</u> writer than Sara Teasdale. (superlative)

   <u>I think Lewis Carroll is the best writer in this selection.</u>

   _____

2. My house is <u>far</u> from our school. (comparative)

   _____

3. Eddie's cough is <u>worse</u> today than yesterday. (superlative)

   _____

4. <u>Many</u> people arrived at the end of the bake sale. (superlative)

   _____

"The Walrus and the Carpenter" by Lewis Carroll (text page 713)
"February Twilight" by Sara Teasdale (text page 716)
"Jimmy Jet and His TV Set" by Shel Silverstein (text page 717)
"The Geese" by Richard Peck (text page 718)

Reading Strategy: Identifying the Speaker in a Poem

Sometimes a poem is in the first person, using words such as *I, we,* and *my.*

"February Twilight": "*I* stood beside a hill"
"Jimmy Jet and His TV Set": "*I'll* tell you the story of Jimmy Jet"
"*We* all sit around and watch him."
"Geese": "*My* father was the first to hear"

The person referred to by pronouns such as *I* and *my* in a poem is not necessarily the poet, but an imaginary character, or **speaker**, who says the words made up by the poet. For example, in "Jimmy Jet and His TV Set," the speaker tells a story about someone he or she knew. Usually, a poem contains clues about the speaker. For example, in "February Twilight," you can tell that the speaker is a person who appreciates the beauty of nature.

DIRECTIONS: Fill in the chart below to identify the speaker in the poems. Include the clues that helped you write your answers. The first row in the chart has been filled in for you. (You may not have something to fill in under every heading for both poems.)

	What relationships does the speaker have with others?	Can you tell if the speaker is male or female?	In what kind of place does the speaker probably live?	Do you think the speaker is an older person or a younger person?
"Geese"	The speaker has a relationship with his or her father, because the poem tells how the speaker remembers the father.			
"Jimmy Jet and His TV Set"				
"February Twilight"				

"The Walrus and the Carpenter" by Lewis Carroll (text page 713)
"February Twilight" by Sara Teasdale (text page 716)
"Jimmy Jet and His TV Set" by Shel Silverstein (text page 717)
"The Geese" by Richard Peck (text page 718)

Literary Focus: Narrative and Lyric Poetry

There are two main kinds of poetry—narrative poetry and lyric poetry. Narrative poetry tells a story with a setting, characters, a plot, and an outcome. Some **narrative** poems, such as "The Walrus and the Carpenter" contain dialogue between the characters. **Lyric** poetry puts less emphasis on actions and more on the speaker's feelings and thoughts. For example, the main idea of the poem, "February Twilight" is the speaker's reaction to a beautiful winter night, not a sequence of events that may have occurred that night.

DIRECTIONS: Fill in the graphic organizer below for each of the poems.

Title of Poem	Narrative or Lyric?	How can you tell?
"The Walrus and the Carpenter"		
"February Twilight"		
"Jimmy Jet and His TV Set"		
"The Geese"		

"The Sidewalk Racer" by Lillian Morrison (text page 724)
"Concrete Cat" by Dorthi Charles (text page 725)
Two Haiku by Matsu Bashō and Mus-Soseki (text page 726)
Two Limericks Anonymous (text page 727)

Build Vocabulary

Using Homophones

Homophones are words that sound exactly the same but have different meanings. The words are often spelled differently as in the words flea and flee. The noun flea refers to a tiny insect. The verb flee means "to run away."

Occasionally homophones are spelled the same. For example, the word *can* may mean "a metal cylinder-shaped container," as in "Please open the can of peas." Can may also mean "able to," as in "I can do that math problem." The following words are homophones:

be / bee   flea / flee   flue / flew   through / threw

A. DIRECTIONS: Complete the following sentences with the correct homophone from the list above.

1. The skateboard _____ up in the air.

2. He skated _____ the tunnel.

3. I want to _____ a professional athlete.

4. It is wise to _____ from danger.

5. Sam _____ a rock into the pond.

6. Smoke drifted from the _____.

7. A _____ hummed over the fragrant flower.

8. The _____ bite was itchy and painful.

Using the Word Bank

skimming	flue	flee	flaw

B. DIRECTIONS: In the limerick below, fill in the blanks with the correct words from the Word Bank.

A crow on a _____ belching smoke

Said, "Something's amiss, that's no joke.

What a _____ in the day.

I'll go _____ away

And _____ this flue, else I will choke."

C. DIRECTIONS: Choose the lettered pair of words that best expresses a relationship similar to that expressed by the words in CAPITAL LETTERS.

1. SMOKE : FLUE ::   a. water : spout   b. house : chimney   c. bird : flight

2. SKIMMING : LIGHTLY ::   a. skating : running   b. skiing : jumping   c. tramping : heavily

3. FLEE : DANGER ::   a. avoid : attraction   b. escape : harm   c. run : walk

4. FLAW : CORRECTED ::   a. mistake : fault   b. stain : cleaned   c. perfect : sentence

Selection Support **259**

"The Sidewalk Racer" by Lillian Morrison (text page 724)
"Concrete Cat" by Dorthi Charles (text page 725)
Two Haiku by Matsu Bashō and Mus-Soseki (text page 726)
Two Limericks Anonymous (text page 727)

Build Spelling Skills: The *oo* Sound

Spelling Strategy The *oo* sound can be spelled a number of ways. Here are some of them: *u*, as in *exclude*, *ue* as in *flue*, *o* as in *to*, *oo* as in *fool*, and *ew* as in *flew*. Usually, when the *oo* sound is spelled with the letter *u*, the *u* is followed by a consonant and a silent *e*, as in *exclude*, or *rule*.

Exception: A few words, such as *haiku* and *flu* spell the *oo* sound with the letter *u* alone. The following words have the *oo* sound. Notice the different ways in which the sound is spelled.

| haiku | two | flue | drew | through | mood | humor | unusual |
| school | too | flew | attitude | cool | | | |

A. Practice: Complete the sentences below with the correctly spelled word. If you are not sure of the spelling, check the list above.

1. I like the way the poet (drew, driew) _____ the cat with words.

2. The skateboarder had some (attitude, attitood) _____.

3. Olivia loved that (haikue, haiku) _____.

4. The poet created a (mude, mood) _____ using just a few words.

5. A (flu, flue) _____ leading to the outside released steam.

6. Meeka liked limericks because of their (humor, hiewmer) _____.

7. The answer (fliew, flew) _____ right out of my mind.

Challenge: A number of words that have the *oo* sound are spelled *ous* and *oux*. These are French words that are also used in English. When pronouncing French-derived words spelled *ous* and *oux*, the *s* and the *x* are silent.

The word *rendezvous*, pronounced "rahn-day-voo," can be used as a noun or a verb. When used as a noun it means "an agreed upon meeting place," as in "Tim and I made the library our *rendezvous*." Rendezvous can also be used as a verb, meaning "to meet at an agreed upon place," as in "We agreed to rendezvous at noon." The word *bijoux*, pronounced "bee-joo," means "precious trinkets," as in "My grandmother had some antique *bijoux*." The word *billet-doux*, pronounced "bee-yay doo," means "love letters," as in "Before my parents married they sent each other *billet-doux*."

In the paragraph below, fill in the blanks correctly with one of the following French-derived words: *rendezvous, bijoux, billet-doux*.

In the romantic poem, the prince and princess would _____ by the

wishing well, or send messages to each other in _____. Each had given

the other tiny _____ as tokens of love.

"The Sidewalk Racer" by Lillian Morrison (text page 724)
"Concrete Cat" by Dorthi Charles (text page 725)
Two Haiku by Matsu Bashō and Mus-Soseki (text page 726)
Two Limericks Anonymous (text page 727)

Build Grammar Skills: Comparisons With *more* and *most*

The comparative form of an adjective has the meaning, "more," for example, *happier* means *more happy*. The superlative form of an adjective has the meaning, "most," for example, *happiest* means *most happy*. While many comparative and superlative adjectives are formed by adding *-er* or *-est* to the positive, or basic, adjective, the comparatives and superlatives of longer adjectives and most adverbs are formed by adding **more** or **most**.

In the sentences below, see how **more** and **most** are used to form the comparative and superlative of the three-syllable adjective *humorous*:

Comparative: Tess thought the limerick was *more humorous* than the other poem.
Superlative: Tess thought the limerick was the *most humorous* of all of the poems.

In the sentences below, *more* and *most* are used to form the comparative and superlative of the adverb *quickly*:

Comparative: Julian ran *more quickly* than the other racers.
Superlative: Julian ran *most quickly* of all the racers.

A. Practice: In each sentence below, underline the comparative or superlative form. Write **C** in the line provided if it is a comparative, or **S** if it is a superlative. The first sentence has been completed as an example.

_S_   1. He was the most daring skateboarder of them all.

____   2. The black cat was the most curious one in the litter. _____

____   3. A fly can fly more easily than a flea. _____

____   4. The concrete poem was more enjoyable than the others. _____

____   5. The haiku is the most beautiful of all the poems. _____

____   6. I think this song is the most interesting of them all. _____

B. Writing Application: Form the comparative or superlative by adding *more* or *most* to the positive form of the adjective or adverb in italics in each sentence below. Then add your own words to complete the sentence. Write the new sentence on the line provided.

1. Noah skated *gracefully*. (superlative)

   Noah skated most gracefully of all the hockey players.
   _____

2. Limericks can be *ridiculous*. (superlative)

   _____

   _____

3. Cats are *independent*. (comparative)

   _____

   _____

4. Sports are *exciting*. (superlative)

   _____

"The Sidewalk Racer" by Lillian Morrison (text page 724)
"Concrete Cat" by Dorthi Charles (text page 725)
Two Haiku by Matsu Bashō and Mus-Soseki (text page 726)
Two Limericks Anonymous (text page 727)

Reading Strategy: Use Your Senses

You will experience a poem more fully if you **use your senses** when you read it. The first sense you use when you read a poem is your sense of *sight*, as you look at the way the words are arranged on the page. As you continue to read, you can use all your senses to almost *see, hear, touch, smell,* and *taste* the images the poem describes. Look for words that appeal to your five senses. The passages below are examples of how words in poems can appeal to your senses:

Sight: "an asphalt sea" ("The Sidewalk Racer")
Hearing: "winds howl in a rage" ("Haiku" by Soseki)

Then use your senses to *experience* the poem rather than simply read the words.

A. DIRECTIONS: Use the chart below to help you **use your senses** as you read the poems. The limerick line "A fly and a flea in a flue" has been charted as an example.

Sight	Hearing	Smell	Touch	Taste
darkness bricks covered with soot	sound of fly buzzing	the smell of soot	hardness of brick	

B. DIRECTIONS: Match the poems, numbered on the left, with one of the senses you might use to experience them, lettered on the right.

_____ 1. "Haiku" by Bashō

_____ 2. "A flea and a fly " limerick

_____ 3. "Concrete Cat"

_____ 4. "The Sidewalk Racer"

_____ 5. "Haiku" by Soseki

_____ 6. "There was a young fellow—" limerick

a. taste of an icicle hanging from a snow covered tree

b. hearing the sound of wheels on concrete

c. smell of cat food in cat's dish

d. sight of a man as he stumbles and falls

e. hearing the splash of water

f. feeling the closeness of being inside a chimney

"The Sidewalk Racer" by Lillian Morrison (text page 724)
"Concrete Cat" by Dorthi Charles (text page 725)
Two Haiku by Matsu Bashō and Mus-Soseki (text page 726)
Two Limericks Anonymous (text page 727)

Literary Focus: Special Forms of Poetry

Poets sometimes use **special forms** of poetry that put words into action in specific, and sometimes new and inventive ways. Here are three examples of special forms of poetry:

Concrete poems: Words are arranged in a shape on paper to reflect the subject of the poem.

Haiku: This unrhymed and deeply expressive Japanese form of poetry has only three lines, with a pattern of five syllables in the first line, seven in the second, and five in the third.

Limerick: In this short, humorous form of poetry, the first, second, and fifth lines rhyme, as do the third and fourth lines. The lines that rhyme have the same rhythm. Limericks are named for the county of Limerick in Ireland.

A. DIRECTIONS: Answer the question about each form of poetry below by circling the letter of the most important fact about that poem's special form.

1. Why is the concrete form important to "The Sidewalk Racer?"
   a. The skateboard shape of the poem catches the reader's eye and intensifies interest in the poem's subject.
   b. Skateboards are used on concrete.
   c. The concrete form is a unique way to write poetry.

2. Why is the concrete form important to "Concrete Cat?"
   a. The words are still, like concrete.
   b. The arrangement of the words completely changes their meaning.
   c. The arrangement of words creates a picture and adds to the subject's liveliness and humor.

3. Why is the haiku form important for the two poems by Basho and Soseki?
   a. The haiku form uses five, seven, and five syllables in its three lines.
   b. The form's few words create deeply expressive images.
   c. Haiku is a Japanese verse form.

4. Why is the special form of the two limericks important to these two poems?
   a. In order to be funny, a poem has to have rhyming lines.
   b. The rhythm and rhyme of the words add to the silliness and fun of the poem's subjects.
   c. Language serves many purposes in limericks.

B. DIRECTIONS: Decide whether the statements below about special forms of poetry are true or false. In the line following each statement write **T** if the statement is true and **F** if it is false.

1. In a concrete poem, words are arranged so that the lines rhyme. _____

2. A haiku poem has three lines and does not have to rhyme. _____

3. Limericks are often sad or serious. _____

4. A concrete poem uses words arranged in a special shape that reflects the subject of the poem. _____

5. Haiku is a form of Irish verse. _____

6. The limerick form uses a specific pattern of rhythm and rhyme. _____

"Parade" by Rachel Field (text page 738)
"Cynthia in the Snow" by Gwendolyn Brooks (text page 739)

Build Vocabulary

Using the Suffix -*ly*

The suffix -*ly* is an ending for many adverbs, words that describe verbs, adjectives, and other adverbs by answering the questions *when*, *how*, or *in what way*. In many cases, when added to an adjective, the suffix -*ly* turns the adjective into an adverb.

Examples:

Adjectives	*bright*	*tender*	*foolish*	*sad*
Adverbs	*brightly*	*tenderly*	*foolishly*	*sadly*

A. Directions: Change each adjective in the following list to an adverb by adding the suffix -*ly*. Then fill in the blank in each sentence below with the adverb that best completes the following sentence.

slow   brisk   handsome   wild   loudly

1. The horses trotted _____ and soon passed the lumbering elephants.

2. Their riders were dressed _____ in red or blue costumes.

3. The crowd cheered _____ as the parade went by.

4. Several camels at the end of the parade strolled _____ by us.

5. The parade master had to shout _____ above the noise of the crowds.

Using the Word Bank

gilded	leisurely	gild	leisure

B. Directions: Use your understanding of the Word Bank words to complete this exercise. Circle the letter of the choice that best completes each sentence.

1. A person with *leisure* is probably one who
   a. has a lot of free time
   b. must work hard
   c. is always hurrying
   d. never has enough money

2. An object that is *gilded*
   a. sparkles like diamonds
   b. has a golden appearance
   c. is dull and dark
   d. is painted white in color

3. A person who walks at a *leisurely* pace on a spring day
   a. has no time to slow down
   b. moves at a fast pace
   c. moves in an unhurried way
   d. moves almost as quickly as a jogger

4. To *gild* an object, you would use this metal:
   a. platinum
   b. copper
   c. bronze
   d. gold

Name _____ Date _____

Build Spelling Skills: *ei* and *ie*

Spelling Strategy Remember these rules to spell words with the letter combination *i* and *e*.

- The letter *i* usually goes first when *i* and *e* come together.

    Examples: n<u>ie</u>ce, p<u>ie</u>ce, retr<u>ie</u>ve, ch<u>ie</u>f

- Write *e* before *i* if the letter combination comes after *c*

    Examples: re<u>ce</u>ive, <u>ce</u>iling,

- Write *e* before *i* when the letter combination spells the long *a* sound

    Examples: n<u>ei</u>ghbor w<u>ei</u>gh

- **Exceptions:** Certain words do not follow the above rules:

    Examples: h<u>ei</u>ght, n<u>ei</u>ther, s<u>ei</u>ze, w<u>ei</u>rd, l<u>ei</u>surely

A. Practice: The following words are missing the letters *i* and *e*. Write the words, with the missing letters in the correct order, in the blanks next to their definitions below.

l___ ___surely   h___ ___ght   c___ ___ling   w___ ___rd   p___ ___ce   retr___ ___ve

1. overhead surface of a room _____

2. strange _____

3. part of a whole _____

4. in an unhurried way _____

5. to bring back _____

6. measurement from bottom to top _____

B. Practice: The following words are missing the letters *i* and *e*. Write the words, with the missing letters in the correct order in the blanks; then complete the sentences below.

n___ ___ther   w___ ___gh   n___ ___ce   rec___ ___ve   s___ ___ze

Example: (to make a hole with a sharp object) Dan used a sharp stick to <u>pierce</u> holes in the baking potatoes.

1. (female child of a person's brother or sister) I wonder if the Cynthia of the poem is the writer's daughter or _____ .

2. (not one or the other) Maybe the child in the poem is _____ one of these.

3. (get) The amazing floats in the parade would probably _____ a lot of applause.

4. (grab) The clashing cymbals would certainly _____ people's attention.

5. (be heavy as) I can only imagine what one of those elephants might _____ .

"Parade" by Rachel Field (text page 738)
"Cynthia in the Snow" by Gwendolyn Brooks (text page 739)

Build Grammar Skills: Double Negatives

Negatives are words such as *never, no, nobody, none, not, nowhere, barely, scarcely.* Contractions ending in the letters *n't,* meaning *not,* such as *couldn't, isn't,* and *don't,* are also negative words. Using a **double negative**, or two negative words together, is incorrect. Look at the examples below:

Incorrect: The poet <u>doesn't</u> <u>never</u> tell us who Cynthia is.

Correct: The poet <u>doesn't</u> <u>ever</u> tell us who Cynthia is.

The poet <u>never</u> tells us who Cynthia is.

The poet <u>doesn't</u> tell us who Cynthia is.

A. Practice: Rewrite each of the following sentences so that it contains only one negative.

1. It doesn't never snow in this part of the country until November.

_____

2. Nobody hasn't seen a snowfall this early in the year before.

_____

3. There is never no point in guessing the weather too far in advance.

_____

4. My little sister could scarcely not stop playing in the snowdrifts.

_____

5. Didn't you never see the advertisements this week?

_____

6. The parade isn't not starting until ten o' clock.

_____

B. Writing Application: On the lines provided, write five sentences about an exciting event you wish you had seen—but didn't! Use the negative provided. Be sure to avoid double negatives.

Example: *not:* I could not leave my house, even though there was a fun street fair. _____

1. nothing: _____

2. never: _____

3. hardly: _____

4. wasn't: _____

5. nowhere: _____

"Parade" by Rachel Field (text page 738)
"Cynthia in the Snow" by Gwendolyn Brooks (text page 739)

Reading Strategy: Read According to Punctuation

Sometimes, when people read poetry aloud, they stop or pause at the end of every line. This makes the poem difficult for listeners to understand. Poetry makes more sense and is more enjoyable to listen to if the reader avoids these pauses, pausing instead at punctuation marks only, as if he or she were reading a prose passage. For example, try reading the following lines from the poem, "Parade," in two different ways. First pause at the end of each line. Then read the lines again, with no pause after lines 1, 3, or 4, and only a slight pause after the comma following "drums" at the end of line 2.

Line 1: This is the day the circus comes

Line 2: With blare of brass, with beating drums,

Line 3: And clashing cymbals, and with roar of wild beasts never heard before

Line 4: Within town limits.

Even when you read poetry silently to yourself, it will make better sense and sound better if you follow these rules:

- **Slight pause** after a comma

- **Longer pause** after a colon, semicolon, or dash

- **Stop longest** for end marks such as periods, question marks, or exclamation points

- **Don't stop** at all at the ends of lines where there is no punctuation.

A. DIRECTIONS: Below is the poem, "Cynthia in the Snow." At the end of each line, write SP for *slight pause*, SL for *stop longest*, or DS *for don't stop*.

It SUSHES, _____

It hushes _____

The loudness in the road. _____

It flitter-twitters, _____

5 And laughs away from me. _____

It laughs a lovely whiteness, _____

And whitely whirs away, _____

To be _____

Some otherwhere, _____

10 Still white as milk or shirts. _____

So beautiful it hurts.

B. DIRECTIONS: Explain briefly why you should not pause between lines 8 and 9 ("To be" and "Some otherwhere"). Tell why a good reader would not pause at this point.

_____

_____

Unit 9: Poetry

Literary Focus: Sound Devices

Onomatopoeia (ah nuh mah tuh PEE uh) and alliteration are two **sound devices** used in poetry and other types of writing. **Onomatopoeia** is a way of using words to imitate sounds.

Examples from "Parade":   clashing   roar

Examples from "Cynthia in the Snow":   sushes   hushes

Notice that *sushes* is a word made up by the poet to imitate the sound of falling snow.
Alliteration is a way of giving words a musical sound by repeating sounds at the beginnings of words.

Example from "Parade":   blare of brass

Examples from "Cynthia in the Snow":   laughs a lovely whiteness whitely whirs

A. DIRECTIONS: Underline the examples of onomatopoeia and alliteration in the following sentences. On the line following each sentence, write O for onomatopoeia or A for alliteration. (For the one sentence that uses both, write both O and A on the line.) The first sentence has been done for you.

1. The big, brown bear stood on its hind legs. __A__

2. The sound of bells jingling in the distance let us know the parade was approaching. _____

3. The drip, drip, drip of the rain on the roof finally put me to sleep. _____

4. His long, graceful fingers made the piano keys tinkle. _____

5. I was startled when the car behind me honked loudly. _____

6. As she rode, her long, lovely hair streamed out behind her. _____

B. DIRECTIONS: Find one example of onomatopoeia and one example of alliteration in the following lines. Write the examples on the lines below.

When our cat had her first litter, the kittens were so tiny, you could hold them in the palm of your hand. But as tiny as they were, when their mother licked them to give them a bath, their purring sounded like a motor boat. As the kittens grew older, they became more playful. They looked like little balls of fluff chasing each other around in circles and pouncing on one another. I loved watching our funny, fluffy kittens as they grew.

1. Example of onomatopoeia: _____

2. Example of alliteration: _____

"Simile: Willow and Ginkgo" by Eve Merriam (text page 744)
"Fame Is a Bee" by Emily Dickinson (text page 745)
"April Rain Song" by Langston Hughes (text page 746)

Build Vocabulary

Using Musical Words

As in other fields, music has its own special words and terms. Read the following examples of **musical words**:

soprano: high in pitch   The *soprano* voices are the highest.

chorus: a large group of people singing together; a piece of music sung by a *chorus*

I hope I will be chosen to sing in the school *chorus*.

orchestra: a large group of musicians who play together

Our school *orchestra* gave a concert.

crescendo: a gradual increase in loudness in a musical composition

The symphony ended in an exciting *crescendo*.

fanfare: a short, loud piece of music, usually played by trumpets to introduce an important person or event

The trumpets announced the entrance of the queen with a loud *fanfare*.

Some musical are to describe things that are not musical. For example, notice how the italicized musical words are used in the following sentences:

When mom asked if we wanted popcorn, we answered 'Yes!' in *chorus*.

Everyone turned around as my brothers' argument came to a *crescendo*.

A. DIRECTIONS: Complete each sentence below, using one of the words above.

1. The band greeted the winning team with a loud _____ .

2. I heard the high _____ voice of the child calling her mother.

3. The music rose to a _____, then became very quiet and peaceful.

4. Before the concert, the audience sang the national anthem along with the _____ .

5. There were so many birds singing in the tree, they sounded like an _____ .

Using the Word Bank

soprano	chorus

B. DIRECTIONS: Circle the letter of the pair of words that expresses a relationship most similar to that expressed by the pair in CAPITAL LETTERS.

1. SOPRANO: HIGHEST :: a. bass: lowest   b. tenor: mellow   c. voice: opera

2. CHORUS: MANY :: a. song: group   b. solo: one   c. refrain: singers

Unit 9: Poetry

"Simile: Willow and Ginkgo" by Eve Merriam (text page 744)
"Fame Is a Bee" by Emily Dickinson (text page 745)
"April Rain Song" by Langston Hughes (text page 746)

Build Spelling Skills: Forming the Plural of Words that End in *o*

Words that end in an *o* preceded by a consonant usually form the plural by adding *s*. Most musical words that end in *o* follow this rule. For example, the plural of *alto* is *altos*. The plural of *soprano* is *sopranos*. All of the following words form the plural by adding *s*: *pistachios, photos, radios, portfolios, pianos, solos, videos, zeros.*

Exceptions: Some words that end in *o* preceded by a consonant form the plural by adding *es*. For instance, the plural of *tomato* is *tomatoes*. Other exceptions include *potatoes, echoes,* and *heroes.*

A. Practice: The words in parentheses following each of the sentences below end in *o*. For each sentence, change the word in parentheses to its plural form.

1. We took _____ of all the relatives at the family reunion. (photo)

2. We could hear the _____ of our voices in the canyon. (echo)

3. The _____ were tuned to different stations. (radio)

4. We kept eating _____ until all that was left was a pile of shells. (pistachio)

5. The two students who helped the firefighters were treated like _____ . (hero)

B. Practice: Proofread the paragraph below. Watch for misspelled plurals of words that end in *o*. Cross out each incorrectly spelled word and write the correctly spelled word above it.

Everyone was eager to hear which team would win the game. Radioes were turned on in

every home. Some people watched on TV and recorded vidoes for friends who couldn't be home

to watch. When the game was over, the players on the winning team were cheered like heroes.

It still seems that I can hear the echoes of the cheering crowds. Newspaper photographers took

photoes of the star players.

"Simile: Willow and Ginkgo" by Eve Merriam (text page 744)
"Fame Is a Bee" by Emily Dickinson (text page 745)
"April Rain Song" by Langston Hughes (text page 746)

Build Grammar Skills: Correct Use of *Its* and *It's*

Its is the possessive form of the pronoun *it*. For example, "As the cake was baking, *its* aroma was heavenly." The word *it's*, however, is a contraction of *it is* or *it has*. In the sentence, "**It's** my favorite flavor," *it's* means "it is." In the sentence, "**It's** been a long time since we talked," the word *it's* means "it has."

See how *its* and *it's* are used differently in the sentences below.

Possessive: We looked at the tree and saw <u>its</u> graceful leaves and branches.

I love to watch the rain and listen to <u>its</u> sound.

Contraction for *it is*: <u>It's</u> interesting that fame can make people happy or unhappy.

<u>It's</u> nice to listen to the sound of the rain.

Contraction for *it has*: <u>It's</u> been raining all night.
<u>It's</u> never rained so hard before.

A. Practice: In each sentence below, identify the italicized word as the possessive form of *it*, or as a contraction of *it is* or *it has*. Write **P** for possessive or **C** for contraction in the space provided.

1. Fame has *its* sting. _____

2. *It's* raining outside. _____

3. The bee buzzed over the flowers, *its* wings whirring. _____

4. I never know where *it's* going to land. _____

5. The insect never made *its* intentions known. _____

6. The tree rustled and *its* branches bent in the breeze. _____

7. *It's* been a nice, long walk. _____

8. The jar was missing *its* lid. _____

9. When *it's* time to go, don't forget your hat. _____

10. *It's* the red hat with blue trim. _____

B. Writing Application: In the paragraph below, chose either its or it's to correctly complete the sentences. Write the correct word in the space provided.

(It's/Its) _____ interesting to compare other kinds of trees. Think about a maple tree. (Its/It's) _____ leaves turn bright shades of red and orange when (it's/its) _____ Fall. (It's Its) _____ branches look rather forlorn once all the leaves have fallen from them. A fir tree, on the other hand, never loses (its/it's) _____ leaves. (Its/It's) _____ called an evergreen, because it stays green, even in Winter. (It's/Its) _____ leaves, called needles, smell wonderful.

"Simile: Willow and Ginkgo" by Eve Merriam (text page 744)
"Fame Is a Bee" by Emily Dickinson (text page 745)
"April Rain Song" by Langston Hughes (text page 746)

Reading Strategy: Respond

Did you ever stop to think that, when you read, you sometimes have a conversation with the author in your mind? As you read a particular passage, you might think to yourself, "I know just what you mean. I've felt the same way," or "I remember when the same thing happened to me." On the other hand, you might be thinking, "I totally disagree." In poetry, especially, an important part of appreciating what you read is reacting or **responding** personally to what the poet has to say.

DIRECTIONS: To help you think of ways to **respond** to the poems in the selection, fill in the leaves on the branch below. On the leaves, write answers to the questions as you read the poems.

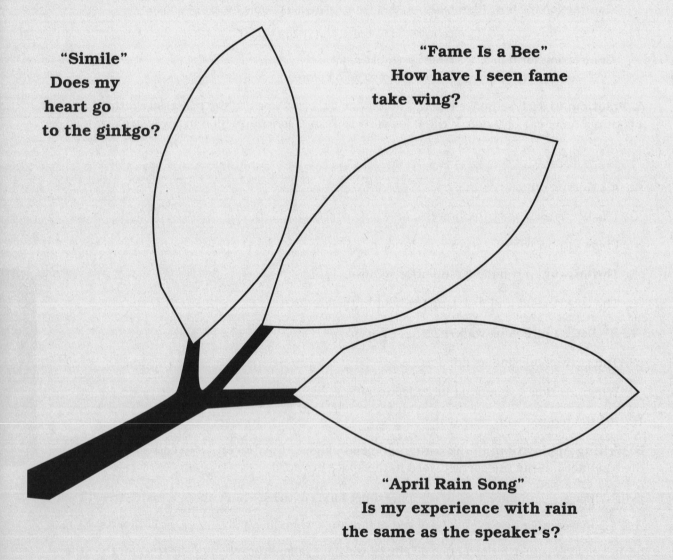

"Simile"
Does my
heart go
to the ginkgo?

"Fame Is a Bee"
How have I seen fame
take wing?

"April Rain Song"
Is my experience with rain
the same as the speaker's?

"**Simile: Willow and Ginkgo**" by Eve Merriam (text page 744)
"**Fame Is a Bee**" by Emily Dickinson (text page 745)
"**April Rain Song**" by Langston Hughes (text page 746)

Literary Focus: Figurative Language

Poems often express thoughts and feelings by using **figurative language**. The use of *simile, metaphor and personification* help you to see and feel things in a new way. Figurative language can also make complicated subjects and emotions easier to understand or imagine.

- **Simile** uses the words *like* or as to compare two things that, at first, do not seem alike. "The willow is **like** a nymph with streaming hair."

- **Metaphor** directly compares seemingly unlike things by describing one as if it were the other, without using the words *like* or *as*. "Fame **is** a bee."

- **Personification** gives human qualities to non-human things. "Let the rain **sing** you a lullaby."

A. DIRECTIONS: Circle the letter of the sentence that correctly answers each question below.

1. Which of the following sentences contains a simile?

   a. The willow branches embraced me.

   b. The poem was a ripe apple.

   c. Anna was as frisky as a colt.

2. Which of the following sentences contains an example of metaphor?

   a. The rain was as soft as silken threads.

   b. The halfback was a charging bull.

   c. The wind wrestled with the trees.

3. Which of the following sentences contains an example of personification?

   a. The sun embraced the sea.

   b. She uses words as a sculptor uses clay.

   c. Her greeting was a bouquet of wildflowers.

B. DIRECTIONS: In the following paragraph, identify the figurative language. Circle each example of figurative language and decide whether it is simile, metaphor or personification. Write **S** for simile, **M** for metaphor and **P** for personification above the circled word or words. The first use of figurative language has been identified for you as an example.

P
It began to drizzle as we walked home. The rain (tapped me on the shoulder.) Gentle raindrops fell like flower petals upon our heads and shoulders. The soft downfall was a surprising gift. We had been working like machines, trying to finish our homework, and now, the little shower was a kindly messenger telling us to forget our worries and cares.

"Exclamation" by Octavio Paz (text page 751)
"Wind and Water and Stone" by Octavio Paz (text page 752)

Build Vocabulary

A. DIRECTIONS: Use each word in the box twice in the following crossword puzzle.

dispersed sculpted murmurs

Across:

2. carved out of wood or stone

4. scattered

5. whispers

Down:

1. carved out of wood or stone

3. scattered

5. whispers

B. DIRECTIONS: Complete each sentence below by writing the correct word from the box in the blank space.

1. The artist _____ a beautiful statue out of marble.

2. The crowd _____ when the meeting was over.

3. The audience was quiet, except for a few low _____ .

Recognizing Synonyms

C. DIRECTIONS: Circle the letter of the word that is closest in meaning to the word in CAPITAL LETTERS.

1. SCULPTED

   a. carved

   b. caved in

   c. crooked

   d. hard

2. MURMURS

   a. gurgles

   b. giggles

   c. whispers

   d. hums

3. DISPERSED

   a. kept quiet

   b. scattered

   c. disappeared

   d. stuck together

Name _____ Date _____

"Exclamation" by Octavio Paz (text page 751)
"Wind and Water and Stone" by Octavio Paz (text page 752)

Connecting a Poem to Social Studies

The poem "Wind and Water and Stone" builds on details from the widely varied geography of Mexico. Mexico is divided, geographically, into six land regions. They are the **Pacific Northwest**, which consists mostly or rolling or mountainous desert; the **Plateau of Mexico**, which is Mexico's most varied region, ranging from flat to mountainous; the **Gulf Coastal Plain**, which is largely covered by tangled forests of low, thorny bushes and trees to the north, and rain forest to the south; the **Southern Uplands**, which sonsist largely of steep riedges and eep gorges cut by mountain streams; the **Chiapas Highlands**, which have great blocklike mountains; and the **Yucatan Peninsula**, a low plateau covered, to the south, by tropical rain forests.

DIRECTIONS: Look in an atlas for maps of Mexico and the Pacific Northwest that show climate conditions. Use the maps to answer the following quesitons.

1. Which land region of Mexico receives more rain, the Yucatan Peninsula or the Plateau of

   Mexico? _____

2. Which land region of Mexico is almost completely dry? _____

3. What is the average rainfall in inches in most of the Pacific Northwest? _____

   _____

4. Would you call the climate in the Chiapas Highlands moist or dry? _____

5. What is the average rainfall in inches on the Yucatan Peninsula? _____

"The Kitten at Play" by William Wordsworth (text page 756)
"Child on Top of a Greenhouse" by Theodore Roethke (text page 757)
"The Shark" by John Ciardi (text page 758)
Two Riddles by Ian Serraillier and Mary Austin (text page 759)

Build Vocabulary

Using the Word Ending -est

When you add the word ending -est to a descriptive word, you show that it is the *most* of what that word describes. For example, when you add -est to the adjective *tall*, you get the word *tallest*, which means "the most tall."

A. DIRECTIONS: Form new words by adding -est to the word in italics.

1. the most *small* _____smallest_____   5. the most *soft* _____

2. the most *smart* _____   6. the most *dark* _____

3. the most *hard* _____   7. the most *long* _____

4. the most *slow* _____   8. the most *narrow* _____

Using the Word Bank

withered	prey	feats	devours	swiftest

B. DIRECTIONS: For each of the following definitions, write the correct Word Bank word in the spaces provided. Then write the letters in the *circled* spaces on the line below, and you will find a word that describes many kittens.

1. remarkable deeds   __ __ __ __(__)

2. dried up   (__) __ __ __ __ __ __ __

3. eats whole   __ (__) __ __ __ __ __ __

4. animals hunted by other animals   __ __(__)__

5. the most rapid   __ __ __ __(__)__ __ __

A word that describes kittens: __ __ __ __ __

Sentence Completions

C. DIRECTIONS: Complete each of the sentences below with a word from the Word Bank.

1. When our dog gets her dinner, she _____ it in a few seconds.

2. The _____ runner usually wins a race.

3. The plants looked _____ because no one had watered them for a week.

4. Many spiders spin webs to trap their _____ .

"The Kitten at Play" by William Wordsworth (text page 756)
"Child on Top of a Greenhouse" by Theodore Roethke (text page 757)
"The Shark" by John Ciardi (text page 758)
Two Riddles by Ian Serraillier and Mary Austin (text page 759)

Build Spelling Skills: Spelling the *ay* Sound as *ey*

Spelling Strategy Sometimes the *ay* sound is spelled *ey*, as in *prey*. However, in many words, the *ay* sound is spelled *ay*, as in *tray*. If you are not sure of the spelling of a word that uses the *ay* sound, look it up in a dictionary.

A. Practice: Each of the sentences below has a word that uses the *ay* sound, but the letters that spell the sound have been left out. In the space after each sentence, write the word with the correct letters filled in. If you are not sure of the correct spelling of any word, look it up in a dictionary. The first one has been done as an example.

1. A good driver must ob__ the law. _____obey_____

2. The class went outside to pl__ during recess. _____

3. Little Miss Muffet sat on a tuffet, eating her curds and wh__ . _____

4. If you drop a carton full of eggs, th__ will probably break. _____

5. She likes to make little statues out of modeling cl__ . _____

6. Gr__hounds are among the fastest of all dogs. _____

B. Practice: In each of the following sentences, if the word in italics is misspelled, write the correct spelling of the word in the space provided. If the italicized word is spelled correctly, leave the space blank.

1. Sharks are *alweys* hungry and will eat almost anything. _____

2. Kittens are usually very *playful.* _____

3. The child on top of the greenhouse must have *disobayed* a rule not to climb so high.
_____

4. "*Hay!*" the adults shouted to the boy on top of the greenhouse, "how did you get up there?"
_____

Challenge: The word *greenhouse*, used in the title of a Theodore Roethki's poem, is a compound word that is made up of *green* and *house*. Below are other compound words that use the word *house*. Write each word next to its definition.

housefly   playhouse   powerhouse   lighthouse

1. _____ a tall, round building with a powerful lamp at the top to help steer
ships away from rocks

2. _____ a small insect that is often found indoors

3. _____ a building in which machinery for making electricity is kept

4. _____ a building that is used for presentation of theater pieces

"**The Kitten at Play**" by William Wordsworth (text page 756)
"**Child on Top of a Greenhouse**" by Theodore Roethke (text page 757)
"**The Shark**" by John Ciardi (text page 758)
Two Riddles by Ian Serraillier and Mary Austin (text page 759)

Build Grammar Skills: Correct Use of *Good* and *Well*

Good is an adjective, which modifies a noun. *Well* is usually an adverb that modifies a verb. It answers the question, *how*?

Examples:

Sharks are *good* swimmers. (*Good* modifies "swimmers.")

He's quiet—that speaks *well* of him. (*Well* modifies "speaks" and answers the question, "*How* does it speak of him?")

A. Practice: Complete each of the following sentences correctly by writing either *good* or *well* in the blank provided.

1. My cousin is a _____ cook.

2. She cooks _____ .

3. He made us a _____ dinner.

4. I don't feel very _____ .

5. You did very _____ on your test.

6. The picture looks _____ on that wall.

7. My parents play the piano very _____ .

8. It would be a _____ idea to get plenty of sleep tonight.

9. He played the game very _____ .

10. You look _____ in that color.

B. Writing Application: Complete each of the following sentences using *good* or *well* where appropriate.

1. Bats are _____ fliers, even though they cannot see _____ .

2. He spoke _____ when he gave his report, but his writing was not _____ .

3. The author started with a _____ subject and wrote a _____ book about it.

4. He spoke _____ of you and said that you were a _____ student.

5. I was afraid that our show would not be very _____ , but it turned out _____ .

6. She is a very _____ dancer and sings _____ , too.

7. "_____ done," she said, "you did a _____ job!"

8. It's a _____ thing that I had your help, or the report would not have been _____ .

"The Kitten at Play" by William Wordsworth (text page 756)
"Child on Top of a Greenhouse" by Theodore Roethke (text page 757)
"The Shark" by John Ciardi (text page 758)
Two Riddles by Ian Serraillier and Mary Austin (text page 759)

Reading Strategy: Paraphrase

When you **paraphrase** a piece of writing, you restate it in your own words, keeping the meaning but not the style of what the author wrote. You may find paraphrasing especially helpful when you read poetry, because the language and images in poems can sometimes make the author's meaning hard to understand. When you find such a passage, write a paraphrase of it, using clear language to summarize the sense of the poet's words. Reread the poem, keeping your paraphrase in mind, and you are likely to find the poem easier to follow. A chart such as the one below can be useful when you paraphrase.

DIRECTIONS: In the left column of the following chart are some passages from the poems in this grouping. For each passage, write a paraphrase in the right column. The first one has been done as an example.

Poem	Paraphrase
1. See the kitten on the wall, Sporting with the leaves that fall.	Look at the kitten as it sits on top of the wall and plays with the falling leaves.
2. The half-grown chrysanthemums staring up like accusers / Up through the streaked glass, flashing with sunlight	
3. Yes, his manners are drab. But his thought is drabber. / That one dark thought he can never complete / Of something—anything—somehow to eat.	
4. I come more softly than a bird / And lovely as a flower	

Unit 9: Poetry

"The Kitten at Play" by William Wordsworth (text page 756)
"Child on Top of a Greenhouse" by Theodore Roethke (text page 757)
"The Shark" by John Ciardi (text page 758)
Two Riddles by Ian Serraillier and Mary Austin (text page 759)

Literary Focus: Poetic Image

A **poetic image** is a picture you have in your mind, created by the words that a poet writes. In order to create that picture, the poet carefully chooses words that help you see, in your imagination, what she or he is describing. In the example below, from "The Kitten at Play," the poet helps you see the playful movements of the kitten with the following words:

Crouches, stretches, paws and darts

To create a more complete image, poets often use words that help you do more than see—they help you hear, smell, taste, and touch as well. In other words, a poetic image can appeal to any or all of your five senses. For example, in the lines below, from "Child on Top of a Greenhouse," the poet appeals to several of your senses in order to create an image:

The wind billowing out the seat of my britches,

My feet crackling splinters of glass and dried putty

The half-grown chrysanthemums staring up like accusers

The following chart helps you see which of the poet's words appeal to which of your senses:

Sight   chrysanthemums staring up like accusers

Touch   wind billowing, splinters of glass and dried putty

Sound   wind, crackling

DIRECTIONS: Fill in the following chart with images from the poems in the selection. Not every box will be filled in.

Sight	Sound	Touch
"The Kitten at Play"		
"Child on Top of a Greenhouse"		
"Shark"		
Riddles		

"The Emperor's New Clothes" by Hans Christian Andersen (text page 775)

Build Vocabulary

Using the Suffix *-ful*

The suffix *-ful* indicates that something is "full of" or characterized by the word to which the suffix is added. For example the word *dreadful*, which appears in the Word Bank, means "characterized by dread, or extreme fear." The word *joyful* means "full of joy." The word *dutiful* means "characterized by duty."

A. DIRECTIONS: Complete each sentence by adding the suffix *-ful* to each word in parentheses.

1. The town where the emperor lived was a lively and (cheer) _____ place.

2. Two rascals offered to weave some (delight) _____ and (color) _____ fabric.

3. The king asked two of his most (faith) _____ and (duty) _____ ministers to check on the weavers' progress.

4. Each man was unable to face the (fright) _____ possibility that he was either stupid or unworthy because he was unable to see the cloth.

5. Neither one was being (truth) _____ when he told the king that the cloth was splendid and (beauty) _____.

Using the Word Bank

exquisite	property	dreadful	rogues	becoming

B. DIRECTIONS: Choose the word from the Word Bank that answers each question below. Write your answers on the lines.

1. Which two words might appear in an ad for an elegant and expensive dress?
   _____

2. Which word is close in meaning to the word *characteristic*? _____

3. Which word might you use to refer to characters who are scoundrels or rascals?
   _____

4. Which word might you use to describe a terrible mistake? _____

Analogies

C. DIRECTIONS: Circle the letter of the pair of words that expresses a relationship similar to that expressed by the words in CAPITAL LETTERS.

____ 1. BECOMING : ATTRACTIVE ::
    a. dreadful : terrible
    b. large : elephant
    c. exquisite : ugly
    d. tired : refreshed

____ 2. ROGUES : HEROES ::
    a. racers : jumpers
    b. writers : authors
    c. destroyers: builders
    d. teachers : principals

Name _____ Date _____

"The Emperor's New Clothes" by Hans Christian Andersen (text page 775)

Build Spelling Skills: Spelling the z Sound With an s

Spelling Strategy The z sound is sometimes spelled with an s, as it is in the Word Bank word *exquisite*. Following are some more words in which the z sound is spelled in this way. Pronounce each one to yourself.

revise   reside   president   advertisement   opposition

A. Practice Finish the incomplete words in each of the following sentences. Each word will contain an s pronounced as z.

1. When you oversee someone's work, you sup_____ it.

2. Television commercials, billboards, and movie posters are all types of ad_____.

3. A person who lives in a town is a re_____ of that town.

4. If you are not absent, then you must be pre_____.

5. Someone who swims, bicycles, and jogs gets plenty of ex_____.

6. The Sahara is a de_____.

B. Practice: Choose the correctly spelled word to complete each sentence. Write the words on the lines provided. *Hint:* The z sound is spelled with an s in some but not all the words.

1. The emperor's greatest (dezire, desire) _____ was to have beautiful clothes.

2. The rogues promised to make him an (exquisite, exquizite) _____ new outfit.

3. Two of the king's (advisors, advizors) _____ went to see the weavers at work.

4. Although they (realized, realised) _____ that the looms were empty, they were afraid to tell the king.

5. Only one person (recognized, recognised) _____ the truth and did not (hezitate, hesitate) _____ to speak up.

"The Emperor's New Clothes" by Hans Christian Andersen (text page 775)

Build Grammar Skills: Commas in Compound Sentences

A compound sentence consists of two simple sentences joined by one of these coordinating conjunctions: *and, but, for, nor, or, so,* and *yet.* The two parts of a compound sentence are separated by a comma. Look at the following examples. Notice that the comma comes just before the conjunction.

> The emperor could not meet with his ministers, **for** he was in his dressing room.
> The weavers were greedy, **so** they asked for more money and more silk.

A. Practice: Combine each pair of simple sentences to form a compound sentence. Use the coordinating conjunction indicated in parentheses. Write the new sentence on the line, putting a comma where needed.

1. The emperor was vain. He loved showing himself off in new clothes. (and)

   _____

2. The two men who came to the palace were lazy rascals. They said that they were famous weavers. (but)

   _____

3. The emperor believed the swindlers. He paid them a handsome amount of money for a new set of clothes. (so)

   _____

4. The prime minister did not tell the king that there was nothing on the loom. He did not want the king to think that he was stupid or unfit. (for)

   _____

   _____

5. The courtiers had to say the new clothes were magnificent. They would be considered stupid or unfit for their posts. (or)

   _____

6. It seemed that everyone was afraid. One person managed to speak up. (yet)

   _____

B. Writing Application: Write a compound sentence about each topic provided below, using coordinating conjunctions as suggested. Be sure to use commas correctly in your sentences.

1. Write a sentence in which you state your name and hometown. Use the conjunction *and.*

   _____

2. Write a sentence about one of your likes and one of your dislikes. Use the conjunction *but.*

   _____

3. Write a sentence about what you might do with your family or friends this weekend. Use the conjunction *or.*

   _____

Unit 10: The Oral Tradition

Reading for Success: Strategies for Reading Folk Literature

Folk Literature is older than recorded history: Its tales, stories, legends, and myths have been passed down for many generations. Because these stories were often told orally, they often contain repetition (making them easier to remember) and dialect (specialized vocabulary and grammar of the region).

- **Understand the cultural background.** You will better understand the actions and characters of a story if you know the culture from which it comes.

- **Recognize the storyteller's purpose.** Remember that these tales are traditional stories that people used to communicate shared beliefs and to explain their world. Try to identify the original storyteller's audience.

- **Predict. Folk literature is predictable.** Good characters and deeds are rewarded; bad characters are either banished or reformed This pattern makes it easy for you to predict the instructional message.

DIRECTIONS: Read the following passage from "The Wise Old Woman," retold by Yoshiko Uchida, and use the reading strategies to increase your comprehension. In the margin, note where you understand the cultural background, recognize the storyteller's purpose, and predict. Finally, write a response to the passage on the lines provided.

from **"The Wise Old Woman"** retold by Yoshiko Uchida

The following passage is the beginning of a folk tale from Japan,
where the elderly are respected for their wisdom and experience.

Many long years ago, there lived an arrogant and cruel young lord who ruled over a small village in the western hills of Japan.

"I have no use for old people in my village," he said haughtily. "They are neither useful nor able to work for a living. I therefore decree that anyone over seventy-one must be banished from the village and left in the mountains to die."

"What a dreadful decree! What a cruel and unreasonable lord we have," the people of the village murmured. But the lord fearfully punished anyone who disobeyed him, and so villagers who turned seventy-one were tearfully carried into the mountains, never to return.

Gradually there were fewer and fewer old people in the village and soon they disappeared altogether. Then the young lord was pleased.

"What a fine village of young, healthy and hard-working people I have," he bragged. "Soon it will be the finest village in all of Japan."

Now there lived in this village a kind young farmer and his aged mother. They were poor, but the farmer was good to his mother, and the two of them lived happily together. However, as the years went by, the mother grew older, and before long she reached the terrible age of seventy-one.

"If only I could somehow deceive the cruel lord," the farmer thought. But there were records in the village books and everyone knew that his mother had turned seventy-one.

Each day the son put off telling his mother that he must take her into the mountains to die, but the people of the village began to talk. The farmer knew that if he did not take his mother away soon, the lord would send his soldiers and throw them both into a dark dungeon to die a terrible death.

"Mother—" he would begin, as he tried to tell her what he must do, but he could not go on.

(continued next page)

Then one day the mother herself spoke of the dread lord's decree. "Well, my son," she said, "the time has come for you to take me to the mountains. We must hurry before the lord sends his soldiers for you." And she did not seem worried at all that she must go to the mountains to die.

"Forgive me, dear mother, for what I must do," the farmer said sadly, and the next morning he lifted his mother to his shoulders and set off on the steep path toward the mountains. Up and up he climbed, until the trees clustered close and the path was gone. There was no longer even the sound of birds, and they heard only the soft wail of the wind in the trees. The son walked slowly, for he could not bear to think of leaving his old mother in the mountains. On and on he climbed, not wanting to stop and leave her behind. Soon, he heard his mother breaking off small twigs from the trees that they passed.

"Mother, what are you doing?" he asked.

"Do not worry, my son," she answered gently. "I am just marking the way so you will not get lost returning to the village."

The son stopped. "Even now you are thinking of me?" he asked, wonderingly.

The mother nodded. "Of course, my son," she replied. "You will always be in my thoughts. How could it be otherwise?"

At that, the young farmer could bear it no longer. "Mother, I cannot leave you in the mountains to die all alone," he said. "We are going home and no matter what the lord does to punish me, I will never desert you again."

So they waited until the sun had set and a lone star crept into the silent sky. Then in the dark shadows of night, the farmer carried his mother down the hill and they returned quietly to their little house. The farmer dug a deep hole in the floor of his kitchen and made a small room where he could hide his mother. From that day, she spent all her time in the secret room and the farmer carried meals to her there. The rest of the time, he was careful to work in the fields and act as though he lived alone. In this way, for almost two years, he kept his mother safely hidden and no one in the village knew that she was there.

_____

_____

_____

_____

_____

_____

_____

_____

"The Emperor's New Clothes" by Hans Christian Andersen (text page 775)

Literary Focus: Characters in Folk Literature

Like most characters in folk literature, the emperor, his courtiers, the weavers, and other characters in "The Emperor's New Clothes" represent qualities or types of people. Readers can learn lessons about life by focusing on the qualities that these characters display and then watching for the results of their actions.

A. DIRECTIONS: Read the following passages. Then write a sentence or two explaining what each passage reveals about the characters indicated.

1. "I should like to know how those weavers are getting on with the stuff," thought the emperor. But he felt a little queer when he reflected that those who were stupid or unfit for their office would not be able to see the material. He believed, indeed, that he had nothing to fear for himself, but still he thought it better to send someone else first, to see how the work was coming on.

The emperor: _____

_____

2. "Heaven save us!" thought the prime minister. "Is it possible that I am a fool! I have never thought it, and nobody must know it. Is it true that I am not fit for my office? It will never do for me to say that I cannot see the stuff."

Well, sir, do you say nothing about the cloth?" asked the one who was pretending to go on with his work.

"Oh, it is most elegant, most beautiful!" said the dazed old man, as he peered again through his spectacles. "What a fine pattern, and what fine colors! I will certainly tell the emperor how pleased I am with the stuff!"

The prime minister: _____

_____

B. DIRECTIONS: Use the organizer below to keep track of the characters' qualities as you read "The Emperor's New Clothes." In each section, jot down your thoughts about the types of people these characters represent.

Character	Characters' Qualities and What They Represent
Ministers and Statesmen	
Emperor	
Child Who Speaks Out	

"The Ant and the Dove" by Leo Tolstoy (text page 784)
"He Lion, Bruh Bear, and Bruh Rabbit" by Virginia Hamilton (text page 785)
"Señor Coyote and the Tricked Trickster" by I. G. Edmonds (text page 789)

Build Vocabulary

Using Forms of *dignity*

The word *dignity* means "the quality of being worthy." Words that are related to dignity include the idea of worthiness. For example, the Word Bank word *indignantly* means "angrily; as if not worth a response." A *dignitary* is a person worthy of respect. An indignity is something that insults one's worth.

A. DIRECTIONS: Choose the correct word to complete each sentence. Write your answers on the lines.

1. He Lion thought of himself as a (dignitary, dignity) _____ among animals.

2. When Bruh Rabbit politely asked him if he could try being more quiet, he Lion considered the question an (indignity, indignantly) _____.

3. He (indignity, indignantly) _____ reminded Bruh Rabbit of his high rank.

4. He lion expressed his belief in his own (dignitary, dignity) _____.

Using the Word Bank

startled	lair	cordial	gnaw	reproachfully	indignantly

B. DIRECTIONS: Answer each of the following questions to demonstrate your understanding of the Word Bank words. Circle the letter of your choice.

1. Which of the following would be considered a *lair*?

   a. a fox's den   b. a fox's cub

2. In which of the following situations does someone answer *indignantly*?

   a. Bill asked Mary how much money she made, and Mary answered "None of your business."

   b. Susan asked Tom if he would like half of her sandwich, and Tom answered, "Yes. Thank you very much."

3. Which of the following statements would someone make *reproachfully*?

   a. "I think you are very kind."   b. "I think you are very ungrateful."

4. Which of the following words might you use instead of *gnaw*?

   a. crawl   b. chew

5. Which of the following might you describe as *cordial*?

   a. a smile   b. an insult

6. Which of the following is more likely to have startled someone?

   a. the sound of a soft rainfall   b. the sound of a car alarm

"The Ant and the Dove" by Leo Tolstoy (text page 784)
"He Lion, Bruh Bear, and Bruh Rabbit" by Virginia Hamilton (text page 785)
"Señor Coyote and the Tricked Trickster" by I. G. Edmonds (text page 789)

Build Spelling Skills: Spelling the *j* Sound With *di*

Spelling Strategy Sometimes the *j* sound is spelled with *di*, as it is in the Word Bank word *cordial*. Another word in which the *j* sound is spelled in this way is *soldier*. In certain other words, the *j* sound is spelled with a *d* followed by a *u*. Say the following words to yourself. Notice the *j* sound in each one.

educate   gradual   graduate   individual   schedule

A. Practice: Use one or more of the words listed above to answer each question. Write your answers on the lines.

1. Which word could be used to describe the movement of a glacier? _____

2. Which two words have to do with school? _____

3. Which word names something you might make if you were planning a large project?

   _____

4. Which word means "a single person"? _____

B. Practice: Proofread the following sentences, looking for the errors in the spellings of words that contain the *j* sound. When you find a misspelled word, cross it out, and write it correctly above the line. Write **C** next to the sentence if the there are no errors.

____ 1. After Leo Tolstoy gradjuated from law school, he served in the army.

____ 2. His experiences as a soljier taught him a great deal about life.

____ 3. Tolstoy wrote books and essays about religion, philosophy, and education.

____ 4. Many Russians wanted to meet this fascinating and influential indivijual.

____ 5. Although Tolstoy was extremely busy, he received his visitors cordially.

Challenge: In "Señor Coyote and the Tricked Trickster," the mouse *gnaws*, or chews, a piece of leather to free Coyote from a trap. In the word *gnaw* and several other words, the *n* sound at the beginning is spelled *gn*.

Match each meaning in the left column with the correct word in the right column. Write the letter of your choice on the line next to each meaning. Use a dictionary if you are not sure of any of the words.

____ 1. to grind one's teeth together   a. gnarl

____ 2. an imaginary troll-like creature   b. gnash

____ 3. a large animal from the antelope family c. gnat

____ 4. a tiny insect   d. gnome

____ 5. to snarl; to growl   e. gnu

"The Ant and the Dove" by Leo Tolstoy (text page 784)
"He Lion, Bruh Bear, and Bruh Rabbit" by Virginia Hamilton (text page 785)
"Señor Coyote and the Tricked Trickster" by I. G. Edmonds (text page 789)

Build Grammar Skills: Commas in a Series

A sentence can list a number of items, which may be single words or groups of words. When three or more items are listed, the list is called a **series**. Look at the examples below. Notice that the words in the series are separated by commas.

The <u>rabbits</u>, <u>squirrels</u>, and <u>chipmunks</u>, were afraid of the man.

The man <u>looked around</u>, <u>listened carefully</u>, and <u>took aim</u> at He Lion.

A. Practice: In the following sentences, place commas where needed in a series . If the sentence does not contain items in a series, write *no* on the line.

_____ 1. "He Lion Bruh Bear and Bruh Rabbit" is an amusing folk tale.

_____ 2. The story is about a conceited lion a thoughtful bear and a clever rabbit.

_____ 3. Every morning, He lion would stretch walk around and roar.

_____ 4. The animals heard him repeating, "ME AND MYSELF. ME AND MYSELF."

_____ 5. They were afraid to come out to hunt fish or play because of the terrible noise.

_____ 6. One day, the little animals decided to go to Bruh Bear and Bruh Rabbit for help.

_____ 7. They knew that these two were wise experienced and resourceful.

_____ 8. Bruh Bear and Bruh Rabbit agreed to go and have a talk with He Lion.

_____ 9. They visited Bruh Bear's lair chatted cordially with him and tried to tell him that Man was the real king of the forest.

_____ 10. By the end of the story, He Lion roars less frequently more quietly and almost peaceably.

B. Writing Application: Write a sentence about each topic suggested below, using items in a series. Be sure to use commas where needed.

1. Write a sentence in which you name your three favorite sports.

_____

2. Write a sentence that tells about a project you completed with two or more classmates.

_____

3. Write a sentence in which you name three things that you do every day.

_____

4. Write a sentence in which you describe a favorite animal of yours. Use three different adjectives.

_____

"The Ant and the Dove" by Leo Tolstoy (text page 784)
"He Lion, Bruh Bear, and Bruh Rabbit" by Virginia Hamilton (text page 785)
"Señor Coyote and the Tricked Trickster" by I. G. Edmonds (text page 789)

Reading Strategy: Recognize the Storyteller's Purpose

You will increase you understanding and enjoyment of folk tales if you **recognize the storyteller's purpose**—that is, if you understand the storyteller's reason for sharing the tale.

Many folk tales have more than one purpose. For example, in "He Lion, Bruh Bear, and Bruh Rabbit," certain descriptions, events, and details are included to amuse and entertain readers. Other details are included to teach a lesson in life.

DIRECTIONS: Use the chart below to help you recognize the storyteller's purpose as you read these tales. First, jot down details from the tale. Then, note whether each detail teaches, entertains or both. One example is given.

	Detail	Entertains	Teaches
"The Ant and the Dove"	Humorous description of the quarrel between Coyote and Mouse		
"He Lion"			
"Señor Coyote and the Tricked Trickster"			

"The Ant and the Dove" by Leo Tolstoy (text page 784)
"He Lion, Bruh Bear, and Bruh Rabbit" by Virginia Hamilton (text page 785)
"Señor Coyote and the Tricked Trickster" by I. G. Edmonds (text page 789)

Literary Focus: Folk Tales

Folk tales are the stories that the people, or "folk," of a country or culture have passed down from generation to generation. These tales may entertain, teach a lesson, or explain something in nature. Through their details and their messages, these stories also reflect the cultures in which they originated.

DIRECTIONS: Read each of the following passages. Then write your answers to the questions.

"The Ant and the Dove"

A thirsty ant went to the stream to drink. Suddenly it got caught in a whirlpool and was almost carried away.

At that moment, a dove was passing by with a twig in its beak. The dove dropped the twig for the tiny insect to grab hold of. So it was that the ant was saved.

A few days later a hunter was about to catch the dove in his net. When the ant saw what was happening, it walked right up to the man and bit him on the foot. Startled, the man dropped the net. And the dove, thinking that you never can tell how or when a kindness may be repaid, flew away.

1. Do you think the purpose of "The Ant and the Dove" is to teach a lesson in life or to explain something in nature? Why?

   _____

   _____

2. Do you think that the people who passed the story along through the years thought that kindness toward others is important? Why?

   _____

   _____

"Señor Coyote and the Tricked Trickster"

One day long ago in Mexico's land of sand and giant cactus, Señor Coyote and Señor Mouse had a quarrel.

None now alive can remember why, but recalling what spirited caballeros these two were, I suspect that it was that some small thing that meant little.

Be that as it may, these two took their quarrels seriously and for a long time would not speak to each other.

3. Identify three details that are related to Mexican culture.

   _____

   _____

4. Which of these details do you think adds a humorous and entertaining touch to the story? Why?

   _____

   _____

"The Gorgon's Head" by Anne Terry White (text page 799)
"How Coyote Stole Fire" by Gail Robinson and Douglas Hill (text page 804)

Build Vocabulary

Using the Suffix -ous

The Word Bank words *perilous*, *venomous*, and *valorous* all contain the suffix *-ous*, which means "having" or "full of." Something that is *perilous* is full of peril, or danger. How would you express the meanings of *venomous* and *valorous*?

A. DIRECTIONS: Use the clues to complete each sentence with a word that contains the suffix *-ous*.

1. Perseus is a _____ hero from Greek mythology. (having fame)

2. Polydectes resents him and sends him on a _____ mission. (full of peril)

3. He assigns Perseus the _____ task of cutting off the Medusa's head. (full of danger)

4. With the help of Hermes and Athene, the _____ young man finds the Medusa and cuts off the grisly head. (having courage)

5. As Perseus flies over the Lybian desert with the head, drops of blood fall down and turn into _____ snakes. (full of venom)

6. The _____ creatures would inhabit the desert forever. (full of poison)

Using the Word Bank

evade	perilous	venomous	abashed	valorous	rivulets

B. DIRECTIONS: Match each word in the left column with its definition in the right column. Write the letter of the definition on the line next to the word it defines.

____ 1. venomous   a. dangerous

____ 2. rivulets   b. escape or avoid

____ 3. evade   c. brave

____ 4. valorous   d. little streams or brooks

____ 5. abashed   e. ashamed

____ 6. perilous   f. poisonous

Recognizing Antonyms

C. DIRECTIONS: Circle the letter of the word or phrase that is most nearly *opposite* in meaning to the word in CAPITAL LETTERS.

1. PERILOUS: a. risky   b. ridiculous   c. ancient   d. safe

2. ABASHED: a. destroyed   b. new   c. proud   d. ashamed

3. VALOROUS: a. gallant   b. fearful   c. expensive   d. heroic

"The Gorgon's Head" by Anne Terry White (text page 799)
"How Coyote Stole Fire" by Gail Robinson and Douglas Hill (text page 804)

Build Spelling Skills: Words Ending With -ous

Spelling Strategy Many adjectives, such as *valorous*, *perilous*, and *famous*, end with -*ous*. When spelling words that end with *ous*, remember to include the *o*, even though you don't hear it.

A. Practice: Unscramble each group of letters to spell a word that matches the clue.

1. extremely angry   (oofrsui) ___ ___ ___ ___ ___ ___ ___

2. wonderful; extraordinary   (noudrows) ___ ___ ___ ___ ___ ___ ___ ___

3. valorous; brave   (ogsuuroaec) ___ ___ ___ ___ ___ ___ ___ ___ ___ ___

4. extremely ugly; horrible   (iduheso) ___ ___ ___ ___ ___ ___ ___

5. full of glory; splendid   (orloisgu) ___ ___ ___ ___ ___ ___ ___ ___

6. unknown; suspenseful   (smueriotys) ___ ___ ___ ___ ___ ___ ___ ___ ___ ___

7. full of virtue; noble   (usurotiv) ___ ___ ___ ___ ___ ___ ___ ___

8. perilous   (dosugersan) ___ ___ ___ ___ ___ ___ ___ ___ ___

B. Practice: Using the number given in parentheses as a clue, write one of the words that you unscrambled to complete each sentence. For example, if (6) appears before a blank, write the word that you unscrambled in number 6 above.

1. Some myths explain events that were (6) _____ to ancient people.

2. Others tell of the (5) _____ deeds of daring heroes.

3. Sympathetic gods often help (3) _____ figures like Perseus.

4. Gorgons, serpents, and other (4) _____ monsters act as foes.

5. In "The Gorgon's Head," for example, Hermes and Athena approve of Perseus, and they help the (7) _____ youth.

6. The serpent that threatens Andromeda, on the other hand, becomes (1) _____ when Perseus tries to help the princess.

7. The hero fights and wins another (8) _____ battle.

8. What (2) _____ adventure will he have next?

Challenge: In "How Coyote Stole Fire," the Fire Beings stamp out *rivulets*, or little streams, of flame so that their fire does not spread out of control. Words that, like *rivulet*, end in *let* often include the idea of littleness. Some examples are *booklet*, *cloudlet*, and *droplet*.

Match each word ending in *let* to its meaning.

____ 1. piglet   ____ 2. islet   ____ 3. eaglet   ____ 4. playlet

a. a little play   b. a little eagle   c. a little pig   d. a little island

Unit 10: The Oral Tradition

"The Gorgon's Head" by Anne Terry White (text page 799)
"How Coyote Stole Fire" by Gail Robinson and Douglas Hill (text page 804)

Build Grammar Skills: Commas With Interrupters

Interrupters are words, phrases, or clauses that interrupt a sentence to add information not essential to the meaning of the sentence. The following chart shows examples of common kinds of interrupters. Notice that the interrupters are set off by commas.

The Name of a person being addressed:	Only you, <u>Coyote</u>, can help us.
Phrases that rename or describe a noun:	Chipmunk, <u>chattering with fear</u>, threw the fire to Frog.
Common expressions:	Frog, <u>on the other hand</u>, showed no fear.

A. Practice: Underline the interrupter in each of the following sentences. Insert commas where needed to set off the interrupting word or phrase.

1. Anne Terry White who was born in Russia has retold many Greek myths.

2. She has for example written a version of the adventures of the Greek hero Perseus.

3. Perseus the son of Zeus and Danae set off to find and slay the Medusa.

4. The Medusa one of the Gorgons had snakes instead of hair.

5. This mythical being was needless to say a horrible monster.

6. Gail Robinson and Douglas Hill have like Anne Terry White published many myths.

7. The myths that Robinson and Hill retell though come from Native American cultures.

8. "How Coyote Stole Fire" is of course a favorite of many people.

9. Coyote clever and compassionate manages to steal fire from the selfish Fire Beings.

10. "How sister did this happen?" shouted one of the Fire Beings.

B. Writing Application: Write a sentence about each topic below, using interrupters as indicated. Be sure to use commas to set off your interrupters.

1. Write a sentence in which you ask a question or make a request. Address a friend or family member within your question or request.

_____

2. Write a sentence about a book or movie that is meaningful to you. Include an interrupter that renames or describes the book or movie.

_____

3. Write a sentence about a hero from literature, history, the arts, sports, or your community. Use a common expression such as *for instance, of course, as many people know,* or *needless to say.*

_____

"The Gorgon's Head" by Anne Terry White (text page 799)
"How Coyote Stole Fire" by Gail Robinson and Douglas Hill (text page 804)

Reading Strategy: Understand Cultural Background

    Myths such as "The Gorgon's Head" and "How Coyote Stole Fire" reflect the cultures from which the stories come. The heroes of these myths embody qualities that are highly valued by people within the culture. For example, the ancient Greeks, who were often at war, placed a high value on strength and valor in battle. Perseus, the hero of "The Gorgon's Head," shows these qualities as he confronts and defeats one of the Gorgons. In a similar way, you can conclude from the Coyote's qualities that bravery and compassion were valued by the Crow people.

DIRECTIONS: Use the graphic organizer below as you read "The Gorgon's Head" and "How Coyote Stole Fire." On each point of the flame jot down a quality that shows what each culture valued in a hero.

Crow Heroes

Greek Heroes

"The Gorgon's Head" by Anne Terry White (text page 799)
"How Coyote Stole Fire" by Gail Robinson and Douglas Hill (text page 804)

Literary Focus: Myths

"The Gorgon's Head" and "How Coyote Stole Fire" are **myths**—ancient stories that relate the actions of gods or heroes or explain events in nature. "The Gorgon's Head" recounts the adventures of the Greek warrior Perseus and includes details that explain something in nature. "How Coyote Stole Fire" explains how ancient people came to have fire through the help of a kind and cunning hero.

DIRECTIONS: Read each passage. Then write a sentence or two to summarize the adventures that it recounts or the event in nature that it explains.

1. **"The Gorgon's Head"**

"Enough of tears!" Perseus said to them sternly. "I am Perseus, son of Zeus and Danae. Now I will make this contract with you—that Andromeda shall be mine if I save her from the serpent."

"Indeed, indeed, valorous youth, she shall be yours! Only save her from the monster, and you shall have our kingdom as well as our daughter."

The monster was coming on, his breast parting the waves like a swift ship. Suddenly Perseus sprang into the air and shot high up in the clouds. Seeing the youth's shadow upon the sea, the monster attacked it in fury. Then Perseus swooped like an eagle from the sky and buried his sword up to the hilt in the beast's right shoulder. The creature reared upright, then plunged beneath the water, and turned around like some fierce wild boar in the midst of baying hounds.

_____

_____

_____

2. **"The Gorgon's Head"**

Over lands and people the hero flew, on and on. He had lost his way now, for Hermes had left him. Below, the Lybian desert stretched endlessly. Perseus did not know what those sands were, nor did he guess that the ruby drops falling from Medusa's head were turning into venomous snakes that would inhabit the desert forever.

_____

_____

3. **"How Coyote Stole Fire"**

As the Beings came after him again, Frog flung the fire on to Wood. And Wood swallowed it.

The Fire Beings gathered round, but they did not know how to get the fire out of Wood. They promised it gifts, sang to it and shouted at it. They twisted it and struck it and tore it with their knives. But Wood did not give up the fire. In the end, defeated, the Beings went back to their mountaintop and left the People alone.

But Coyote knew how to get fire out of Wood. And he went to the village of men and showed them how. He showed them the trick of rubbing two dry sticks together, and the trick of spinning a sharpened stick in a hole made in another piece of wood. So man was from then on warm and safe through the killing cold of winter.

_____

_____

_____

"Why Monkeys Live in Trees" by Julius Lester (text page 820)
"Arachne" by Olivia E. Coolidge (text page 822)
"A Crippled Boy" by My-Van Tran (text page 826)
"The Three Wishes" by Richard E. Alegría (text page 828)

Build Vocabulary

Using the Word Root -mort-

The Word Bank word *mortal* contains the word root -*mort*-, meaning "death." Here is a list of words with the word root -*mort*-:

mortal: able to die, or a person who will not live forever

immortal: able to live forever, or a being (such as a god) who will live forever

mortician: person who prepares the dead for burial

mortify: make feel humble and ashamed

mortuary: building where the dead are kept until buried

A. DIRECTIONS: Use one of the words above to complete each of the sentences below.

1. The captain will _____ me if she yells at me in front of the whole team.

2. The god granted three wishes to the worthy _____.

3. The _____ helped to plan my great-grandmother's funeral.

4. The body was laid in the _____ until the funeral.

5. The ancient Greeks believed their gods were all-powerful and _____.

Using the Word Bank

bellowed	obscure	immortal	mortal
obstinacy	foliage	embraced	covetousness

B. DIRECTIONS: Match each word in the left column with its definition in the right column. Write the letter of the definition on the line next to the word it defines.

_____ 1. bellowed   a. stubbornness

_____ 2. obscure   b. wanting what another person has

_____ 3. immortal   c. not well known

_____ 4. mortal   d. to cry out loudly

_____ 5. obstinacy   e. leaves of trees and bushes

_____ 6. foliage   f. clasped in the arms

_____ 7. embraced   g. living forever

_____ 8. covetousness   h. referring to humans who will die

Unit 10: The Oral Tradition

"Why Monkeys Live in Trees" by Julius Lester (text page 820)
"Arachne" by Olivia E. Coolidge (text page 822)
"A Crippled Boy" by My-Van Tran (text page 826)
"The Three Wishes" by Richard E. Alegría (text page 828)

Build Spelling Skills: -cy and -sy

Spelling Strategy Many words end in the letters -cy or -sy. The two word endings are spelled differently and have different meanings but the same pronunciation. It might help to remember that the suffix -cy often means "the quality or state of." Here are several examples:

obstina<u>cy</u> the state of being obstinate or stubborn

accura<u>cy</u> the quality of being accurate

courtesy politeness

controversy argument

prophecy prediction of the future

A. Practice: Write the word from the list that above that best completes each of the following sentences.

1. In my family _____ is expected of everyone.

2. Often in myths, a character makes a _____ about the future.

3. We questioned the _____ of the news report.

4. Our class had a _____ over where to go on our class trip.

5. Because of his _____, he would not change his mind, no matter what.

B. Practice: Complete the following letter. Using the context clues, choose four words from the list above to fill in the blanks.

Dear Helen,

   I went to visit our old friend Arachne the other day. I was worried, because I'd heard that she has gotten into a _____ with the goddess Athene about who is the better weaver. I've always thought Arachne could use a lesson in _____, especially when talking to goddesses. Although she weaves with amazing _____, I would make a _____ that her rudeness will get her into trouble some day. She wasn't at home when I got there, but in the place where she usually sits and weaves, I saw a large spider spinning a web. What do you think happened to Arachne?

                                              Your friend,
                                              Iris

Challenge: The Word Bank word *bellowed* contains several smaller words not related to its meaning. One example is owe. Can you find at least five other small words in *bellowed*? Write your answers on the lines provided.

_____ _____ _____ _____ _____

"Why Monkeys Live in Trees" by Julius Lester (text page 820)
"Arachne" by Olivia E. Coolidge (text page 822)
"A Crippled Boy" by My-Van Tran (text page 826)
"The Three Wishes" by Richard E. Alegría (text page 828)

Building Grammar Skills: Varying Sentence Beginnings

Variety is the spice of life. It's also the spice of good writing. If every sentence in a story began with the subject, the story would sound monotonous, and the reader would get bored. By beginning sentences in other ways, writers keep their writing fresh and interesting. Here are four examples of different sentence beginnings from the selections:

Subject: <u>He</u> was crippled in both legs and could hardly walk.

Prepositional phrase: <u>At that exact moment</u>, one of Leopard's children ran up to him.

Adverb: <u>Suddenly</u>, he realized that his wife, without stopping to think, had used one of the three wishes...

Verb: <u>Rest</u> content with your fame of being the best spinner and weaver that mortal eyes have ever beheld.

A. Practice: Read each sentence and identify its beginning. Write *S* if the sentence begins with the subject, *V* if it begins with a verb, *P* if it begins with a prepositional phrase, and *A* if it begins with an adverb.

____ 1. "Live on, wicked girl," she said.

____ 2. After that he always treasured Theo's presence and service.

____ 3. The family lived happily all the rest of their lives.

____ 4. Finally only Monkey remained.

____ 5. From his limb high in the tree Leopard could see into the tall grasses where Monkey went to rest.

B. Writing Application: All of the sentences below begin with a subject. Rewrite the sentences so that each one begins in a different way—with, a verb, a prepositional phrase, or an adverb.

1. Leopard gazed at his reflection, admiring his beautiful coat and whiskers.

_____

2. A huge mound was in the middle of the clearing.

_____

3. Arachne said, "Accept my challenge, Athene."

_____

4. Athene stepped forward angrily.

_____

5. A woodsman and his wife lived in a little house in the forest.

_____

Unit 10: The Oral Tradition

"Why Monkeys Live in Trees" by Julius Lester (text page 820)
"Arachne" by Olivia E. Coolidge (text page 822)
"A Crippled Boy" by My-Van Tran (text page 826)
"The Three Wishes" by Richard E. Alegría (text page 828)

Reading Strategy: Predict

When you read a story or book it is fun to **predict** what is going to happen next. Many times the author will give you clues as to what will happen. For example, when you read in "Why Monkeys Live in Trees" that the mound of black dust is a mound of black pepper, you might predict that the other animals won't have any easier time eating it than Hippopotamus.

You can base your predictions on what you have already read. Often, folk tales are more predictable than other kinds of stories because they usually follow a pattern. You can be fairly certain that kind and generous characters will be rewarded, whereas wicked or greedy characters will most likely be punished.

DIRECTIONS: Read each passage below. Then, on the lines provided, write a prediction about what will happen and your reasons for making the prediction.

1. "Why Monkeys Live in Trees"
   From his limb high in the tree Leopard could see into the tall grasses when Monkey went to rest. Wait a minute! Leopard thought something was suddenly wrong with his eyes because he thought he saw a hundred monkeys hiding in the tall grass.

Prediction:_____

Reason for Prediction:_____

2. "Arachne"
   Thus as Athene stepped back a pace to watch Arachne finishing her work, she saw that the maiden had taken for her design a pattern of scenes which showed evil or unworthy actions of the gods, how they had deceived fair maidens, resorted to trickery, and appeared on earth from time to time in the form of poor and humble people.

Prediction:_____

Reason for Prediction:_____

3. "The Three Wishes"
   "It doesn't seem possible that you could be so stupid! You've wasted one of our wishes, and now we have only two left! May you grow ears of a donkey!"
   He [the woodsman] had no sooner said the words than his wife's ears began to grow, and they continued to grow until they changed into the pointed, furry ears of a donkey.

Prediction:_____

Reason for Prediction:_____

"Why Monkeys Live in Trees" by Julius Lester (text page 820)
"Arachne" by Olivia E. Coolidge (text page 822)
"A Crippled Boy" by My-Van Tran (text page 826)
"The Three Wishes" by Richard E. Alegría (text page 828)

Literary Focus: Oral Tradition

Myths and folk tales are stories that people have told other over and over again down through generations. They are created from what is called the **oral tradition**. These stories often reflect the traditions, beliefs, and values of the people who created them. Many myths and folk tales are told for the purpose of teaching an important lesson about life.

DIRECTIONS: Read the following passages from the selection. Then fill in the blanks by answering the questions, basing your answers on details in the passage.

1. "Why Monkeys Live in Trees"
The monkeys ran in all directions. When the other animals saw monkeys running from the grasses, they realized that the monkeys had tricked them and started chasing them. Even King Gorilla joined in the chase. He wanted his gold back.
The only way the monkeys could escape was to climb to the very tops of the tallest trees where no one else, not even Leopard, could climb.
And that's why monkeys live in trees to this very day.

What lesson about life does this tale teach? _____

2. "Arachne"
At that the body of Arachne shriveled up, and her legs grew tiny, spindly, and distorted. There before the eyes of the spectators hung a little dusty brown spider on a slender thread.
All spiders descend from Arachne, and as the Greeks watched them spinning their thread wonderfully fine, they remembered the contest with Athene and thought that it was not right for even the best of men to claim equality with the gods.

What lesson about life does this tale teach? _____

3. "A Crippled Boy"
For once the king could speak as much as he wanted without being interrupted. The King was extremely pleased with his success and the help that Theo had given him.

What lesson about life does this tale teach? _____

4. "The Three Wishes"
The old man left, but before going, he told them that they had undergone this test in order to learn that there can be happiness in poverty just as there can be unhappiness in riches.

What lesson about life does this tale teach? _____

"Loo-Wit, the Firekeeper" retold by Joseph Bruchac (text page 833)

Build Vocabulary

In "Loo-Wit, the Firekeeper," the old woman lives in a lodge, which is a type of dwelling used by some Native Americans of North America. Other Native American dwellings include the hogans, wigwams, teepees, and long houses.

A. DIRECTIONS: Using a dictionary or other reference source, write a description of each of the Native American dwellings indicated and name at least one tribe or nation associated with the dwelling.

1. hogan _____

_____

2. wigwam _____

_____

3. teepee _____

_____

4. long house _____

_____

B. DIRECTIONS: Other meanings of the word *lodge* include "hut," "cabin," and "inn." Complete each of the following sentences with the most appropriate synonym for *lodge* from the preceding list. Check a dictionary if you're not sure of the different shades of meaning.

1. The charming _____ served large, family-style meals.

2. The hikers managed to find shelter in a primitive _____ just off the trail.

3. At scout camp, there were six girls to a _____.

C. DIRECTIONS: Look up *lodge* in a dictionary to find one of its meaning as a verb. Then write a sentence that demonstrates that meaning.

_____

_____

"Loo-Wit, the Firekeeper" retold by Joseph Bruchac (text page 833)

Connecting a Myth to Social Studies

The three mountains in the story belong to the **Cascade Range,** a chain of mountains in the Pacific Northwest region of the United States. Many of the peaks in the Cascades were once active volcanoes. The tallest mountains in the Cascades are Mount Rainier, in Washington, and Mount Shasta, in northern California. Other mountains in the range include Mount Adams, which, according to the story was once the chief of the Klickitats; Mount Hood, which was, in the story, the chief of the Multnomahs; and Mount St. Helens, which the story tells us was once the beautiful maiden Loo-Wit. Mount St. Helens is still an active volcano, having erupted several times since 1980.

DIRECTIONS: In an atlas, find a map of the Pacific Northwest, and locate three mountains in the story, as well as the Columbia and Willamette Rivers, which divided the lands of the Klickitats and the Multnomahs. Then answer the questions below.

1. In which state is Mount Adams located? _____

2. In which state is Mount Hood located? _____

3. In which state is Mount St. Helens located? _____

4. Write one or two sentences telling why the story developed so that Mount St. Helens was

   once the maiden who kept the fire. _____

   _____

   _____